Adolf Hitler
and the
German Trauma

1913-1945

AN INTERPRETATION
OF THE NAZI PHENOMENON

Adolf Hitler and the German Trauma

1913-1945

AN INTERPRETATION OF THE NAZI PHENOMENON

by

Robert Edwin Herzstein

Capricorn Books, New York
G. P. PUTNAM'S SONS, NEW YORK

PREFACE

MY book is an interpretive introduction to the Nazi experience. In part it is biography, in part social and political history. I attempt to relate the personal and political career of Adolf Hitler to the course of twentieth-century German history. I hope that a study of the dynamic interaction between Adolf Hitler and Austro-German history may aid both students and general readers in understanding the man and his adopted fatherland.

This volume is not a survey of contemporary German history; it is a study of Adolf Hitler and National Socialism's role in the social aberrations and disintegration that I call the German trauma. Thus, I do not try to cover the entire political and social history of the period since 1913, or even that of the Third Reich. I am highlighting the role of the National Socialist leadership as a way of understanding the agonies and contradictions of German society.

The literature on National Socialism has indeed become voluminous, and I hope that my book reflects a thorough but critical familiarity with the most important works in that literature. The emphases of the book mirror both my own approach to Nazism and what I take to be the concerns of the latest scholarship.*

---

*I have assembled and edited a collection of documents and interpretations that some readers may wish to use in conjunction with this book: *Adolf Hitler and the Third Reich 1933-1945* (Boston, Houghton Mifflin, 1971).

I would like to thank several individuals who by their work, interest, and criticism aided in the creation of this book. Professor Theodore H. Von Laue of Clark University read the manuscript. His comments were both encouraging and critical, and I have benefited from them. My study of the Nazi phenomenon has been influenced by my participation, at the kind invitation of Professor Stanley Hoffmann of Harvard University, in the Peace and War Interdisciplinary Colloquia of the American Psychoanalytic Association (1970-1971). My friends Mr. Donald R. Koenig of the Trinity School in New York and Professor Harry Cliadakis of the University of South Carolina have listened with patience to many of my monologues on the subject at hand. Their criticisms and suggestions have been valuable to me.

By way of illustration of Hitler's conduct of the Second World War, I include a number of photographs which have never before been published. I would like to thank Mr. Patrick Sheehan of the Library of Congress Film Division, Washington, D.C., for his help and unfailing courtesy in making available to me the German films from which these photographs were made. The Photoduplication Department of the Library of Congress made the photographs for me, and for this I would like to thank their skillful technicians. Permission to use these photographs was graciously granted by Transit Films GMBH, Munich; photos from UFA newsreels (1940-1945).

My friend Wendy Wilkens helped type the manuscript. Her encouragement made a major contribution to the creation of the book. My literary agent and friend, Ms. Susan Ann Protter, and my editor, Mr. Edward T. Chase of G. P. Putnam's Sons, made the decision to publish my book in this form, and I am grateful for their confidence. Ms. Anne Gordon of Putnam's played a major role in seeing this book through the press. Mrs. Terry Dokus also contributed to the physical preparation of the manuscript. Ms. Sally Connelly prepared the index, and for this I am most grateful.

All of these fine people contributed to the book in their own way. I am, of course, solely responsible for all statements of fact and all interpretations put forth in these pages.

ROBERT E. HERZSTEIN

Columbia, South Carolina
August, 1973

Contents

CONTENTS

Illustrations will be found following page 163

Adolf Hitler
and the
German Trauma

1913-1945

AN INTERPRETATION
OF THE NAZI PHENOMENON

CHAPTER I

Prelude: Portrait of the Führer As a Young Austrian, 1889-1913

1. Adolf Hitler: The Early Years

ADOLF HITLER was born in the Lower Austrian village of Braunau-am-Inn on April 20, 1889. This part of Lower Austria had been Bavarian until the late eighteenth century, and it was very close to the German frontier. The area around Braunau was an impoverished agricultural region at the time of Hitler's birth. To a person of ambition Braunau offered few opportunities, but a provincial capital such as Linz or the great cosmopolitan center of the Habsburg monarchy, Vienna, offered much more both in potential opportunity and disappointments. Hitler was to discover this as an adolescent. His father, Alois Hitler, was a minor Austrian customs official who prided himself on his service to the Habsburg monarchy. He dreamed of filling out his last days as a prosperous farmer. In this aspiration he was to be bitterly disappointed.

Hitler's father was considerably older than Klara, his mother. In addition, Alois Hitler was illegitimate, though he legally bore his stepfather's name, Hitler, rather than his mother's maiden name, Schicklgruber. Satirical opponents of Hitler in the 1930's joyfully pointed out that his "real" name was Schicklgruber, and one can hardly imagine the future German Führer having had such a

1

meteoric rise if his followers had to greet him with "Heil Schicklgruber!" Despite this engaging bit of political satire, Adolf Hitler's name was never Schicklgruber, rather, he was born with the surname Hitler. Illegitimacy was quite common in the Austrian countryside and little stigma attached to Hitler's father because of the circumstances of his birth. Incest, too, seems to have been common in that part of the country. This latter became one of Adolf Hitler's pet phobias later in life, along with venereal disease. Indeed, Adolf Hitler may have been acquainted with both of these dread phenomena from his own personal experience, indirectly in one case and directly in the other.

Once Hitler had discovered that the Jew was the source of everything diabolic in his own life and in the world, he transferred his phobias about incest and syphilis to the Jews, making them the purveyors and benefactors of both. Hitler does seem to have been haunted by the possibility that his father's natural father was a Jew, although there is little factual evidence for this assumption. Since Hitler's own SS insisted that its members be able to trace their Aryan ancestry back to 1750, Hitler himself was much concerned about whether a non-Aryan ancestor would be discovered in his own family tree as late as the mid-nineteenth century. We are told by one source that even as Führer, Hitler would stand pensively staring at vials of his own blood, presumably searching for traces of a "Jewish taint" in it. As far as incest goes, Alois Hitler married Hitler's mother despite the fact that as Catholics they needed special dispensation, since their blood relationship was within the prohibited degree of consanguinity.

From the records that have been preserved, there seems to have been little that was remarkable about Adolf Hitler's early life. Like most German-speaking boys of that age, he was much taken with the wild west novels of Karl May. Indeed, he continued to read them even as an adult, and told generals fighting on the eastern front that May's cowboys and Indians were a good analogy for the future relationship between Germans and Slavs. Hitler may have been more introverted and moody than the average child, but even this is difficult to determine from existing historical materials. And in dealing with such a sensational figure, we must be wary of doctored reminiscences.

After his retirement Alois Hitler engaged in a series of restless moves in the region around Linz, all of them failed attempts to realize his dream of becoming a prosperous country gentleman. Adolf Hitler registered for school in Linz, and the one subject which seems to have made a profound impression upon him was history, as taught by a Doctor Leopold Poetsch. Poetsch taught history not as the patriotic story of various Habsburg monarchs and their battles, but as the story of an endless German struggle against the Slavic menace. Years later, Hitler would recall the impression that Poetsch's history had made upon him, and after the Führer had become a famed Chancellor he presented the old man with a special copy of *Mein Kampf*.

It may be from this early period, at the turn of the century, that Hitler acquired his conflicting viewpoints on Germany and Austria. He began to see Austria as a multinational state, a ramshackle empire in which the naturally superior Germanic ruling race was being threatened by the revolt of more numerous Slavic underlings. To the north, the great new Germany of Bismarck and Wilhelm II represented strength, military success, and the Germanic future. Indeed, it may have been this early that Hitler perceived the division of the German people into Austrian and German states as a tragedy for his race. According to what he says in *Mein Kampf*, however, he had not yet picked up another ingredient of his ultimate world view—anti-Semitism. That was to come later, in Vienna.

In Linz Hitler quarreled more frequently with his father about his future. He was a dreamy, melancholy youth, and at this point, when he was perhaps thirteen or fourteen, he began to fancy that he would become an artist. Alois Hitler's provincial ideas of security and success led him to look upon this plan of his son as madness. He vowed that he would never let Adolf become an artist. Such encounters, as later described by Hitler, show important qualities in both father and son: insensitivity on the part of the father, stubbornness and sullen determination on the part of the son. The relationship between the two was an extremely distant, if not hostile one. Hitler had little to say about his father later in life. Indeed, we may speculate that Hitler saw his father much as he was coming to see Austria: ramshackle, unimaginative, and destructive of the healthiest impulses of the young Germanic people. His mother he may have seen in terms of an idealized Germany, beautiful, strong, worthy of love. Biographers of Hitler who are in the process of applying psychoanalytical theory to the study of his upbringing and career note that later in life he had a penchant for relations with women who were at least twenty years younger than himself, that is, at least as young as his mother was in relation to his father, or as young as the new Germany was compared with decrepit Austria.

The sudden death of Hitler's father early in 1903 removed one obstacle to his future plans. Already, Adolf was dreaming of going to the cosmopolitan city of Vienna, the capital of a disturbed but still powerful Habsburg monarchy. As a semi-orphan he would receive a pension from the Austrian state, and he now had to deal with an indulgent, harried, and ill mother rather than with a dictatorial father. Hitler left school in Linz in 1905 at the age of sixteen. The immediate cause for this dropping out was a lung ailment, though Hitler may have seized upon this in order to end a nagging quarrel with his mother. She had wanted him to continue his studies so that he might follow in the footsteps of his father.

The next few years were extremely happy ones for Hitler. His indulgent mother did not force him to work, and he was able to roam around the Danubian countryside to his heart's desire. Hitler could dream about his future as an artist while not having to go through the boring drudgery of school in Linz. Relatives helped his ailing mother, and thus the young Hitler did not have the natural responsibility of caring for the household. Eventually, he scraped together enough money in 1906 to visit Vienna, and with periodic interruptions he remained there until 1913.

2. Country Boy in the Big City: Vienna

At first, Hitler was ecstatic at the sight of the great Ringstrasse, the circular boulevard along which were found so many of the great imperial structures in this autumn of the Habsburg monarchy. Hitler acquired a taste for neoclassical architecture, along with a liking for the Austrian baroque and romantic styles. He was overwhelmed by the sight of these great buildings, and when an acquaintance or friend from the country would come into town, young Adolf would show him around the buildings of the city with a glowing look in his eyes. Perhaps as early as 1906 and 1907 he was thinking of a future career as an architect. For the time being, however, he tried to get admitted as an artist to the Vienna Academy of Fine Arts. He failed both in 1907 and 1908, and Hitler's second attempt met with even more contempt than his first. To Hitler, a sensitive, poorly trained peasant boy, these rebuffs from a great institutional center of the cultural life of the Habsburg monarchy must have indeed been painful. One can well imagine his resentment against his social betters and their conservative "rules." Hitler carried this social resentment with him throughout his life.

If there is one thing that Hitler disdained in life it was regular, methodical work. This he associated with his father, mediocrity, and lack of imagination. Despite his rebuffs, it was clear that Hitler would rather live in misery in Vienna than return to the placid countryside of

Braunau or Linz. When his mother died in 1907, Hitler became entitled, along with his sister, to a more generous pension from the Austrian state, and he frittered this away over the next few years. Where did Hitler sleep during this "time of struggle" in Vienna? In flophouses, occasionally in rooms co-rented with his friend August Kubizek, and at times probably on benches.

The outstanding characteristic of young Adolf's personality in these years was a strange combination of extreme romanticism with an increasingly heavy burden of social resentment and anxiety. For years, we are told, Hitler was in love at a distance with a beautiful Austrian girl of upper-class background named Stephanie, and he would have to gaze on in despair as she drove off in a coach with handsome young officers of the Imperial Guards. He was much taken with the music of Wagner as well as with popular Viennese operettas. Kubizek tells us that although Hitler totally lacked any technical knowledge of music, he at one point attempted to compose an opera along Wagnerian lines.

There is some circumstantial indication that Hitler may have contracted syphilis during this period. It is true that when he was Führer and Reich Chancellor venereologists were attached to his medical staff, and that in 1942 Heinrich Himmler, his police chief and Reichsführer of the SS, showed *his* physician a secret report implying that Hitler was in the last stage of paralytic syphilis. Much of the information about Hitler in this period, however, has to be studied with a great deal of caution. Here is an example of the problem. On the one hand, we have overwhelming evidence for a portrait of Hitler as the type of aimless, lonely vagabond and dreamy romantic whom we have just portrayed. On the other hand, August Kubizek says that Hitler would go to an opera, and despite his shabby appearance, women of good social standing would be so taken with his profound gaze that they would send him notes during intermission suggesting assignations. Too often, historians of National Socialism have portrayed the political genius of a later period as a complete break with the aimless vagabond of this period, suggesting that it was enough that Hitler discovered politics in 1919 for him to become what he did. It is difficult to believe that Hitler had no intimation of his amazing charismatic powers, even during this shabby stage of his life. It is far more plausible that his very understanding of his own unrealized potential fed the resentment which so twisted his character in these early years.

During these decades the Habsburg monarchy was in the autumn of its existence. It was racked by conflicts among different nationalities, as long-dormant Slavic peoples rediscovered a militant sense of their own national identity. In Bohemia, Czechs struggled with the powerful German minority over the use of Czech in schools and the administration. South Slavs battled Germans in Carinthia and Carniola. Poles struggled to suppress the aspirations of the Ukrainian peasantry in eastern Galicia, and Hungarians attempted to repress their Rumanian and Slovak subjects in the eastern or Transleithian part of the monarchy. There was universal manhood suffrage in the Austrian part of the monarchy after 1907, and this turned the Austrian Reichsrat or Lower House into an absurdly undignified carnival involving the deputies of different nationalities. They would sometimes blow horns, throw inkwells at each other, and shout obscenities. In seeing this spectacle the young Adolf Hitler must have been profoundly unimpressed with the glories of parliamentary democracy. The more he saw of Vienna, the more Hitler became enamored of chauvinist German culture and German nationalism. The more he saw, the more contempt he had for this ramshackle Habsburg monarchy, for its aged, peculiarly beloved Emperor Franz Joseph, and for its squabbling Slavic and non-Germanic minorities. The Germans were but a third of the population in the Cisleithian (or Austrian) part of the monarchy. The western part of the monarchy, which was dominated by the Germans, was increasingly beleaguered by the demands of South Slavs and Czechs.

In the eastern or Transleithian part of the monarchy, the Magyars of Hungary were the ruling ethnic group, though comprising less than 50 percent of the population. They lorded it over a majority or near majority of Slovaks, Rumanians, and South Slavs. It was during this period that Hitler acquired his contempt for the aristocratic pretensions of these Hungarians. On the surface, the Magyars and the Germans seemed to be allies in their work of suppressing the aspirations of the Slavic peoples of the monarchy. In fact, the struggles between the Magyars in Budapest and the German authorities in Vienna had gone on since the eighteenth century, and the *Ausgleich* or "compromise" of 1867, which divided the monarchy, had not resolved important questions. Among these was the amount to be donated by Budapest to Vienna for expenses incurred by matters of common constitutional interest, such as foreign affairs and defense. Hitler saw the Magyar gentry and magnates as irritating factors undermining German hegemony in western Austia, thereby aiding the Slavic hordes.

While Germany was seemingly on the road to world power, about to challenge Great Britain on the high seas and achieve imperialist status, Austria was prey to the type of conflict which we have described. Franz Joseph had reigned since 1848, and he had presided over the gradual disintegration of the monarchy and the rise of peoples such as the Czechs and the South Slavs. He had lost territory to the despised Italians. It was freely booted about in Vienna that when Franz Joseph died the Habsburg monarchy, despite the mournful glow of a great Indian summer, would be buried with him.

In coming to Vienna, Hitler came to a city which was undergoing the agonies of modern social change. Industry was developing in many parts of the monarchy, particularly in Bohemia, while Vienna itself was the great center of Central European trade and commerce. This

was a different world from the simple pastoral setting of
Hitler's youth. In the world of Vienna he learned that
life was a brutal series of disappointments, a constant
struggle. Hitler saw class conflict everywhere, not least of
all in the great parades of workers on May Day as the
Social-Democratic Party began to agitate more and more
openly for the demands of the proletariat. The worker
at least had his trade union and the Social-Democratic
Party; he also had a trade. Hitler, the petit bourgeois vagabond from the Lower Austrian countryside, had refused
at an earlier age to do what most youths in Austria and
Central Europe did: follow in the footsteps of their
fathers. He disdained regular work, feeling himself an
artist, daydreaming week after week and month after
month. Hitler belonged to no class or profession, he was
rootless. This alone was a major factor in his adherence
to racial ideology at this time. Here was a theory which
made part of a greater whole, one which gave him roots.
Hitler was impressed by the solidarity of the Socialist
movement in Austria, but given his social background
and lack of regular habits, his thinking in terms of *personal* resentment rather than collective *social* conflict,
young Adolf could only resent and fear the Marxism
which he saw in the streets. He saw it reflected in the
impressive lines of workers marching abreast in endless
columns in various demonstrations and celebrations.

Hitler had wanted to be an artist, but he had been
turned down by the Vienna Academy of Fine Arts. He
was also rejected by the architectural faculty. Hitler was
a member of the *Lumpenproletariat* during this period. He
earned a meager living in a variety of ways after his pension ran out in 1910. Hitler may have cleaned carpets,
done some house painting, sold handpainted postcards
of scenes in Vienna to tourists. In this latter enterprise
he had a partner by the name of Hanisch, with whom
he later had a falling out. He caused Hanisch to be put
in jail for a week for cheating him. Hitler would paint
the postcards and Hanisch would sell them on the streets.
Presumably, the profits would be split. It is interesting

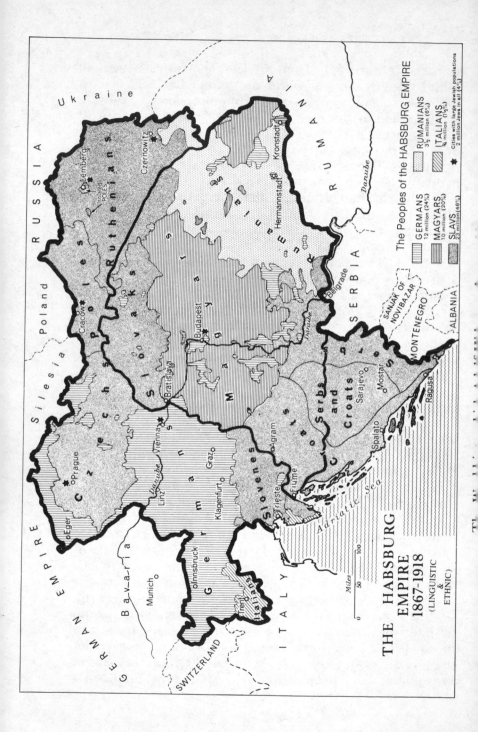

The Peoples of the HABSBURG EMPIRE

GERMANS 12 million (24%)
MAGYARS 10 million (20%)
SLAVS 23 million (48%)
RUMANIANS 3½ million (6%)
ITALIANS ¾ million (1%)
★ Cities with large Jewish populations
2 million Jews in all (4%)

THE HABSBURG EMPIRE
1867-1918
(LINGUISTIC & ETHNIC)

Miles
0   50   100

that Hitler's artwork, even at this stage, was extremely antihumanistic. His cold scenes of great buildings, devoid of human images, were done in the impressionist manner so popular during that epoch. The sugary impressionism of Hitler's painting paralleled the escapist operettas that were so popular at the time. Hitler was enamored of these operettas during his whole life.

This combination of sentimentality, starkness, and misery left an indelible imprint upon Hitler's character. He set up psychological defense mechanisms around himself so that later in life few individuals could say they were his friend. Even Albert Speer only went so far as to say that if Hitler had been capable of true friendship, Speer would have been his first friend. In the true petit bourgeois manner, Hitler saw the forces around him as personalized and conspiratorial. He saw himself victimized at every turn in the great metropolis, thwarted by decadent Establishment institutions such as the Academy of Fine Arts. Hitler hated the Establishment because it was not protecting the Germanic race, nor was it furthering his own aspirations. Later, while writing *Mein Kampf* in the 1920's, Hitler looked upon the pre-1914 leadership in the German Reich as a failure. At this time, however, before the First World War, he seemed to look enviously upon his great Germanic neighbor to the north. In this he was not alone in Austria.

3. The Austrian Caldron

Numerous conflicting social forces emerged in late-nineteenth-century Austria-Hungary. The rise of an industrial proletariat in Bohemia and the greaterVienna area presaged an era of social conflict, but even the Social-Democratic movement in Austria was to be torn by the thorny nationalities question. The Czech workers in 1910 probably wanted Czech independence as much if not more than they wanted class solidarity with the Austro-German proletariat. Certain Marxist and Social-

Democratic leaders like Otto Bauer and Karl Renner tried to come to grips creatively with the nationalities question; indeed, such Marxists did not necessarily see the Habsburg monarchy as a retrogressive factor. Some Socialists felt that it might become the nucleus of a vast economic unit in Central Europe. Marx and Engels themselves had, in Greater-German nationalist fashion, been most suspicious of the aspirations of "backward" peoples such as the Czechs and the South Slavs. A rising Socialism was one of the major forces in the Vienna which Hitler knew before 1913.

The rise of Austrian Socialism late in the nineteenth century weakened liberalism, which, in however inadequate a fashion, might have made some attempt to come to grips with the forces which disrupted Europe in the twentieth century. As early as 1882, leading Austrian liberals, meeting in the city of Linz—Georg von Schoenerer, Viktor Adler, and Heinrich Friedjung—reexamined classical liberalism and found it wanting. Liberalism was everywhere dependent upon the favor of the new middle classes of the nineteenth century, but this urban middle class was weak in the overwhelmingly rural, patriarchal Habsburg monarchy. In addition, in Vienna it was largely Jewish. Its future was in any case limited, for liberalism had long been associated with Greater-German domination of the Danubian basin, and hence was unacceptable to the rising national minorities of the empire. In addition, the creation of Bismarck's Prussian-German Reich cut off the Austrian liberal middle classes from their somewhat more influential German equivalent. The Catholic Church was still extremely powerful in Austria, and Franz Joseph was a pious believer who preferred to govern with the approbation of the Church against the liberals, rather than vice versa. The Church was hostile to the new developments of late-nineteenth-century Austria—the great cities, the Jewish liberal press, the industrial transformation—and the liberals were involved in all of these forces. As national and class tensions increased, liberals, particularly those of Jewish origin, were vulnerable targets for the despair of different groups. Viktor Adler abandoned liberalism after 1882 for Marxian Socialism while Friedjung still considered himself a liberal. But this brilliant historian became a strident Greater-German nationalist, thus associating Austrian liberalism more closely than ever with German domination in the western half of the Habsburg monarchy.

Georg von Schoenerer broke with liberalism after 1882, becoming the founder of Austrian Pan-Germanism. Hitler had some kind things to say about him in *Mein Kampf,* though he criticized his heavy-handed anti-Catholic propaganda. Georg von Schoenerer, who had a patent of nobility due to his father's pioneering work in the development of the Austrian railroad system, was a violent opponent of the Habsburg monarchy. He was also an early racial anti-Semite of whom Hitler was to write glowingly in *Mein Kampf.* Von Schoenerer was a product of the emerging struggle between Czech and German in Bohemia. He felt that the Habsburg monarchy was throttling the natural hegemony of the Germans in Central Europe. "Knight George" despised the Habsburgs and praised the Hohenzollerns. He hated the Catholic Church, coining the phrase "*Los von Rom*" or "away from Rome." His followers at times went so far as to practice a sort of "Wagnerian," neo-Germanic paganism, something which was politically stupid in pious, Catholic Austria (as Hitler pointed out in *Mein Kampf*). Von Schoenerer's Pan-German followers often behaved in the manner of future storm troopers or gangsters, breaking up the presses of publishers who had supposedly insulted "His majesty the German Emperor." They sang "Deutschland über Alles" and greeted each other with the Germanic "Heil," something they may have inherited from the German nationalist "Turnvater" Jahn, who had flourished early in the nineteenth century. The vision of von Schoenerer's followers was apocalyptic, a sure sign of what was coming in Central Europe. They saw the battle between German and Slav not as the political history of a struggle for hegemony, but as a blood struggle for existence. This impressed Hitler mightily. When von Schoenerer died, his group seemed to fade with him, but the ideas he had implanted were to bear fruit in Austria in the chaotic days after the collapse of the Habsburg monarchy in 1918. This was most true in the "Sudetenland" in Bohemia, which became part of the hated Czech state.

Georg von Schoenerer was not the only politician in the Habsburg monarchy whom Adolf Hitler later praised. He had great respect for Karl Lüger, mayor of Vienna in the first decade of this century. Lüger was in part the type of urban social reformer who was to be found in other areas at the time. One thinks, for example, of the Chamberlain family in Birmingham, England, or of urban progressives in the United States. Lüger municipalized many of the essential services of the city of Vienna, taking them out of the hands of foreign capitalists. He was a friend of the Viennese little man, of the petty bourgeoisie. Lüger was a pious Catholic who was violently opposed to liberalism, which in Vienna seemed largely to be in the hands of upper-middle-class Jewish capitalists. This won him great popularity at a time when liberalism was increasingly vulnerable. Lüger showed Hitler how to use anti-Semitism as a political device, but it must be said that Hitler later found Lüger's anti-Semitism somewhat wanting since Lüger, as he himself once put it, decided "who was a Jew." In other words, Lüger was not a racial anti-Semite. His anti-Semitism was an economic and electoral device, not a genocidal racial concept. In this Hitler saw him as inferior to von Schoenerer. Hitler disdainfully wrote in *Mein Kampf* that, given Lüger's anti-Semitism, if things really got bad for the Jews, "a few drops of baptismal water" would take care of the problem. Thus, the liberalism that Hitler saw in Vienna was to a great extent Jewish; further, it was anticlerical and urban, it represented successful elements in

a changing society. For Socialism Hitler could have little
use, given his class background and psychological pro-
pensities. Hitler appreciated von Schoenerer's *racial* anti-
Semitism and fervent German nationalism, and he
respected Lüger both for his attempt to help the little
man and for his electoral use of anti-Semitism.

What was Hitler's Vienna like? For Hitler the Vienna
of 1912 was largely a gloomy, overcast place in which he
lived in misery. It was a place of great beauty and great
frustrations. Hitler was later to write that Vienna was the
hard school of life for him, one in which he learned the
basic lessons of his ideology and his struggle. Yet this
does not seem to have been so much a time of struggle
for Hitler as a time in which he was buffeted about by
an indifferent fate. He nursed resentments which were to
later explode into war and murder. There was a great
cultural revival in Vienna in this period. This was the
civilization, after all, which produced or nurtured men
such as Sigmund Freud, Gustav Mahler, Arthur
Schnitzler, and Hugo von Hofmannsthal. This high culture, however, was not what Hitler came into contact with
during these years. He saw the grim side of Vienna,
counting himself lucky when he could afford to stand at
a popular operetta or a Wagnerian tragedy. Hitler saw
the misery of the streets, and one can image the psychic
dislocation that such a rural boy might suffer, given these
new surroundings.

4. Adolf Hitler at Twenty-four

There was no city in the world in which popular anti-
Semitism was more deeply rooted than in Vienna. Hitler
later said that he was at first repelled by the violence of
the popular anti-Semitic publications in the city. According to his own account, he had known Jews in Linz, but
they had looked more or less like everybody else. In
Vienna he came into contact with Jews in the long black

garb of their Eastern European or Galician brethren. This repelled him. He tells us that he said to himself, "Can this be a German?" In Vienna, as in many other Eastern European cities, the Jews played a major role in retail trade and the media. Although Hitler seems at one point to have gotten his one shabby overcoat as a gift from a Jewish merchant named Neumann, his contacts with individual Jews appear to have been very few. One theory, later recounted by flophouse intimates of the future Führer, suggests that Hitler may have contracted syphilis around 1912 from a Jewish prostitute named Hannah. True or not, this was the low type of association which Hitler conceivably may have had with Jews during this period. Anti-Semitic material in Vienna was often pornographic. If we consider that Hitler was going through a period of severe adolescent and early-manhood sexual stress and quest for identity, the impact of such an obscene portrayal of the diabolical Jewish stranger male whom Hitler saw all around him may indeed have been profound.

Hitler later said that behind every filthy business in Vienna was a Jew. He saw the Jew as undermining the morality of the German people. The Jew was an urban force, a liberal presence, a force for progressive social change. Hitler, by contrast, came from the Austrian countryside, and despite his later "Nietzschean" cynicism, he was a profoundly conservative petit bourgeois in his public social and sexual mores. He saw the Jew behind every disintegrative aspect of contemporary life: socialism, prostitution, pornography, the collapse of Germany. The Jew was the alien stranger upon whom Hitler could project all of his own fears and fantasies. Did Hitler fear incest because of the degree of consanguinity between his father and his mother? Well, everyone "knew" that the Jews were products of incest, of close inbreeding, or as Hitler put it, of *"tiefe Inzucht,"* in the teeming, filthy ghettos of Galicia and Poland. Did Hitler fear venereal disease with a particular horror possibly because he had con-

tracted it at the age of twenty-three? Then the Jew was
the pimp behind the prostitute, the "bacteria of decom-
position" attempting to destroy the moral and physical
health of the German people by infecting them. There
may thus have been a strong psychotic element in Hitler's
acquisition of anti-Semitism. According to his own
account, he must have acquired this anti-Semitism
between the ages of seventeen and twenty-four, that is,
during the time of what Erik Erikson calls the "crisis of
identity" in late adolescence and early manhood.

This crisis was only the second part of a continuing
period of turmoil in Hitler's adolescent life. The first part
had been the revolt against his father, and his subsequent
feelings of guilt. Erikson has gone so far in his study of
Hitler's childhood as to say that there was a peculiarly
Central European pattern to it: revolt, guilt, atonement,
then a sense of purity in sexual matters. This would fit
Hitler's adolescence. It would not be surprising if he had
visited a prostitute in Vienna in 1912. If Hitler thus contracted syphilis, one can only imagine his shamed feelings
of guilt. These feelings of guilt, needing an outlet, would
find the Jew ready at hand.

In 1913 Hitler was a man of twenty-four. He had
absolutely no prospects in life, no trade, no future. The
army was after him, for there was conscription in the
Habsburg monarchy. He crossed the frontier to Munich
in this same year, possibly to avoid military service.
Things did not go much better for him in Munich, at
least until August of 1914. Hitler had left the Habsburg
monarchy behind him, though the despised derelict
would return to Vienna in triumph in the spring of 1938.
He had already acquired the fundamentals of his world
view. Hitler had spent many hours in coffeehouses and
canteens in Vienna reading newspapers and arguing
about politics. Even at this point he seems to have been
extremely intolerant of others' opinions. There is something about Hitler's mind which is typical of a modern
popular newspaper reader. Hitler showed quickness in

picking up concepts, but much more hesitation about making a careful study of them. Hitler claimed that he read widely in the public library of Vienna during this time. How widely we will probably never know, but he seemed to have bits of information about everything. In this Hitler was the proverbial arrogant, self-taught individual. He typically displayed open contempt but secret respect for that formal education which he had never enjoyed.

Hitler emerged from his Vienna years a sort of vagabond for all seasons, a man with ideas about many things but totally lacking in preparation for any one thing. He came into Vienna a dreamy, romantic, repressed, proud, involuted adolescent. He left with an ideology of racial hatred and a more pronounced personal neurosis. Hitler believed in idealized romantic love for woman, but he learned in Vienna that life is a sewer, a scramble for bare existence. He believed in the Greater German idea, but he saw Jews and Slavs undermining it everywhere. He believed in a natural racial aristocracy, but saw a corrupt Reichsrat making a laughingstock out of the Germans.

Hitler was probably influenced by some of the Nordic racialism floating about in this period, but to what extent it is difficult to say. He, like many other serious Nazi ideologists, seemed to take the virtues, goodness, and martial prowess of the Germans for granted. These "thinkers" spent much more time elaborating the counter-evil of the Jew. Unlike Himmler, who waxed poetic and romantic over the Nordic ideal, Hitler was always more interested in projecting inherent evils onto the Jews than in celebrating the greatness of the Teutonic race. In Munich in 1913 and 1914 Hitler led an uncertain, irregular life, ever in fear that the police authorities would ultimately ship him back to Austria for military service or jail.

His life suddenly took on meaning in late July and early August of 1914, when an international crisis, having its origins in the faraway Balkans, shook Europe and changed both its history and the life of Adolf Hitler. Hitler's career and Europe's destiny began a union which was to end in the *Reichsbunker* under Berlin almost thirty-one grim years later.

CHAPTER II

War and Politics as Salvation, 1914-1924

1. Corporal Adolf Hitler

WHEN Hitler was already famous as a leader of the National Socialist movement, an enterprising observer went over photographs of the cheering Bavarian crowd in the Odeonsplatz in Munich in early August, 1914. Using a magnifying glass, he discovered the enchanted face of the twenty-five-year-old Adolf Hitler, his expression transfixed by ecstasy as the royal declaration of war was read to the happy crowd. Adolf Hitler had not yet found his calling in life, but soon he volunteered for the Royal Bavarian Army, which under the German constitution came under German Imperial command in wartime. Hitler served in the army until the spring of 1920.

Adolf Hitler's life and that of Europe were forever altered by the events of 1914. In war Hitler found what he had never found in peace. He became a whole human being, for his life took on meaning. Unlike most soldiers, Hitler had little use for furlough, for he had no one at home he wanted to see, nor anywhere to go. The danger of combat put him into a state of exultation, and the aimless, skinny private of 1914 became a man in whom idea and reality finally merged. The phlegmatic German nationalist of 1910 became the brave runner of messages between trenches on the western front. Hitler received the Iron Cross twice, once in 1914 and again in 1918. He was always extraordinarily proud of his Iron Cross, First Class and wore it most of the time after he became Chancellor of the German Reich on January 30, 1933. When a political opposition newspaper once accused him of having been a coward in World War I, Hitler was so enraged that he brought a libel suit against it. Although the precise record of his military accomplishments seems to have mysteriously vanished from the Defense Ministry after he became Chancellor, there is little reason to doubt that Hitler was a brave soldier in the Great War. What is peculiar is that given the high mortality rate among German officers, this brave lance corporal was never considered for promotion to officer status. However, it is highly possible that Hitler did not push for such a promotion, but was so happy in his work and in the sense of shared purpose with his plebeian comrades that he never wanted it.

We must try to imagine the exultation that Adolf Hitler felt in war, however repugnant it may be to us. For over forty years the German nation had been schooled in the victories of 1864, 1866, and 1871. To be a reserve second lieutenant in the Royal Prussian or Imperial German army was a sign of tremendous social status for the rising bourgeois. In 1914 Germany was a society which still had enormous respect for feudal social mores, though it had gone far on the road to industrial capitalism. Hitler had a love for Germany before he came to Munich in 1913, and being part of the German military machine, however indirectly, he was under the command of titans such as Ludendorff and von Hindenburg. This alone must have given him an overwhelming sense of well-being. Hitler worshiped the German military machine during these years, especially the German General Staff, about which he was later to say many unkind things.

There is a scene in Jean Renoir's 1938 film *The Grand Illusion* which may give us some insight into the way Hitler, the new German, felt during the Great War of 1914-1918. In this film a group of French prisoners sees a German military band and troops march by its barracks. All talking and joking stop, and the men are transfixed by the serried ranks and the rousing marches with their musical touch of heroism and pathos. This is what Hitler found in the Great War, and this is what he never forgot. Such indeed was the widely shared experience that the Germans called the *Fronterlebnis* or "front experience." It transformed the life of many individuals. We are accustomed to talking about the pacifist literature, such as Erich Maria Remarque's *All Quiet on the Western Front,* which emerged in Germany after the First World War. Yet there was another side to the story, the side which concerned a man like Hitler. This was the feeling that the great trials of trench warfare truly tried men's souls, and made individuals who had been aimless in civilian life heroes in military uniform. Ernst Jünger and Ernst von Salomon reflected this sense of the *Fronterlebnis* in post-1918 Germany. Men like Hitler felt no regrets over their service in the war; indeed, it had been the most meaningful *spiritual* experience of their lives. Hundreds of thousands of such men went about Germany in the early 1920's with pins on their lapels which read *Im Felde niemals besiegt* or "never conquered in the field."

Hitler later affirmed that a good German march was worth more than any modern "musical trash," by which he presumably meant twelve-tone or atonal music. In this Hitler was also saying that the sentimentality of an Austrian march such as the "Radetzsky March" or even Austrian waltz music was inferior to rousing German marches such as the "Hohenfriedberger" or the "King Frederick the Great," which he heard so often after 1913. Hitler associated himself fully with the fate of the German Reich from August, 1914, and it is interesting that at no later point, according to his recorded statements, did he feel any sense of superiority or sentimentality about his Austrian origins. Despite his continued love for rich pastry and waltz music, Hitler turned his back on the Habsburg monarchy. This is indeed unusual, since he had come to Germany in his mid-twenties. His emotional break with old Austria was complete.

In the trenches Hitler fortified some of the hatreds which he had acquired long before 1914: hatred for the French, who thwarted Germany in its European ambitions, and hatred for the British Empire, which blocked Imperial Germany's drive for a place in the sun. England, after all, was a "Nordic" power which had stabbed Germany in the back in 1914 by allying herself with the decadent French. *Gott strafe England* or "May God punish England" was a popular slogan in Germany during the Great War. Hitler's sense of the eastern front and of the peoples to the east, particularly those in Russia, was probably vague at this point, though it would be fortified by contact with White Russian émigrés after 1920.

On November 11 or 12, 1918, Adolf Hitler was in a military hospital in Pasewalk, recovering from blinding due to a mustard gas attack, when he learned of Germany's armistice with the Allies. He tells us in *Mein Kampf* that this was the blackest hour of his life. The German war, which had given his life meaning, had suddenly ended in a horrible defeat. In 1902 he thought that being an artist would give meaning to his life, and his father had attempted to thwart him. In the following year, however, his father had died and his life again took on substance. In 1918 Hitler felt himself at one with the German national idea, the idea that had seemingly been defeated. But it is possible that Hitler, drawing upon emotional analogy, felt that from within himself he would muster the strength that would raise Germany from the ashes and smite her enemies. This would give Germany and her son, Adolf Hitler, life once again.

2. Versailles and Weimar

Hitler, enamored with the front, had had little contact with the home front during the past four years. He knew that the German army had not been totally smashed in the field, but had seemingly suffered a few "tactical" defeats in the autumn of 1918. Hence, he could not see that the German military defeat was a result of collective forces beyond the control of any individual. The British blockade, superior Allied might due to the arrival of troops from the associated power, the United States; these, plus internal exhaustion in Germany, both military and civilian, accounted for the defeat of the Second Reich. A mere forty-seven years before Bismarck had founded this Reich, a mighty German state. These were not forces which Hitler, who as a petit bourgeois personalized everything, could comprehend. He was a prey to early rumors about stabs in the back and conspiracies.

In 1914, the blustering yet frightened Emperor Wilhelm II had proclaimed that "I no longer recognize any political parties, only Germans." This civil peace or *Burgfrieden* lasted well into 1917, when parties and interests began squabbling among themselves over war aims and peace strategies. There was widespread famine and misery in Germany from 1917 to 1919 due to the Allied blockade. Left-wing and revolutionary pacifist groups attracted broad support, even in military and naval ranks, for a speedy end to the war. There was a great deal of suspicion of the imperialist war aims of the real leaders of the German war effort, Hindenburg and Ludendorff. The Social-Democrats, who had overwhelmingly gone along with the government in the war effort until the spring of 1917, finally grew restless. This was largely as a result of pressure from below. The successful Bolshevik Revolution in Russia in the autumn of 1917 further encouraged the Socialist and pacifist aspirations of large segments of the German population. Hitler was totally blind to these objective historical factors. He came to believe in a conspiracy by Bolsheviks, Jews, and Social-Democrats. Blind to the incompetence of the Imperial leadership, Hitler felt that this conspiracy had cheated Germany out of her victory, and had wasted the blood of two million of her finest sons. Hitler felt that the blackest hour of his life, the day of the Armistice, must have been the result of a conspiracy, the type of conspiracy which had victimized him in his artistic and architectural ambitions in Vienna before 1913.

Adolf Hitler saw the collapse of Austria, which preceded that of Germany, as a further case of conspiracy and treason. Much later, in February of 1938, when he had a stormy interview with his archenemy Chancellor Schuschnigg of Austria, Hitler told that hapless man that the whole history of Austria "was one long treason." Austria, like his father, represented the betrayal of a creative idea, in this case, of the German national idea. This idea involved the survival of the German nation and its ultimate triumph in Europe.

The armistice of November 11, 1918 had come as a profound shock to German public opinion. Most Germans did not know that their great war leader Ludendorff had told the Kaiser weeks earlier that the war was lost and that the politicians must seek terms from the Allies. When the armistice came, most Germans assumed that the ultimate peace treaty would be based upon Woodrow Wilson's relatively lenient Fourteen Points, first drafted in January of 1918. One of the cruelest disappointments for them was the harshness of the Treaty of Versailles, which was signed on June 28, 1919, over the protest of German groups ranging from majority Social-Democrats to right-wing militarists. Yet military defeat (and such it was) was not the only shock that German public opinion had had to bear in the months before the armistice. In October and November of 1918 the collapse of Germany's allies Bulgaria and Austria-Hungary had weakened the Reich's position in critical areas of Central and Southeastern Europe.

After four years of privation, grumbling over the shortage of food, coal, and other vital items turned into strikes and revolution. The sailors in Kiel mutinied, fearing that their officers would send them out in a last vain attempt to cover the German Navy with honor in a hopeless clash with the Royal Navy. Militant German Marxists, organized in the Spartakusbund and in some cases in the Independent Social-Democratic Party of Germany, were thinking about violent revolution. They were in part inspired by Lenin's example in Russia. Revolutions broke out all over Germany in November of 1918. Hastily formed soldiers' and workers' councils took pacifist, republican, and antimilitary positions. A revulsion against militarism swept through many parts of the land. Against this chaotic background Wilhelm II, King of Prussia and German Emperor, abdicated and fled in a heavily guarded car to the Dutch frontier. He died in Dutch exile in 1941, but not before congratulating Hitler upon the collapse of France in the summer of 1940.

The German revolution of November, 1918 was hardly that. The majority Social-Democrats, long pariahs in Imperial Germany, had proven their patriotism by their steadfast support of the war since 1914. They now inherited power in the weakened German state, but they took it over against the background of internal chaos and external defeat. Germany had been a semiabsolutist, semiconstitutional state since 1871. Since 1890 it had lacked consistently strong leadership. The Social-Democrats had mistaken parliamentary strength for revolutionary power, and now in 1918 they fatally mistook a vacuum for a revolution. By this time it was clear that the German Socialists were split into at least two camps. There were the radical revolutionaries, led by individuals such as Rosa Luxemburg, a remarkable Marxist theoretician, and Karl Liebknecht, the son of one of the founders of German Marxism. The majority Social-Democrats were men who had usually supported the war and had often endorsed the imperial war aims of the German government. They came to power in November, 1918, and consolidated that power in the cruel winter of 1918-1919.

To Adolf Hitler, the collapse of the empire revealed that it had been a hollow shell all along. Nevertheless, Hitler was profoundly shocked by military defeat and by the sudden accession to power of Socialists such as Friedrich Ebert and Philipp Scheidemann, the proclaimers of the November Republic. Hitler forever after considered these men the "November criminals," individuals who had benefited from a stab in the back on the home front and an external military crisis. They did this in order to bring themselves to power and inaugurate a decadent, pacifist republic. Early in 1919, Adolf Hitler must have been deeply disturbed by the antimilitarist tendencies abroad in the population. Although these tendencies were largely a passing phase, decorations were ripped off the breasts of German officers as they returned from four years at the front. Left-wing pacifist propaganda was everywhere. The German middle class was frightened that the Bolshevik revolution, which had received much attention in Germany, might be repeated in the Reich.

In this situation, the German army, limited by the Allies in 1919 to about 100,000 men, came to the fore as the defender of the established order. The Social-Democrats were too powerful to challenge at this point, and with allies such as the German Democratic Party they were able to preserve a semblance of political continuity and order in the crisis years 1918-1920. The Social-Democrats collaborated with the Reichswehr in order to maintain order and crush the extreme left in cities such as Berlin and Hamburg. This was an unholy alliance, fatal to the progressive aspirations of the Socialists, but in the chaotic situation of 1919 men like Ebert, Scheidemann, and Hindenburg found out that they had more in common than they would have once believed. Ebert once said, "I hate social revolution, I hate it like sin." These majority Socialists had in part degenerated into middle-aged bureaucratic hacks, men who vaguely wanted to bring about reforms in German society. They feared disorder more than they desired social change. They were afraid of Lenin and Leninism, indeed their chief theoretician, Karl Kautsky, wrote several pamphlets against Lenin and Trotsky. Rosa Luxemburg had done the same thing, but from a democratic and radical viewpoint, not from the viewpoint of the preservation of the established (supposedly democratic) order.

The majority Socialists, the German Democratic Party, and liberal elements in German society drafted the constitution of the German Republic in Weimar in 1919. The Weimar assembly consisted of some of the best legal brains in German society, including a key figure such as Hugo Preuss. The document that they put forth was an extremely liberal one, borrowing from the American Constitution and the French Declaration of the Rights of Man. In an ultrademocratic mood, it provided for proportional representation, thus aiding ideological minorities in their quest for seats in the German Reichstag. This proved to be of dubious value in the 1920's, when extremist groups were thereby able to achieve a national platform and some prestige despite local and limited electoral strength. Further, the constitution had the famous Article 48, which allowed the Chancellor dictatorial powers in the time of a crisis as proclaimed by the Reich President. His decrees would have the force of law if countersigned by the President.

The Weimar constitution was a federal one, leaving a great deal of power to the individual states, many of which had a feeling of revulsion towards the Prussian domination that they had undergone since 1866 or 1871. This federalism was a double-edged sword, because it meant that reactionary, separatist forces could use a state such as Bavaria with relative impunity as a base for attacking the Republic in the years immediately after 1919. In effect, the Socialists helped bring about a middle-class republic in Germany. On the surface, 1918 was Germany's equivalent to France's 1789, for it made good the failed revolution of 1848. It was certainly not a Socialist revolution, though it did bring about certain reforms. The great landholders in East Elbia, the backbone of the reaction, maintained their control over their land and their peasants. The great industrialists of Saxony, Silesia, and the Ruhr were ultimately untouched by the vague Socialism of the Weimar constitution, and they survived the speeches of its creators. The bourgeois democracy brought about by the Weimar constitution came into being against an unhealthy background of defeat and repression. Despite the hopes of some of its creators in 1919, it was the product of despair and bitterness.

3. Freikorps and Reichswehr

Misery and despair were universal in Germany after the First World War. For many men, especially young officers, the Great War had been the great life. They now felt aimless in the Allies' 100,000-man German Reichswehr. Many of these men joined the Freikorps, answering the desperate appeal of adventurers and patriots to defend Germany's beleaguered frontiers against inferior breeds such as the Poles and the Czechs. The Freikorps men were adventurers who loved war for its own sake, men answering the patriotic call to defend Silesia and other areas against the resurgent Slavic menace. The Freikorps was a universal phenomenon in Central Europe in this period, though it went under different names. The Heimwehr in Austria, for example, owed its origins to the struggle with the South Slavs in the area beyond Klagenfurt. The Freikorps could also be used internally against left-wing enemies of the republic and German society. To the Freikorps men, such as a former officer like Captain Ernst Röhm, the German Republic was a treasonous farce to be attacked and overthrown with impunity. To many Germans, the Freikorps was an outlet for frustrated militaristic and patriotic sentiments. Thousands of men flocked into it, not wanting to give up the heroic, virile life of the battlefield.

The Freikorps was used in the bloody suppression of the Communist republic in Munich in April, 1919. Wherever it went in Germany, it brought about a white terror before which the so-called red terror paled in intensity. These men had been brutalized by years of war-fare, and they now used their weapons against their own suspected left-wing countrymen. The German middle class had been frightened by the sudden appearance of a Soviet republic under Bela Kún in Hungary early in 1919. At about the same time, Kurt Eisner, the Inde-pendent Socialist Prime Minister of Bavaria, who had led the revolution there in November of 1918, was assas-sinated. After a great deal of political infighting, a Com-munist republic emerged in Munich for a short period of time. The Freikorps helped to crush this "menace," but many elements of the German bourgeoisie never for-got this immediate threat of "Bolshevism."

This, then, was the Germany to which Adolf Hitler returned when he was released from the hospital at Pasewalk. Hitler was in no hurry to leave the army. He had no civilian career or family to which to return. So he carried out or volunteered for various assignments such as guarding the prisoner-of-war camp at Traun-stein, near the Austrian frontier. Pictures of Hitler dur-ing the First World War show him as a young man of average height, rather thin, with a shaggy mustache. Except for his eyes, he bears little resemblance to the paunchier, better-groomed figure of the late 1920's. De-spite Hitler's undoubted oratorical potential the relatively (if deceptively) stable German society of the prewar period would have offered little scope for his activities. Demagogues preaching similar messages had occasionally been elected to the Reichstag or had been the authors of best-selling books, but in the long run their careers in Imperial Germany had not been successful.

In the demoralized, hysterical atmosphere of the immediate postwar period, Hitler was to seize his oppor-tunity. His interest in politics had increased with the war, and in the collapse of Germany he had seen the great political catastrophe of the age. He could not accept this collapse as a military one because this would imply that both the German army and Adolf Hitler had failed. He saw the collapse as the result of revolution and sabotage by Jews and Bolsheviks. This was an attitude furthered soon after the war by respectable figures such as Erich Ludendorff, the great strategist, who had been Quartermaster General of the German army. Eventually, Hitler's interest in politics led him to small-scale work for the Reichswehr in Bavaria as a political informer and educator *(Bildungsoffizier)*. This was the great age of the drifting ex-soldier in many parts of Europe. One need only think, for example, of the *squadristi* or Black Shirts of Mussolini's Fascist movement, formed in Italy in 1919.

The Reichswehr was interested in various fringe political groups on the right, especially in Bavaria. It wanted to see if they might be useful in subverting the Treaty of Versailles and in keeping alive extreme nationalist sentiment. All over Germany right-wing societies of a nationalist and racialist stamp sprang up. They shared in common a hatred of the Versailles treaty and of the "November Republic." Such ideological groups, made up of social misfits, spokesmen for special interests, and isolated publicists, had existed in Germany well before 1918. They now took on respectability, however, and they were patronized by official organizations such as the Reichswehr. This was only natural, for their ranks were swollen with ex-soldiers and officers. In Bavaria, public opinion after the Soviet Republic and the White Terror was especially favorable to any actions which would circumvent the Treaty of Versailles. Furthermore, Bavaria was a natural homeland for "anti-Prussian," anti-Berlin, anti-German Republic sentiments, for it was basically Catholic and conservative. In Bavaria powerful military groups marched about openly, despite protest from the Allies and the Berlin government. The local command of the Reichswehr was later in the hands of men such as von Lossow, who was sympathetic to the extreme nationalist cause.

4. The German Workers' Party

On a fateful day in September, 1919, the Bavarian Reichswehr command ordered Adolf Hitler to go to a meeting of the German Workers' Party (DAP), which was holding one of its periodic assemblies in Munich. This party, which was led by Karl Harrer and Anton Drexler, consisted of a very small membership. Its few adherents were to be found almost entirely in the city of Munich and its environs. Almost every political group, no matter how insignificant, considered itself "radical" in the uneasy social and political situation of 1919. This, after all, was the great age not only of the front-fighter, but. also of the worker. The proletarian had seemingly come into his own with the new democratic order prevailing in the world. All parties considered themselves "parties of the workers." The German Workers' Party was no exception. Karl Harrer had been a member of the *Thule Gesellschaft,* a racialist society whose ideas would not have shocked Adolf Hitler in 1919. Hitler had been exposed to similar concepts in the publication *Ostara* in the Vienna of 1912. Anton Drexler was a locksmith who worked in a railroad yard. He had the typical petit bourgeois hostility towards trade unionism and Marxism. These men, along with four others, made up the steering committee and regular membership of the German Workers' Party in 1919.

After going to another meeting, Hitler was impressed by the faith and determination of the small group. Soon after becoming acquainted with it, he became Party member #555 and seventh member of the Party steering committee. Because of this, the rumor later spread that Hitler was #7 in Party membership. On his own party card the 555 was ultimately rubbed out and the 7 substituted for it. While Hitler was not the seventh Party member, neither was he merely #555, for the membership numbers had been inflated by the small Party in order to give an impression of greater size. There may have been fifty or a hundred members of the Party who preceded Hitler in joining it.

Hitler was a jumble of confused emotions and political feelings at this time, and 1919 was to be a crucial year in his political education. He read *My Political Awakening* by Anton Drexler, which reads like a confused grab bag of crank economic theories, hostility to big capitalism, fanatic nationalism, and anti-Semitism. In this pamphlet Hitler found a more articulate, ordered statement of his own beliefs. In addition, Hitler was soon exposed to the thoughts of another early member of the DAP, Dietrich Eckart, a racial theoretician and alcoholic who combined mystic Germanic racialism and anti-Semitism with some journalistic and scholarly ability. Eckart was the editor of the *Racial Observer (Völkischer Beobachter)* before Alfred Rosenberg took over that position. His ideas seem to have influenced Hitler, and he authored a pamphlet called *Bolshevism from Moses to Lenin: A Dialogue Between Adolf Hitler and Myself.* The early German Workers' Party was made up of fringe semi-intellectuals and cranks, social misfits, and extremists. In the chaos of contemporary German society they saw an opportunity for personal realization which had been denied to them in a more stable social structure.

Even after Hitler became a member of the DAP, he continued to serve in the army as a lecturer in citizenship extension courses for former soldiers. The Reichswehr had discovered his oratorical ability, as had the DAP, and they both made use of it in this hard winter of 1919-1920. Hitler's first official position as part of the steering committee of the DAP was as *Werbeobmann* or propaganda and recruitment chief. One of the things that probably attracted him to this party, besides its confused ideology, was the opportunity to dominate a small, fragmented group. From its beginnings, there were differences in emphasis among the different members of the DAP. Hitler was concerned about the Jews, the Weimar Republic, and the Treaty of Versailles. Gottfried Feder was more involved with the economics of "interest slavery" than anything else. There was a common hostility to big capitalism among these petit-bourgeois members of the

DAP. They all hated the large department stores and economic concerns which had made life economically untenable for them, or so they thought. Economics was never one of Hitler's major concerns.

5. Adolf Hitler and the Ideology of Agitation

Hitler's role as a speaker gave him tremendous leverage with the other members of the steering committee. He could pack several hundred people into a beer hall in Munich, whereas the first meeting of the DAP that he had attended saw perhaps twenty or twenty-five men sitting about in a desultory manner in an ill-lit hall. Hitler's style of speaking was histrionic. Then and later, he would pose for photographers in a faintly ridiculous theatrical manner. Hitler practiced his speeches before a mirror. There was little doubt about the quality or the timbre of his voice. At times Hitler sounded like a Wagnerian *Heldentenor,* modulating the hysteria in his voice in order to achieve maximum effect. He repeated certain themes over and over again, reinforcing his own certainty and attempting to convert his listeners. In one of the most original passages in *Mein Kampf,* Hitler spoke about the nature of propaganda. He, like Joseph Goebbels, put great faith in the spoken word. Hitler felt that the spoken word was at the root of all successful revolutions in history, from that of Moses to that of Lenin. Indeed, a painting by a Nazi artist in the 1930's showed Hitler addressing an early meeting of the German Workers' Party, with the caption (stolen from the Gospel According to St. John) "In the beginning was the word."

Hitler believed that a political audience did not want to be confused by subtle, contradictory, and overly numerous concepts. He believed that a political audience was "like a woman"—it wanted to be "taken" by a forceful speaker. Hitler had an instinctive way of establishing a rapport with his audience, though he improved on this over the years. Albert Speer recalls that when he first heard Hitler speak it was in an academic setting. The image he had of the fanatical demagogue evaporated as he saw a "rational," calm man address the group. Hitler would modulate his tone and adapt the contents of his talk to suit his audience. The contents appear to be meager enough if one reads the surviving printed versions of those early speeches. Hitler's early speeches emphasized the great miseries in a society torn by terrible tragedy and crisis. This was enough for an oratorical beginning.

In 1920, the small but growing German Workers' Party changed its name to the National Socialist German Workers' Party. The German historian Friedrich Meinecke, writing after the German catastrophe of 1933-1945, argued that some form of a combination of nationalism and socialism was inevitable in Germany in the twentieth century. These were, after all, the two great ideas of the preceding age, one being the property of the bourgeoisie and the other of the proletariat. It was the aim of many groups, ranging from that associated with Pastor Friedrich Naumann around 1900 down to the Nazis themselves, to fuse these two ideas. The socialism of the early Nazis, however, was but a vague, ill-defined hostility to big capitalism. It was really a slap in the face at the respectable Munich bourgeoisie. Early posters announcing Nazi meetings were usually done in red in order to frighten off this timid, "solid" bourgeoisie. Hitler, knowing the type of person attracted to his movement, did at one point say that those whose "major interest is preserving the social order will never come to us." He might also have said the opposite, for he also sensed that serious social revolutionaries would never come to a party based upon militarism, anti-Semitism, and the most irrational forms of social resentment.

The Greater German idea, which had first emerged as a powerful political force in 1848, was widely popular among German youth during and after the First World War. Put briefly, its aim was to unite all German-speaking people in Central Europe, with the possible exception of the Swiss, in one Greater German Reich. This Reich would include Austria, the Sudetenland, and the areas lost to Poland after the World War. It would also include the South Tyrol in Italy. The Nazis took up this radical Greater German idea, borrowing their inspiration more from the fanatical late-nineteenth-century Greater German publicist Paul Lagarde than from the liberal Greater German nationalists of the Frankfurt Parliament of 1848-1849. In yet another respect the Nazis took over an old, dangerous German malady: radical anti-Semitism. The Nazis explicitly stated that entry to their meetings was forbidden to Jews. Such was the ideological radicalism of the early Nazi movement. These considerations should not lead us to overlook the hunger for power which inspired Hitler, since, as he himself said, from 1919 to 1923 he had one aim in mind: the violent overthrow of the Weimar Republic and its sullen Bavarian allies.

By April 1, 1920 Hitler had been mustered out of the Reichswehr. He now became a full-time agitator for the NSDAP. To Adolf Hitler, these years before 1930 were the *Kampfzeit* of Nazi mythology, and the men who joined the party in this period were the *alte Kämpfer*, the old fighters. These were men to whom Hitler was generally grateful, even in cases where they demonstrated their administrative incompetence after 1933.

Between 1920 and 1923 the Nazi Party was but one of many right-wing fringe groups in south Germany. It participated in mass rallies with other such groups, and Hitler, despite his oratorical abilities, did not have the following or the prestige to lay claim to the leadership of the entire south German nationalist movement. Even late in 1923, at the time of his celebrated and failed *Putsch,* he needed a symbolic figurehead. In appearance, Hitler had begun to fill out a bit, though it was only during his jail term in 1924 that he really began to put on weight and become somewhat paunchy. In 1921 and 1922 his appearance was still gaunt. He generally wore a rather shabby raincoat, although for special occasions he would appear decorated with his Iron Cross, First Class. Accounts of this period indicate that Hitler was working as he never had before, traveling about Bavaria, solidifying his control over the small NSDAP, and successfully enticing other right-wing leaders, such as the notorious Nürnberg anti-Semite Julius Streicher, into the Nazi movement. Streicher, who was a leader of the German-Socialist Party (DSP), was convinced that he should bring that party into the NSDAP on Hitler's terms. Although Streicher was a notorious lecher and a man of crude political and personal habits, Hitler never forgot the importance of Streicher's move. It upset a coalition against him among some of the older members of the NSDAP. Even at this time Hitler displayed a fondness for vicarious violence. If he did not, he would not have been able to put up with an individual such as Streicher, later to be Goebbels' "Hero of Nürnberg."

Hitler's speeches became increasingly violent in 1921 and 1922 as Germany was rocked by a series of uprisings and assassinations, usually from the right. In March, 1920, a group of Freikorps men under the nominal command of Wolfgang Kapp had actually seized Berlin. The government had fled, the Reichswehr remained inactive, and it was only the united action of the greater Berlin working class which undid the *Putsch* of Wolfgang Kapp. This example of proletarian unity was sorely lacking when Hitler rose to power in 1930-1933. There was widespread sympathy for Kapp, particularly in separatist Bavaria. In 1921, a leader of the Center Party, Erzberger, was assassinated and in 1922 Foreign Minister Rathenau met a similar fate. The *Fehmemord* in Bavaria, assassinations of supposedly left-wing or "treasonous" figures carried out by right-wing extremists, undermined law and order in that country.

6. The Nature of the Early Nazi Party

Against this poisonous background, Hitler drew into his party men such as Captain Ernst Röhm, still officially with the Reichswehr command in Bavaria, and the former head of the Richthofen air squadron in 1918, Hermann Göring. Göring was a high-living, intelligent, cynical, self-proclaimed Renaissance man, married to a beautiful Swedish wife. Men such as Röhm and Göring wanted adventure—they wanted a nationalist uprising against the Republic. They, in turn, through their military prestige, brought hundreds of other men into the paramilitary arm of the Nazi Party, the Sturmabteilung or SA. Hitler was always troubled by this Freikorps adventurer type. Contrary to what one might assume, he was suspicious of such men. His direction was entirely political and he saw paramilitary groups such as the SA as an arm of his political leadership of the National Socialist German Workers' Party. Men like Röhm and Göring, at least in this period, saw things quite differently. They wished to use the SA and other paramilitary groups as a sort of surrogate army, as an illegal Reichswehr akin to the "Black Reichswehr" flourishing in northern Germany. In this SA they would perpetuate military values, hide weapons, and prepare for the day of reckoning with the Weimar Republic. They hoped to play a major role in obliterating the Treaty of Versailles and its main sponsor, France. Röhm looked more to coordination with other (non-Nazi) paramilitary groups in the Kampfbund, of which he was the head, than to the "political direction" given by windy orators such as Feder, Eckart, and even Hitler. The dispute between Hitler and the SA flared up sporadically between 1924 and 1933. It occurred again after Hitler came to power, and was only settled by the brutal murder of Röhm and his closest colleagues on the Night of the Long Knives, June 30, 1934. Yet Hitler's words were increasingly threatening in 1921 and 1922, and in order to carry out some kind of revolution he needed Röhm, Göring, and the men who had flocked into the SA and the other paramilitary groups in Bavaria.

Several elements made up the early Nazi Party: petit bourgeois, theoretical cranks such as Harrer, Eckart, Feder, and Drexler; ex-servicemen and adventurers such as Göring, Rudolf Hess, and Ernst Röhm; the fanatically ambitious, embittered revolutionary orator, Adolf Hitler; anti-Semitic pornographers and dregs such as Julius Streicher. There is a further problem concerning the early Party which is more difficult to pinpoint, but it is undoubtedly there. The Party spent far more than it took in from selling subscriptions to the *Völkischer Beobachter* and charging admission to Nazi rallies. What was the nature of the financial support for the Party? Certain elements in Munich society, afraid of Bolshevik revolution and hating the Weimar Republic in Berlin, were willing to give money to Adolf Hitler. At first, Hitler bowed and scraped in the presence of such individuals of superior social status. Hitler clearly was ill at ease. He would scream too much and then turn on his heels and take his leave. But individuals such as Bruckmann, the publisher of the racial theoretician Houston Stewart Chamberlain, Helene Bechstein, wife of the famous piano manufacturer, Putzi Hanfstaengl, of the famous art-collecting family, and Winifried Wagner, daughter-in-law of the great composer, took Hitler under their protection in this period, taught him better manners and better dress, and gave the Party some money. At this and later times Hitler seems to have had a particularly winning way with middle-aged women, and he used this charm to the utmost. Some very few industrialists, such as Fritz Thyssen, may have given Hitler some funds early in the 1920's, but it would be absurd to state that Hitler was a tool of the German industrialists during this period. He was not nearly that important until 1931-1932.

Winifried Wagner, who was particularly enamored of Hitler, was an important conquest for him. She had at her disposal the prestige of the Bayreuth shrine. In fact, Hitler visited Bayreuth shortly before the abortive uprising of November 8-9, 1923. It was on paper supplied by Winifried Wagner that Hitler dictated the first draft of Volume I of *Mein Kampf*. Through her he came into contact with the infirm Houston Stewart Chamberlain, archpoet of German racialism, the author in 1899 of the

famous *Foundations of the Nineteenth Century.* How closely
Hitler had read Chamberlain is difficult to determine.
Certainly, the "positive Christianity" point of the 1920
Nazi program reflected Chamberlain's views, though it
hardly reflected Hitler's. In his table talk during World
War II, Hitler criticized Chamberlain for trying to fuse
Germanic and Christian concepts. For Hitler, Christianity
was a part of the Jewish poison which had infected the
Aryan peoples. In this he vulgarized Nietzsche and con-
tradicted Houston Stewart Chamberlain. Nevertheless,
Hitler knew the prestige of this fanatical racial theorist
in right-wing circles, and he paid a symbolic visit to
Chamberlain in Bayreuth in October, 1923. Chamberlain,
in a now famous letter to Hitler, soon thereafter avowed
his belief in the Nazi cause and his personal faith in the
Führer's messianic mission. When Chamberlain died in
1927, the Nazi daily gave him a five-column obituary.

Thus, before 1923 Hitler and the Nazis drew almost
exclusively upon fringe fanatical elements in German
society, elements which were at the time without a
national base. We must question what type of a society
it was in which such elements could eventually mold the
destiny of Europe. But such financial and social contacts
were not the only important new acquaintances made by
Hitler in these early years of the *Bewegung* or the Nazi
movement. Through the agency of Alfred Rosenberg, a
German Balt who had been in Russia during the
Bolshevik Revolution, Hitler met many of the White Russian refugees who flocked to Munich after the failure of
the Russian counterrevolution in 1919-1920. These
individuals, already strongly anti-Semitic, helped convince Hitler that the Russian Revolution was a revolt of
the racial underworld provoked by the Jews in order to
destroy the Aryan peoples. Following Houston Stewart
Chamberlain, Hitler felt that the Slavs had no state-
molding ability of their own, but that the Germanic élite
which had just been exterminated by the Bolshevik Jews
had created the Romanov Russian state. The conviction
that this Bolshevik structure was hollow and decadent

stayed with him at least until 1943. Certain Nazis even mused at times in the 1930's that perhaps Stalin's present hegemony indicated a return to "national Russian" from "Jewish" values.

It is difficult to portray the moral and intellectual atmosphere in Bavaria and indeed in much of Germany during this period. Students went about quoting the "Protocols of the Elders of Zion," a notorious forgery which claimed that a Jewish world conspiracy existed. Anti-Semitism was more rife than ever before and was openly advocated by leading academics. The so-called Revolution of 1918 had not been a revolution in terms of replacing judges and teachers, most of whom stayed on and continued to hold their old imperial, reactionary German attitudes. They often treated the left harshly and the right, however murderous, kindly.

In the midst of all of this decadence and despair, great innovative work flourished in the Weimar Republic. Such creative work, whether in architecture, painting, or literature, tended to have an aesthetically or politically radical impulse behind it. This further annoyed large segments of the frightened German middle class, while the very real decadence of the SA, Freikorps men, and Nazis was successfully concealed behind the torrent of abuse which they visited upon the so-called cultural Bolshevism of the experimental German intellectual scene. As Peter Gay has put it, the artistic outsider of the prewar days was now the artistic insider. The bourgeoisie, however, was troubled by the revolutionary implications of the new art and the new values. Under these unsettled conditions, thousands of men flocked into groups such as the Nazis and the SA in order to reaffirm traditional patriotic virtues. Solidarity as expressed in military music and marching, the use of the Aryan sign or swastika (which had first been used by the Austrian Nazis), parading about in uniforms, and above all, the continuation of the officer-enlisted man relationship—this was the manner in which men like Röhm and Hitler answered the chaos and innovation of the early Weimar period.

The Nazi Party in Germany was not the only National Socialist organization in Europe. The Sudeten Germans and the Austro-Germans had similar if weaker organizations, and at least until the early 1920's there was a sort of Nazi international among the three of them. The German party, however, had by 1923 eclipsed the others in both fame and strength, and Hitler was the undisputed leader of this Nazi Party by 1922. It was clear that the other members of the steering committee could not do without him, that he was the main reason why the halls were filled when the NSDAP held a rally.

7. The Bavarian Right and the Crisis of 1923

There is no question that Hitler's followers wanted to launch a revolutionary uprising during this period, but the thorny questions of Bavarian politics made this course of action difficult. Many reactionary Bavarian politicians wished to use movements such as the SA and the NSDAP for their own ends. They wanted to use them, along with the local Reichswehr, in order to weaken the hold of Berlin over Bavaria. From the very beginning, however, Hitler, despite his Austrian and South German origins, was violently opposed to any form of separatism. One of the basic (and more popular) points of the 1920 Nazi program was the union of all Germans in a Greater German Reich. Hitler did not wish to destroy the Weimar Republic merely in order to restore the reactionary Wittelsbach dynasty in Bavaria. He was, however, willing to keep his own counsel on some of these points, and the tactical opportunism of which he was capable down to his dying days was mirrored in the courteous attention Hitler paid to individuals such as Crown Prince Rupprecht of Bavaria, on the one hand, and Erich Ludendorff on the other. Rupprecht and Ludendorff had been violent enemies since the Great War. Hitler wished to use Bavarian separatist sentiment in order to overthrow the Berlin government and establish his own dictatorship.

This seems staggering, given the relative smallness of the Nazi Party in late 1923. Yet in that year certain events occurred which seemed to make the chances for the overthrow of the republic somewhat better.

Claiming that the Germans had defaulted on reparations payments, the French occupied the industrial Ruhr. The German government decided upon passive resistance. This led to economic chaos and the collapse of the mark. Left-wing elements raised their heads in areas like Saxony and Thuringia, where Communists entered a left-oriented Social-Democratic government. Once again the specter that had given Germany Bavarian Bolshevism in 1919 seemed to be present. To the Munich burghers this brought back memories of the so-called Red Terror of 1919. There was passive and even active resistance to the French in some parts of the Rhineland. Resisters such as Leo Schlageter were killed by the French and proclaimed martyrs by both the Communist Party of Germany and rightist groups such as the Nazis. The lines between the extremes seemed to be erased and once again the peculiar phenomenon of National Bolshevism emerged.

This National Bolshevism, which the Bolshevik theoretician Karl Radek and the German writer Ernst Niekisch developed, argued that both Germany and Russia were the pariahs of the postwar world, and that they were being exploited by the international capitalism of American, British, and French financiers. The Treaty of Versailles was both the agency of Germany's thralldom and the justification for Russo-German collaboration. In fact, this collaboration had been made real in Rapallo by Walter Rathenau in 1922, and it was a factor for the next decade. Hitler had little use for Bolshevism, but given the opposition of the workers and the nation to the occupation of the Ruhr, the radical anticapitalist and anti-French rhetoric and impulses of the Nazis and other paramilitary groups in Bavaria became ever more hysterical late in 1923.

When the Chancellor, Gustav Stresemann, sought a peaceful solution to the problem of the Ruhr and cracked down upon dissident elements in the Reich and Bavaria, the Nazis felt that they had to act. But there were still certain question marks. Would the local command of the Reichswehr, under von Lossow, support a Nazi, paramilitary, Bavarian separatist uprising? Late in 1923, the Berlin government had appointed Gustav von Kahr as *Reichstatthalter* or Regent in Bavaria, giving him dictatorial powers. His separatist sentiments were well known. Could he be trusted? Could he be used? What about the police president, Seisser? How well coordinated would movements be between the SA, the Kampfbund, and the other paramilitary organizations in Bavaria? Who would lead the uprising? These were some of the questions which faced the Nazi leadership in early November, 1923. Thousands of armed men who were members of the SA, the Kampfbund, and other paramilitary organizations wanted action. Hitler had ever more whipped up their passions by his political speeches since the French occupation of the Ruhr. He himself had not planned a move on the night of November 8, 1923, but pressure from below and the fear of missing the great opportunity spurred him on to action. Hitler felt if he did not act he would lose the membership of the SA and of the militant segments of the National Socialist German Workers' Party. Similar pressures confronted him throughout the year of destiny, 1932.

Like other revolutionary leaders in the twentieth century, Hitler was forced to attempt a premature uprising against his own better judgment. But once the uprising had begun, he threw himself into it with the total passionate, political commitment of which few normal individuals are capable. Mussolini, after all, in a daring stroke in October of the preceding year, had gathered together his militant followers and had succeeded in so bluffing and intimidating the royal Italian government that he became Prime Minister. The analogies between Mussolini's Fascist movement and Hitler's was clear to all in 1923. Thus, Mussolini's mythical march on Rome provided a hopeful model for the Nazi and paramilitary legionaries.

Napoleon appears to have lost his nerve during his own "eighteenth Brumaire" or coup in 1799, an attempt to seize power which was successful only because of the great daring and coolness of his brother, Lucien. Lenin launched the abortive July uprising against the provisional government in Russia in 1917 against his own better judgment, largely due to pressure from below. It failed and the Bolsheviks went through a period of profound danger. Early in 1919, Karl Liebknecht and especially a hesitant Rosa Luxemburg felt propelled by circumstances and militant pressure to launch an uprising against the provisional German republic. The uprising was easily put down and they were murdered. As a revolutionary who staked all on the gamble for power, Hitler always knew there was a chance he might fail and be destroyed. On November 8, 1923, he was willing to take that chance, but largely because he felt he had no choice.

8. Adolf Hitler as Failed Revolutionary: The *Putsch*

Hitler decided to take advantage of a major patriotic meeting to be held in the Bürgerbräukeller on the evening of November 8 at which von Lossow, von Kahr, and Seisser would all be present. He had the SA, under the command of Göring, surround the hall. According to contemporary accounts, Hitler was in a complete nervous frenzy on this night of November 8. He did something extremely uncharacteristic—he drank a couple of mugs of beer in order to raise his courage and steady his nerves. In the midst of the meeting, Hitler fired a shot and jumped onto a table, startling the audience of several hundred. He excitedly announced that the Bavarian and Reich governments had been deposed, that the "November criminals" of 1918 would be brought to justice and a new national government and army had been formed with Ludendorff as head of the army and Hitler as head of the government. Hitler told the crowd that the SA had surrounded the hall and, more importantly, that he was working in agreement with patriots such as von Lossow, Seisser, and von Kahr. After this episode, Hitler retired with these men to a room in the back. He told them that he had four shots in his revolver—three for them and one for himself if the *Putsch* failed due to their refusal to back it. Von Kahr and his colleagues realized that they had little choice but to pretend to play along with Hitler. At this point, the story and the intrigues become quite complicated. Who was double-crossing whom? Hitler was using men like von Kahr, a local hero of the Munich bourgeoisie and the Bavarian separatists, in order to shore up his support for a march on Berlin. Bavarian separatists and monarchists wished to use the Nazi movement, the SA, and groups such as the Kampfbund in order to defy the authority of the Reich, restore the Wittelsbachs, and possibly detach Bavaria from the Weimar Republic. The mood of the beery crowd changed when Hitler returned to the hall with von Kahr, von Lossow, and Seisser. When they shook hands there was tremendous enthusiasm. It indeed looked as if a "national revolution" against the hated republic had begun. Paramilitary and rightist groups began to pour into the area around Munich.

One of Hitler's great coups had been to get Ludendorff to serve as a figurehead for his national revolution. The old quartermaster general was undoubtedly upset at the fact that he had been assigned the leadership of a nonexistent army rather than the dictatorship which Hitler had arrogated to himself. Nevertheless, Ludendorff went along with the revolt. On the next day, Ludendorff, Hitler, Göring, Scheubner-Richter, and other prominent Nazis marched towards the Odeonsplatz in order to seize the Bavarian headquarters of the Reichswehr and liberate Röhm and his followers, who were being besieged there. The attitude of the national leadership of the Reichswehr was quite unclear in situations such as this. Von Seeckt, a leader of the Reichswehr, wished to preserve the discipline of the old German army and prepare it for new tasks such as breaking the "fetters" of Versailles. He would not countenance rowdy revolution from the left nor from the right, but his sympathies were undeniably with the latter. Von Seeckt had expected that von Lossow would use the Reichswehr to preserve the authority of the Reich in Bavaria. Von Seeckt had little sympathy with separatism. He was one of the fathers of the policy of secret military collaboration with Bolshevik Russia, though he had nothing but hatred for Communism. He desired the destruction of Poland, an indirect creation of the Treaty of Versailles, and he had all the social and ethnic prejudices of the North German ruling class. Nevertheless, it was unthinkable to von Seeckt that an ex-corporal such as Hitler (whom he had met in 1922) should, with his Bavarian rowdies, overthrow the government of the Reich.

Von Seeckt had earlier made it clear to von Lossow that if the Bavarian contingents of the Reichswehr did not put down an attempted *Putsch*, Berlin would do it directly. The fact that this was true was to be Hitler's greatest surprise on that fateful day, November 9. He assumed that after seeing him march along beside Ludendorff, the Reichswehr would come over to his side. In this he mistook sentiment for commitment. There was great sympathy for this "national revolution" among the junior officers of the Bavarian Reichswehr, which had no desire to fire upon old trench comrades such as Hitler and Röhm. Such a painful confrontation, however, proved unnecessary. The streets leading to the Feldherrnhalle, or great war memorial in the Odeonsplatz, and from there to the War Ministry, were extremely narrow. Although the Nazis and their followers outnumbered the police, the gendarmes were able to contain them. It is unclear to this day who fired first. Whatever the origin of the first shots, several people were killed, including three police and sixteen Nazis. Hermann Göring was badly wounded, and Hitler himself either fell or ducked, painfully dislocating his shoulder. He was taken away in a waiting limousine. One of the stories that Hitler or his

court later spread in order to counter rumors of cowardice was that he had injured his shoulder while trying to
take a child out of the line of fire. This seems a most uncharacteristic act, though as a sentimental afterthought
it would be typical of the Führer's character.

Ludendorff's contempt for Hitler, already somewhat in
evidence by November 9, grew in the years ahead. He
himself had kept marching boldly through the police
ranks while Hitler fled. He was later arrested—un-
wounded. His break with Hitler was complete by the time
the Führer got out of prison late in 1924. In 1937, when
he was on his deathbed, the old general contemptuously
pushed aside a field marshal's baton that the Chancellor
of the Third Reich had bestowed upon him.

For Hitler and the Nazis, those sixteen who fell on
November 9, 1923 were the martyrs of the *Bewegung,* the
alte Kämpfer who had given their lives to bring about a
purifying revolution amidst the disgusting muck of the
unpatriotic, Jew-ridden Weimar Republic. November 8
and 9 were sacred days in the Nazi pantheon right
through 1944. During the time of the Third Reich, the
holy days of the *Bewegung* were January 30 (Hitler's accession to power), mid-March (Heroes' Memorial Day), April
20 (Hitler's birthday), May 1 (the celebrations of the German Labor Front), early September (the great Nürnberg
party rallies) and finally, November 9, the anniversary of
the *Putsch.* Hitler, exploiting the blood-oriented mysticism of the Nazi movement, had the sole power to conse-
crate new banners for various SA contingents. He would
often do so by touching the new banners with banners
(Blutfahnen) supposedly dipped in the blood of the
November 9 martyrs. This was the *Fahneneid* or "banner
oath" of Nazi mythology.

What practical lessons did Hitler draw from his failure
in the so-called beer-hall *Putsch?* He later said that he now
realized he would have to come to power legally. He
could never come to power through a revolt during
which the army would be either ambiguously neutral or

ranged against the *Bewegung*. Hitler never again trusted Bavarian separatists such as von Kahr and Seisser. Indeed, these men, who against their will had agreed to collaborate with him on November 8, betrayed Hitler on the very next day. This at least is how Hitler saw it. Their role, to say the very least, had been ambiguous. Hitler had von Kahr murdered on the Night of the Long Knives, June 30, 1934.

The temporary eclipse of the Nazi movement in Bavaria—the Party and its organs were made illegal soon after the *Putsch*—gave the smaller North German contingents of National Socialism a chance to organize and exercise greater influence. Hitler's last political success in this period was his trial, which ended early in 1924 with a sentence of five years' imprisonment. Actually, Hitler was imprisoned from November 11, 1923 to December 20, 1924. The judge, a product of the old German Empire, was extremely favorable to the defense, as was the audience. For the first time Hitler became well known outside Bavaria, and newspapers covered the trial in countries such as England, France, and America. Hitler turned the accusations against him into an indictment of the Weimar Republic.

The Nazi movement, though surfacing under different names in different areas, grew rapidly in the first half of 1924. This was reflected in the Reichstag elections of May, 1924, in which the Nazis and their allies captured about two million votes. When Hitler was sent to the Landsberg fortress prison, the Nazis began squabbling among themselves and with fellow travelers such as Ludendorff. Hitler left the direction of the party to a hapless administrator, the pseudointellectual Alfred Rosenberg, editor of the *Völkischer Beobachter*. At Nürnberg, after the war, Rosenberg said this was an unlikely choice, and that Hitler probably did it because he did not want any one individual to exercise real power in the Party while he was in prison. Hitler was afraid that he might lose control of the movement. Actually, if he had, it probably would have disintegrated into a meaningless fringe group, with about the same (nonexistent) level of importance as that which the *Encyclopaedia Britannica* ascribed to Adolf Hitler in its fourteenth edition (1929).

The years 1924 to 1928 were difficult years for the Party, and for Hitler personally, but he had made good use of his time in prison. He was allowed to walk about freely, had comfortable quarters, and was permitted personal secretaries such as Rudolf Hess, Father Bernhard Stempfle, and Max Amann, future Nazi publishing magnate. Hitler drafted or dictated the first volume of *Mein Kampf,* a work which received little notice until the end of the decade. When he emerged from the Landsberg fortress on December 20, 1924, Adolf Hitler reentered a German society which seemed more stable than it had been since before the war, hence one in which the Nazi movement would have a bleak future.

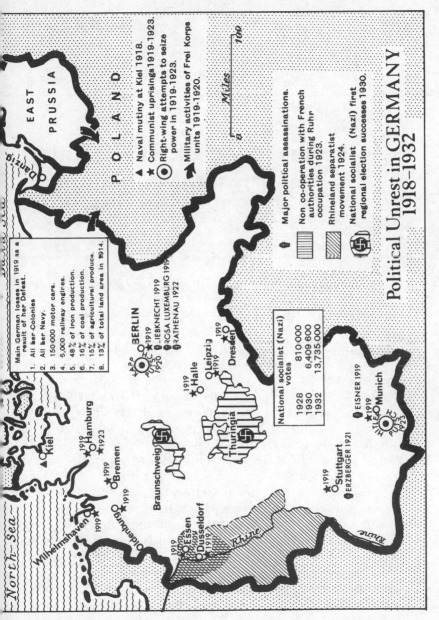

Political Unrest in Germany, 1918-1932

CHAPTER III

The Resurrection of Adolf Hitler, 1925-1933

1. Weimar: A Political Overview

IN the years after 1925 the Nazi Party slowly became a national or Reich party. This geographical expansion paradoxically occurred during the years of its greatest electoral weakness. Slowly but surely, a skeletal structure grew up, the future nucleus of a great organization after 1930. In the first phase of its history, 1919 to 1923, the National Socialist German Workers' Party can only be understood against the background of Bavarian politics and particularism, though some knowledge of the early Weimar Republic is necessary in order to grasp the moral and political atmosphere in which the Party first arose. Hitler's struggle for power between 1925 and 1933 was played out against a broader backdrop.

The history of the Weimar Republic can be divided into three more or less distinct periods. The first is from the November Revolution of 1918 to, for convenience's sake, Hitler's trial in 1924. This was a time of great instability, both political and financial. There were uprisings and *Putsches* of both the left and the right. Frequent political assassinations occurred. 1924 to 1929 was a period of deceptive stability. The republic was firmer in dealing with its more outrageous enemies. The foreign policy of Gustav Stresemann of the German People's Party (DVP) helped bring Germany back into the concert of European nations without sacrificing the friendship of Soviet Russia. This was the age of the "spirit of Locarno," of friendship between Stresemann and the French statesman Aristide Briand, a time when a highly political type of pacifism became almost fashionable in the foreign ministries of countries such as Germany, England, and America.

Europe seemed to be recovering. German heavy industry was producing as never before, and the reparations question had been, if not solved, at least made manageable by the Dawes Plan of 1924. The mark was stabilized, and throughout this period the "Weimar Coalition" in Prussia, consisting of the German Democratic Party, the Social-Democrats, and the Catholic Center Party, provided political stability for two-thirds of Germany. Much of this prosperity, however, was deceptive. It was largely based upon short-term, high-interest loans from Wall Street, loans which often went to German municipalities for public works and beautification projects. In case of a disturbance on Wall Street, these loans might be quickly recalled, thereby wrecking investment in the German economy. Unemployment was high, especially in the winter. Social misery existed side by side with great wealth, while modern currents in music and the arts disturbed the pious traditionalist feelings of many Germans. Even those who had learned to live with the republic (*Vernunftrepublikaner*) were not inspired by it. In a time of crisis they would turn their backs upon Weimar and German political democracy.

Electoral politics in the Weimar Republic was a complicated matter. One of the reasons why the republic was so troubled by violence and street fighting in its later stages was the very fact that its political processes, though evidently the "most democratic in the world," were largely inaccessible to the young and the discontented. The large Social-Democratic Party, a reluctant mainstay of the Weimar Republic, had fallen into the hands of middle-aged bureaucratic hacks who had little ability to inspire the young. Though their party was scarcely orthodox Marxist in nature any longer (it had not been so since the turn of the century), the Marxist rhetoric of the Social-Democratic *Bonzen* or "gurus" still frightened the German bourgeoisie. The predictions of Marx and Engels, that the German proletariat would be an absolute majority of the nation, had not come to pass.

The Social-Democrats were attacked on the left by the KPD or German Communist Party, which was under Stalinist domination after 1925. This party, too, ultimately turned out to be a parliamentary one, though its revolutionary rhetoric frightened the German bourgeoisie during the Depression and induced millions of workers to abandon the more moderate SPD by 1932. Such a split in the German labor movement was disastrous. Both Stalinist hatred of the SPD or "Social Fascists," as the Communist called them after 1928, and Social-Democratic complacency and anti-Communism were to blame for the terrible predicament of the German working class by 1932.

The German Democratic Party started out with millions of supporters in 1919 and 1920 but it collapsed completely during the Great Depression. This was largely a party of middle-class intellectuals, many of them Jewish, and it unreservedly supported the republican idea, but the ideas of 1789 and 1848 could not prevail in the Germany of 1932. The German People's Party (DVP), among whose leaders was the Weimar Foreign Minister Gustav Stresemann, was largely a party of western German entrepreneurs and capitalists. It represented elements which had been largely associated with the right wing of the National Liberal Party before 1918. The DVP supported the Weimar Republic because the German capitalists knew that they had no function within the existing political structure. This did not mean that they would not turn their backs upon both the Party and the republic in a time of economic and political crisis.

The Center Party or Zentrum, growing up in the

1870's during the time of the great struggle between Bismarck and the Catholic Church, had its left and right wings. It had a stable electorate because of its confessional appeal and its association with various Catholic newspapers and youth groups. The Center Party conditionally supported the Weimar Republic, at least until March of 1933. On the right, the DNVP or German National People's Party (German Nationalists), from the 1920's largely led by Alfred Hugenberg, the media magnate, was an extreme rightist party which only on rare occasions considered combining with other parties to form a majority coalition in the Reichstag. It increasingly moved away from right of center toward the Nazis after the stunning Nazi successes in the elections of September 14, 1930. The Nationalists had strong ties with the Stahlhelm, the most important veterans' group, and they were very strong in the backward rural areas of Mecklenburg, Brandenburg, and East Prussia. This party was one of pastors, landlords, and ex-soldiers. It was a true party of social reaction, one which wished to preserve privilege by destroying the Weimar Republic. Its anti-Semitism, so common in German society at the time, was of the traditional religious and social variety. It did not smack of the genocidal psychopathia of the Nazis. Nevertheless, the Nationalists and Hugenberg were essential to Hitler's consolidation of power in Germany.

In addition to these major parties, various special-interest and ideological groups appeared and disappeared throughout the lifetime of the Weimar Republic. Proportional representation gave such parties their opportunity. The Weimar Republic was only stable on the ministerial level from 1924 to 1930. Both before and after that time it proved impossible for the Reichstag to form workable majority coalitions. The last years of the Weimar Republic—1931 to 1933—were in effect a time of Presidential dictatorship. Unlimited authority was conferred upon a Chancellor who had the confidence or at least the grudging support of the President.

The two Presidents of the republic, Friedrich Ebert and

PARTY	NATIONAL ASSEMBLY JANUARY 19, 1919			JUNE 6, 1920			MAY 4, 1924			DECEMBER 7, 1924			MAY 20, 1928		
	Total Votes	%	No. Deputies	Total Votes	%	No. Deputies	Total Votes	%	No. Deputies	Total Votes	%	No. Deputies	Total Votes	%	No. Deputies
No. eligible voters	36,766,500		423	35,949,800		459	38,375,000		472	38,987,300		493	41,224,700		491
No. valid votes cast	30,400,300	82.7		28,196,300	78.4		29,281,800	76.30		30,290,100	77.69		30,753,300	74.60	
Majority Socialists	11,509,100	37.9	165	6,104,400	21.6	102	6,008,900	20.5	100	7,881,000	26.0	131	9,153,000	29.8	153
Independent Socialists	2,317,300	7.6	22	5,046,800	17.9	84				....	...	..	....	...	..
Communist party	....	...	..	589,500	2.1	4	3,693,300	12.6	62	2,709,100	9.0	45	3,264,800	10.6	54
Center	5,980,200	19.7	91	3,845,000	13.6	64	3,914,400	13.4	65	4,118,900	13.6	69	3,712,200	12.1	62
Bavarian People's party	....	...	..	1,238,600	4.4	21	946,700	3.2	16	1,134,000	3.7	19	945,600	3.0	16
Democrats	5,641,800	18.6	75	2,333,700	8.3	39	1,655,100	5.7	28	1,919,800	6.3	32	1,505,700	4.9	25
People's party	1,345,600	4.4	19	3,919,400	13.9	65	2,694,400	9.2	45	3,049,100	10.1	51	2,679,700	8.7	45
Wirtschaftspartei	275,100	0.9	4	218,600	0.8	4	693,600	2.4	10	1,005,400	3.3	17	1,397,100	4.5	23
Nationalists	3,121,500	10.3	44	4,249,100	14.9	71	5,696,500	19.5	95	6,205,800	20.5	103	4,381,600	14.2	73
Christlich-soz. Volksdienst							....	...	..	....	...	..	....	...	..
Landbund							574,900	1.9	10	499,400	1.6	8	199,500	0.6	3
Christlich-natl. Bauern u. Landvolk							....	...	..	....	...	..	581,800	1.8	10
Deutsch-Hannov. Partei	77,200	0.2	1	319,100	0.9	5	319,800	1.0	5	262,700	0.8	4	195,600	0.5	3
Deutsche Bauernpartei							....	...	..	....	...	..	481,300	1.5	8
National Socialists	....	...	..	....	...	..	1,918,300	6.5	32	907,300	3.0	14	810,100	2.6	12
Other parties	132,500	0.4	2	332,100	1.6	..	1,165,900	4.0	4	597,600	2.0	..	1,445,300	4.8	4

Reichstag Elections 1919-1933
(continued on page 70)

Paul von Hindenburg, reflected its contradictory tendencies. Ebert was of proletarian origin, a moderate
Socialist who became a German President standing above
parties, including his own. He saw his task as one of con-
ciliation, a peculiar role for a self-proclaimed Socialist to
follow in a capitalist society. The Social-Democrats, who
did little or nothing to bring about Socialism in Weimar
Germany, thus provided the state with a President who
had proclaimed that he "hated social revolution as he
hated sin." Nevertheless, people came to accept and like
Ebert. When he died and elections had to be held in 1925
it is interesting that Paul von Hindenburg emerged as
Ebert's successor in the second round. He seemed to be
different from Ebert in all respects.

Hindenburg was a military man, though his soldierly
abilities, one must say, have been questioned then and
now. Hindenburg had an uncanny ability (through what
we might call the public relations of his aide, General
Groener) to keep himself above different party squabbles.
He associated himself with the nationalist cause only
when it appeared to be popular and when it had achieved
a consensus, as for example, in the case of the "stab in
the back" myth. He lacked Ludendorff's brains but he
also did not have his colleague's warped character and
malignant hatreds. Hindenburg's social views were reactionary and akin to those of the German Nationalists.
How alert or how senile was he? It is difficult to say. To
most Germans Hindenburg was the greatest living German, the first soldier of the World War. He sincerely
intended to uphold the constitution of the Weimar
Republic when he took his oath of office in 1925. In the
relatively prosperous years that followed, Hindenburg
seemed to be carrying out his position in a dignified and
sympathetic manner, but he was not up to the challenges
of depression and political crisis. Ultimately, there is an
irony in a republic twice having to turn to a military
leader (in 1925 and 1932) in order to stabilize itself. This
was a symptom of the Weimar tragedy.

In its last as in its first years, the Weimar Republic

was troubled by both the random and paramilitary types of violence. In a society which had been extremely militaristic, it was difficult for people to accept an army of 100,000 men, which only existed to preserve internal order. The violence of political combat in Germany had led several political parties to develop their own private armies. The Social-Democrats, for example, had their Reichsbanner, which was committed to the democratic principles of 1848 and the Weimar Republic. The Reichsbanner, however, was usually unarmed and was no match for the more militant groups of the right and left. The Stahlhelm, of which Hindenburg was an honorary member, did not engage in street fighting to any great extent. It did hold frequent parades and rallies, however, and made its presence felt through heavy-handed pro-Imperial and antirepublican propaganda. Some of the people associated with it were active in the secret or "black" Reichswehr. This was the informal name for military activities forbidden to the Reichswehr under the disarmament clauses of the Treaty of Versailles. The Communist Red Veterans' League engaged in defensive and aggressive violence against Social-Democrats and Nazis at an increasing tempo after 1928. It brought down upon itself the wrath of the Social-Democratic Interior Ministry in Prussia in 1929 and was a major target of Nazi violence and counterviolence. This organization, largely illegal after 1929, did more street fighting against the Nazis than any other group in the Weimar Republic.

The Nazis had their Sturmabteilung or SA, which once again came under the command of Ernst Röhm in the last crucial years of the Nazi struggle for power. Röhm had his differences with Hitler. He wanted a more or less independent military striking arm in the SA, the nucleus of a future German army. This difference was to plague Hitler until he had Röhm killed on June 30, 1934. For a few years at the end of the 1920's Röhm went to Bolivia to help train the army there. He returned when Hitler needed him as the final stage in the struggle for power was about to begin. The SA emerged by

1933 with a membership of four to five hundred thousand, by far the largest paramilitary group in the Weimar Republic.

2. The Nazi Party in 1925: Some Personalities

One of the lessons to be learned from a study of twentieth-century revolutionary movements is that those movements which have been able to seize and consolidate power generally built up a structure parallel to that of the state *before* their great hour struck. The National Socialists were no exception to this rule. Between 1925 and 1933 the Nazis developed many of the institutions typical of their party during the period of the Third Reich. The SS, for example, which around 1923 had originated in Hitler's SA bodyguard, the Stosstrupp Adolf Hitler, emerged by 1929 as a small élite group under the command of Heinrich Himmler. Himmler, the son of a tutor to the Bavarian Wittelsbach dynasty, was a taciturn, introverted youth whose great ambition was to be a Germanic hero on the model of King Henry the Fowler or the Emperor Frederick Barbarossa. He was unprepossessing in appearance, bowlegged, round-shouldered, and squinting behind spectacles. Himmler had a receding chin and what German writers like to call slightly "Mongoloid" features.

Heinrich Himmler was in his early twenties when he joined the Nazi movement. He was pedantic but also romantic, dreaming in 1921 of leading German colonization movements to Russia. Himmler had gone to school to study agronomy, hence his later reputation as a failed chicken farmer. His interest in breeding, however, was not restricted to poultry. Himmler was convinced that in nuturing an élite group within the Nazi Party, the SS, he could create the nucleus for a future superior breed of the Nordic race. Such ideas, absurd or obscene as they may appear today, were not considered illicit in respectable intellectual circles in Germany in the 1920's. The racialist writer Houston Stewart Chamberlain had influenced broad strata of the German middle class, and the Nazi anthropologists who emerged in the 1930's were men convinced that National Socialism was not the myth of the twentieth century but, as the late Hajo Holborn put it, the "science of the twentieth century." Himmler's SS was thus part bodyguard, part nucleus for a future German élite. Hitler preferred it to the SA because, unlike Ernst Röhm and the early Hermann Göring, Himmler always assumed that all of his authority came from Hitler. He had no independent authority of his own.

Himmler was not the first Reichsführer of the SS when he was appointed to that post in 1929, but he turned it into a great organization. In 1931 a young, cashiered officer of the German navy, Reinhard Heydrich, became the head of a Security Service or SD within the SS. This was an intelligence organization which compiled dossiers on enemies of the Nazi Party and on its membership. Under Heydrich, it was to be an important part of Himmler's SS. The rivalry between the SA and the SS dated back to this point. Hitler, who liked to concentrate all ultimate power in his own hands, was not unaware of the jealousy which old leaders (Obergruppen-führer) of the SA felt at seeing the rise of Himmler's SS. Indeed, this hostility was to his liking. Heinrich Himmler—policeman, racial élitist, bureaucratic pedant, impractical dreamer—this man represented a major acquisition for the National Socialist movement. Himmler was at this time under the influence of Alfred Rosenberg and Walther Darré, learning from the former's racialist historical mysticism and from the latter's blood-oriented (Blut und Boden) agricultural theories about the peasantry. He did not hesitate, however, to put both in the shadow when he had the power to do so during the Third Reich.

In the internal struggles that racked National Socialism in the late 1920's, Hitler always drew his greatest support from the alte Kämpfer in Bavaria and the south. Men like

Christian Weber, Hermann Esser, and Julius Streicher, individuals of repugnant morals, uncouth and corrupt, these were men who saw in the National Socialist movement possibilities for the realization of their base instincts and lust for power. They followed Hitler blindly. A freebooter like Göring gave the movement a certain prestige. He had been a much-decorated soldier in the World War, achieving the rank of captain. He had contacts in the Reichswehr and with certain German and Swedish business interests. Rudolf Hess, born in Alexandria, Egypt, of German parents, was a student of the famous Munich geopolitician Karl Haushofer. Hess worshipped Hitler from the beginning, served as his loyal secretary in the Landsberg prison, and eventually achieved the position of deputy Führer. In the late 1920's Alfred Rosenberg was working on the turgid book which made him famous, *The Mythos of the Twentieth Century*, a rather stupid compendium of history, racialism, German myth, and National Socialist ideology. Even Hitler later commented that he couldn't get through the book because it was so muddled and abstruse. Rosenberg took himself extraordinarily seriously, and as head of the Foreign Policy Office of the Nazi Party he would harbor great diplomatic ambitions.

In a highly stratified society such as that of supposedly democratic Weimar Germany, the Nazi Party offered an opportunity for upward social mobility to relatively young men of petit bourgeois or proletarian social origin. This is not to say that the Party was without its recruits from higher social strata. It did get an occasional engineer, such as Dr. Fritz Todt, and began to recruit men from the upper middle class, such as the young Albert Speer, after 1930. By and large, however, the Nazi Party was a militarized society in microcosm, which by offering a substitute structure to that of the state, circumvented the social pressure and stratification inherent in German society. This is what led ambitious young men such as Dr. Joseph Goebbels to the Party.

3. "Left-Wing Nazism": The Strasser Crisis

In the middle twenties the Party went through a major crisis. It had split into different segments during Hitler's period in prison in 1924, and it took him some time to reassert his control. In Bavaria certain members of the Party had cooperated with other rightist groups in a "Racialist Bloc." Elsewhere in Germany, figures such as General Ludendorff and the Strasser brothers, originally of Bavarian origin but active in founding North German segments of the Nazi Party, had collaborated in forming a "National Socialist German Freedom Movement." Men such as Goebbels, the son of impoverished Rhenish parents, the Strassers, and even Röhm took the Socialist aspect of National Socialism much more seriously than did Hitler. Hitler's idea of Socialism was a German racialist folk community purged of Jews. He did not define it in terms of social radicalism as did the Goebbels of 1925.

Men such as Goebbels and Gregor Strasser drew certain conclusions from the failure of the *Putsch* of 1923. They felt that it proved you could never trust reactionaries, Bavarian separatists, and people with class arrogance. At this time Goebbels and the Strassers remembered the red field upon which the swastika was imposed in the Nazi Party banners. At a Party congress in Hanover in 1925, Goebbels supposedly got up and demanded that "the petit bourgeois Adolf Hitler be expelled from the Party," for "he has betrayed Socialism." The Strasser brothers, Gregor and Otto, were active in promoting the development of National Socialism in northern Germany during this period. Their ideas seem to have consisted of Socialism, corporativism (largely borrowed from Italian Fascism and from the Viennese theoretician, Othmar Spann), plus a fanatical, militaristic nationalism. They naturally wished to free Germany from the "fetters of Versailles." The Strassers brought into being branches of the Party where they had never before existed, and they were largely responsible for its founding in Berlin.

Hitler had changed a great deal since his days as an army educational officer and Nazi propaganda chief in 1919-1920. He had met some important people, learned better manners, and was having his teeth fixed so that they looked less molelike. He now liked to ride about with a chauffeur in a fast Mercedes, and enjoyed getting away to the country for weekends. Throughout this period Hitler's source of income was unclear, and he flew into a rage when questioned about it. He had met some of the better families in Munich, and he knew very well the constant need of the Party for money. Hitler had no intention of throwing all this away by waving a red flag. It is inaccurate, however, to say that Hitler "betrayed" Socialism. He never had any concept of what it was. In the moves of the Strassers, however, Hitler saw a distinct threat to his own power. In 1926 he rallied the South German party chiefs, men like Streicher, Himmler, Esser, Weber, Rosenberg, and Darré, and welded them into a majority coalition. It carried the day in a Party congress in the South German city of Bamberg. Here the Strassers and their allies were barely but clearly outnumbered, and Hitler's control over the Party was secure for the next nineteen years. As a sop to the radical Socialist elements, the 25-point program of 1920 was declared to be "forever inalterable." Hitler could afford to utter such declarations, since he had successfully buried many of the more radical provisions of that manifesto.

Goebbels, who had been anti-Hitler in 1925, met Hitler for the first time soon after the Hanover congress. He declared in his diary that he was overwhelmed by the Führer's charismatic personality, especially by his "beautiful blue eyes." Goebbels promptly switched sides, betraying the Strassers, and was rewarded by an appointment from Hitler as Gauleiter of Berlin, a dangerous but useful post which he held until his suicide in the spring of 1945. Goebbels was one of the most intriguing figures in the Nazi pantheon. He had a clubfoot due to a bout with polio, hardly a recommendation in circles which prided themselves upon their Nordic physical supremacy. Joseph Goebbels was a man of shrewd intelligence, a brilliant speaker, an indefatigable worker. He was also a total opportunist, a cynic of great magnitude who only knew one loyalty in the last decades of his life—loyalty to Adolf Hitler. Goebbels was a typical tormented product of a lost generation. He was the author of a failed novel, *Michael, A German Destiny in the Form of a Diary,* and in his diary in this period he comes across as an ineffable romantic. Yet Goebbels' attitude towards love was an extremely cynical, manipulative one, as he used his position in the Third Reich to blackmail attractive actresses into his bed.

Goebbels seems to have desired not so much power for himself, but rather the feeling of being part of a great, irresistible movement. He had a knack for coining phrases which made excellent propaganda, but his real sentiments were expressed very frankly in table talk with associates during the war. For example, Goebbels told Wilfrid von Oven that a person of his (Goebbels') social background never would have become a Minister under the class-conscious old regime. He thereby showed that he shrewdly appreciated the prospects for upward social mobility which Third Reich offered. Goebbels was a violent anti-Semite and, although this may not be the whole story, it is significant that Heinrich Himmler told his masseur during the war that Goebbels was more responsible for Hitler's institution of the final solution of the Jewish question (genocide) than any other individual. Goebbels was certainly behind the infamous "Crystal Night" destruction of Jewish properties in the pogrom of November, 1938.

Hitler projected his own psychopathy onto perversions and crimes supposedly associated with the Jews. Likewise, Goebbels may have shuddered whenever he thought of his deformity. He may have decided that in the extermination of the Jews he was extirpating all that was deformed within his body and his soul. If Goebbels differed from Hitler in any important ideological respect, it was in his anticapitalism. During the war he referred proudly to the fact that he belonged to the "left wing" of the movement. Goebbels took Socialism seriously, but not so seriously that he would not betray it for the office of Gauleiter of Berlin. After 1925 he would prize close-ness to the person of Adolf Hitler above all else.

The Strasser brothers reacted to their defeat in Bamberg in different ways. Gregor stayed within the Nazi movement as a sort of "loyal opposition," toying with conspiracies against Hitler as late as 1932, but ultimately remaining loyal to him. For his loyalty he was rewarded by being murdered on June 30, 1934. Otto Strasser, along with other disgruntled Nazis who were unhappy about the Hitler personality cult and the Nazi movement's betrayal of Socialism, left the Party after 1930 and formed his own "Black Front." This movement substituted for the salute "Heil Hitler!" the greeting "Heil Deutschland!" Its membership was never particularly large, and Otto Strasser eventually had to leave Germany. Hitler cannily realized that the Nazi movement had a mystical, emotional appeal for the downtrodden and alienated of *many* social classes and age groups in Germany. He sensed that it could not and should not try to outdo the Communists and Socialists in social radicalism. Further, he knew that the projection of his own charisma, and the irresistible sense of success projected by the Nazi movement were both dependent upon adequate funds and connections. For this he needed the industrial support of men like Fritz Thyssen, men who could not stomach the radicalism of the Strassers or the early Goebbels.

What was Adolf Hitler like during these quietly ominous years of the late 1920's? Though he liked to have his chauffeur drive him about in a fast automobile, he typically would never drive himself for fear of getting into a fatal accident. Hitler always claimed that his concern for his own physical well-being was motivated by a fear of costing the German people his services. Yet when he did take his own life, he blamed other forces for having to do so. There is an ultimate evasion of responsibility and escapism about Hitler which none of his words can cover. Hitler was extremely sentimental. He liked to go on picnics to the country and have young blond women of modest intelligence around him. All sorts of gossip has appeared about Hitler's sexual life, but unfortunately there is little evidence for any particular interpretation. A recent biographer of Eva Braun, Hitler's mistress from 1932 to 1945, finds their relationship banal but more or less normal. Putzi Hanfstaengl, a close associate of Hitler from the early 1920's until 1937, and at one point Hitler's foreign press chief, hints at all sorts of weird perversions on the part of the Führer. Professor Robert Waite has suggested that Hitler was attracted to women who were as much younger than himself as his mother was younger than his father, that is, more than twenty years.

One of Hitler's most sensational affairs during this period seems to bear out Waite's thesis. This was his liaison with his young niece, Geli Raubel, who committed suicide in 1931. On the other hand, Hitler also had tremendous appeal for middle-aged women, and Nazi leaders jokingly referred to such ardent females as their "varicose vein squad." Women and sex, however, were secondary passions to Hitler. His main passion was hatred for the Jews and a related desire for total political power. This is what he understood by self-realization in the service of the *Volk*. Hitler disliked women who were too intelligent and witty, and would tell them so to their faces. He liked to relax by sitting about eating sweets, drinking minted tea, and holding hands and chatting with pretty blond "Nordic" or "Alpine" types of females. Was Geli Raubel the great passion of Adolf Hitler's life? It is hard to say, but when she committed suicide he collapsed completely, and was only saved from utter breakdown by Hermann Göring's steady hand. Hitler never forgot Göring's steadfastness in this great crisis of his life, and from then on he always referred to him as the Iron Man. He showed loyalty to Göring even when the latter's manifest military incompetence had been demonstrated over the skies of Britain in the summer and autumn of 1940.

During these years of relative Weimar stability, Hitler used his leisure to continue the literary pursuits that he had begun in the Landsberg fortress with the first volume of *Mein Kampf*. He completed a second volume, a good part of which was devoted to his foreign policy schemes. Hitler also wrote a third manuscript in 1928, which was only published long after his death as *Hitler's Second Book*. This tome was an amplification of the foreign policy concepts that he had developed in *Mein Kampf*.

4. The Crisis of Weimar and the Appeal of Hitler

Things looked bleak for the movement in 1928, when the Nazis polled under a million votes and won only twelve seats in the Reichstag. Hitler, however, never despaired. He was always sure of his ultimate success, and he communicated this irresistible sense of victory to his followers. Whether he had inner doubts in this period that he suppressed by his own fanaticism, we shall never know. Although parliamentary life in Weimar was never smooth, the years 1928 to 1930 saw Germany governed in relative calm by a "Great Coalition" under the moderate Social-Democratic Chancellor Hermann Mueller. The coalition included the SPD, the German Democratic Party, the Center, and the German People's Party. The prospects for the republic seemed fairly bright, and even a wing of the rightist German National People's Party (DNVP) thought of collaborating with the governmental coalition. Alfred Hugenberg, however, a man of vast ambitions and little political sense, was committed to taking the Nationalists on a violently antirepublican tack in collusion with the Nazis.

Hitler was pledged to a legal course during these years, though it should be pointed out that his concept of legality had nothing to do with Anglo-Saxon legal precepts. By "legality," Adolf Hitler meant that he would not attempt an uprising or commit high treason as he had in November, 1923. He certainly did not rule out intimidation, believing that the forces that controlled the streets would ultimately control the state. Hitler's use of intensive propaganda, scurrilous journalism, and stormtrooper intimidation were all part of his concept of legality. He was in constant trouble with the authorities during these years, being forbidden to speak here or there, seeing his storm troopers occasionally disbanded, even getting involved in tax disputes with the government. National Socialist lawyers, however, such as the *alter Kämpfer* Wilhelm Frick and the ambitious young Hans Frank, and sympathetic officials in various state ministries usually solved these problems for him.

The Great Depression of 1929 favorably altered the prospects for National Socialism in Germany and Austria. The collapse on Wall Street occurred in the latter part of that year. A series of panicky economic measures in Germany and the West ultimately raised unemployment figures in the Reich to six and a half or seven million in 1931-1932. The "permanent" prosperity of the middle Weimar years, which had, anyway, been better for capitalists than for the workers, proved illusory—as Hitler and the Communists had predicted all along. This collapse of the Central European economy was not an isolated factor, for it was part of a world capitalist depression. In 1931 their desperate situations led Germany and Austria into a proposed customs union. They were prevented from realizing it due to French pressure. The collapse by 1931 of the Austrian Credit-Anstalt, or Central Banking Institution, meant that the Depression would spread ever further and deeper. In 1929-1930, the German government had accepted the American Young Plan, considering it a helpful measure in terms of the reparations question. The Nazis joined with the Nationalists in a vigorous attempt to prevent German acceptance of the Plan. This coalition was a sign of things to come. In Prussia, Nazis and Communists in the Landtag or Diet collaborated in an attempt to destroy the democratic Weimar Coalition which had been ruling that vital land since 1919. Although this attempt failed in a great popular referendum in 1931, combined agitation from an ever more powerful left and right made democratic forces in Germany despair.

The last Weimar governments had significant achievements to their credit. In the field of disarmament, for example, Germany had gained the principle of parity by 1932. In addition, German pressure helped bring about a moratorium on reparations payments because of the disastrous world economic situation. Yet the domestic economic policies pursued by these last Weimar chancellors, in particular by Dr. Heinrich Bruening of the Center Party (1930-1932), were deflationary and catastrophic. Bruening feared that another inflation such as that of 1923 would wreck the German middle class and throw it into the arms of the Nazis. He did not seem to appreciate the fact that keeping the mark sound at the expense of governmental expenditures would only exacerbate an already bad situation. The cycle was vicious: People became unemployed, the economy continued to collapse, and the middle class suffered as much if not more than the working class. It was during Bruening's chancellorship, after all, that the Nazis made their most striking gains.

From 1931 Bruening had to rule by decree in a Presidential dictatorship, since he feared new elections and was unable to form a stable majority coalition in the Reichstag. Great masses of people referred to Bruening as the "Hunger Chancellor." He cut social insurance benefits in order to stabilize the mark, thereby augmenting the misery of the nation in this pre-Keynesian age. Bruening was a man of good will and an ardent anti-Nazi, but he had to juggle forces such as unemployment, political chaos on the streets, the increasingly difficult, aged President von Hindenburg, a swing to the right by his own party, and a recalcitrant Reichstag. He

PARTY	SEPTEMBER 14, 1930			JULY 31, 1932			NOVEMBER 6, 1932			MARCH 5, 1933			NOVEMBER 12, 1933		
	Total Votes	%	No. Deputies	Total Votes	%	No. Deputies	Total Votes	%	No. Deputies	Total Votes	%	No. Deputies	Total Votes	%	No. Deputies
No. eligible voters	42,957,700		577	44,226,800		608	44,373,700		584	44,685,800		647	45,141,900		661
No. valid votes cast	34,970,900	81.41		36,882,400	83.39		35,471,800	79.93		39,343,300	88.04		42,988,100*	95.2	
Majority Socialists	8,577,700	24.5	143	7,959,700	21.6	133	7,248,000	20.4	121	7,181,600	18.3	120			
Independent Socialists	......	...	...	......	...	...	......	...	...	......	...	...			
Communist party	4,592,100	13.1	77	5,282,600	14.6	89	5,980,200	16.9	100	4,848,100	12.3	81			
Center	4,127,900	11.8	68	4,589,300	12.5	75	4,230,600	11.9	70	4,424,900	11.7	74			
Bavarian People's party	1,059,100	3.0	19	1,192,700	3.2	22	1,094,600	3.1	20	1,073,600	2.7	18			
Democrats	1,322,400	3.8	20	371,800	1.0	4	336,500	1.0	2	334,200	0.8	5			
People's party	1,578,200	4.5	30	436,000	1.2	7	661,800	1.9	11	432,300	1.1	2			
Wirtschaftspartei	1,362,400	3.9	23	146,900	0.4	2	110,300	0.3	1	......	...	...			
Nationalists	2,458,300	7.0	41	2,177,400	5.9	37	2,959,000	8.8	52	3,136,800	8.0	52			
Christlich-soz. Volksdienst	868,200	2.5	14	405,300	1.1	3	412,500	1.2	5	384,000	1.0	4			
Landbund	194,000	0.5	3	96,900	0.2	2	105,200	0.3	2	83,800	0.2	1			
Christlich-natl. Bauern u. Landvolk	1,108,700	3.0	19	90,600	0.2	1	46,400	0.1	...	......	...	...			
Deutsch-Hannov. Partei	144,300	0.4	3	46,900	0.1	...	64,000	0.2	1	47,700	0.1	...			
Deutsche Bauernpartei	339,600	1.0	6	137,100	0.3	2	149,000	0.4	3	114,000	0.3	2			
National Socialists	6,409,600	18.3	107	13,745,800	37.4	230	11,737,000	33.1	196	17,277,200	43.9	288	39,638,800	92.2	661
Other parties	1,073,500	3.1	4	342,500	0.9	1	749,200	2.2	...	136,646	0.3	...			

* No. invalid votes: 3,849,363

Reichstag Elections 1919-1933

proved unequal to this task, but perhaps there was no one in Germany who would have been more capable of dealing with such vast problems. In the Reichstag elections of September 14, 1930, the economic depression showed its profound political effects. The Nazis made extraordinary gains, winning almost one hundred seats more than they had in 1928. The Communists also gained, though less sensationally. The democratic parties of the center lost.

In these years the Nazis began to spend more and more money on propaganda. Their prospects became national in scope and the seizure of power now seemed a possibility. It is in this period that some of the most famous Nazi propaganda emerged. A young SA street fighter of dubious morals, Horst Wessel, took an old sailor's ditty which had a moving melody and wrote the words that made it the Nazi national anthem, "Raise the Banner," later known as the "Horst Wessel Song." Communists had earlier used the melody for a song of their own. Horst Wessel, a whore's lover and the friend of pimps in Berlin, was murdered in 1930, and promptly became Goebbels' ideal Nazi martyr. One poster showed Nazi mourners around the coffin of Horst Wessel above the caption, "A dead man calls upon us to act!" This was a great age for political poster propaganda. Another famous Nazi poster showed a family in dire need, with the caption, "Against despair and hunger—vote Hitler!" Yet another: "Our Last Hope— Hitler."

These were powerful appeals to the German masses. The Nazis did not have a coherent economic program. They did not want or need one. Had not the government of experts and democrats failed? Hitler blamed the depression upon the "November criminals," the Jews, the Treaty of Versailles, upon those dark, satanic men who had betrayed the German people. The Nazis emerged in 1930 as the second-largest party in the Reichstag, and many twilight conspiracies to bring Hitler to power and/or to use him began. These conspiracies only ended

Germany 1932, 'Mjölnir' (Hans Schweitzer)
Our last hope: HITLER

with Hitler's appointment as Chancellor on January 30, 1933.

5. Hitler and the Antirepublican Right

To some people on the right, such as the Nationalist kingmaker Alfred Hugenberg, the Nazis were a godsend, for they could supposedly be used. Here was a rightist, patriotic party which promised rearmament and had a mass base, something the Nationalists lacked. Could not Hitler be brought into a rightist antirepublican coalition with the blessings of President von Hindenburg? The thinking went that this would tame the Nazis, and the respectable right might steal his mass movement away from Hitler. Conservative propertied circles in Germany were terrified during the Great Depression that Bolshevism might emerge successful. Hitler did play this anti-Bolshevik theme unremittingly, but he had also learned some lessons from the dark events of the *Putsch* of 1923. He would no longer enter into a coalition with any rightist force unless it was clear from the beginning that he controlled it and coordinated its actions. In order not to be used he would have to have power (*i.e.*, the promise of the chancellorship) in such a coalition *before* the "seizure of power."

Adolf Hitler had emerged by 1930 as one of the most important political figures in Germany. Certainly he was ubiquitous. Hitler was one of the first political figures to make use of new forms in transportation and the media. The Nazis, for example, in addition to their famous poster art, soon made use of the sound films that were introduced in Germany at this time. Hitler would fly from rally to rally in an airplane, descending from the clouds like a Chaplinesque Wotan coming down from Valhalla. And in a time of despair, Hitler's constant reaffirmation of traditional German values, ironic against the background of some of the human types in the movement, reassured the German nation that if Hitler were in power all would be well again. Industrialists saw him as a man who would break the trade unions and smash the Bolsheviks, thus opening the way for rearmament. Reactionary nationalists felt that he might restore the old order of 1914.

Hitler was aware of attempts to use him to reestablish an order which he felt had been fundamentally untenable and unhealthy for the German nation. Hitler told Hermann Rauschning that he would never fight a war in order to regain the borders of 1914, and that one of the reasons he was grateful to the "November criminals" of 1918 was that they had at least done away with the Hohenzollern monarchy. Hitler, however, usually kept these points to himself. Undoubtedly, some of the Nationalists who entered into the "Harzburg Front" alliance with Hitler in 1931 felt that the ex-corporal would restore the Hohenzollern monarchy. Interested parties succeeded in October in bringing about a preliminary meeting between Adolf Hitler and von Hindenburg. Hitler, using a more or less reputable officer, Hermann Göring, in order to impress Hindenburg, raved on for some time to the cranky old man. Hindenburg was unimpressed, and later commented that Hitler might be good enough to be Minister of Posts, but never a Chancellor. The meeting was a failure.

During these years before 1933 Party membership went way up, as did the number of volunteers for the SA. The SA, after all, seemed to offer some reason to live, and some means for a subsistence livelihood. It gave a young man a uniform, a couple of meals a day, and even a place to stay in an urban barracks. In addition, the SA offered the opportunity for street violence and homosexual opportunities for those so inclined. This appealed to an enormous number of young Germans in an age of growing despair. Communist and Nazi clashes resulted in many deaths between 1929 and 1933, though occasionally, to the despair of most of the Nazi electorate, they did collaborate. Such cooperation occurred during the Berlin transportation strike in the autumn of 1932.

What was the source of this Nazi upsurge in strength, its influx of new members and new voters? In part it was the despairing youth. Millions of young Germans could vote for the first time between 1930 and 1932. The parliamentary system seemed corrupt, inefficient, and unable to solve the economic and social problems of the Reich. Individuals of all social classes flocked to the Nazis, including a sizable number of proletarians. The Nazis were, after all, creating an alternative state at an ever-accelerating pace. This opened up new positions in various Party organizations to the young and the ambitious. More men than women flocked to the Hitler movement, more young than old.

The existential despair prevalent in German society was graphically illustrated by its art and motion pictures. The movie *M*, starring Peter Lorre, is the story of a child-murderer who ultimately confesses the compulsion that drove him to his acts before a hostile but empathetic audience. Its dark mood was typical of the mood of late Weimar Germany. Political art was ever more sadistic, and not just the art of the Nazis. Mass murderers such as the so-called Düsseldorf Vampire were hailed as heroes by hysterical throngs of people. German society had been in crisis since 1914, a crisis of war and defeat, of political change, of inflation and assassination. When the few Weimar years of stability (1924-1929) proved to have been illusory, the moral fiber of the nation broke. German society, not necessarily due to unique faults of its own, proved unable to cope with the forces unleashed by modernity. In the Hitler movement, essentially a retrogressive tribal reaction, many people saw the source of a new racial folk community and of their own individual redemption. This was Hitler's appeal. Generations of militarism, racialism, and social strain would now yield a grim harvest. A movement which promised everything and was responsible for nothing would come to power against a nihilistic background.

By early 1932, with the Depression raging unabated, various extremist forces in the Weimar Republic began to call for new elections to the Reichstag. They argued that the Reichstag of 1930 was no longer representative, and in this they were proved right. But first an election had to be held for the Presidency of the Reich. After some indecision Hitler decided to run against Hindenburg. Indeed, there was so much pressure from below for the Nazis to do something to seize power that if Hitler had decided to stay out of this contest (although the negative result was clear from the beginning) he might have lost control of the Nazi movement. It would then have disintegrated into warring, conspiratorial factions.

Early in 1932, a group of industrialists, meeting through the offices of men such as Kurt von Schroeder, head of the Stock Exchange in Cologne, and the opportunistic but clever financial wizard Hjalmar Schacht, brought about a meeting between German industrialists, financiers, and Hitler. Hitler came out of this meeting at the Düsseldorf Club with pledges of large-scale financial support—financial support which would be vital in the forthcoming election campaigns. The Nazis spent much more than they received in 1932, and without such financial support the Party would have been in dire straits in that fateful year. If the big capitalists thought that they could buy or control Hitler, they were mistaken, though the full extent of their miscalculation was not clear until long after 1933.

The bankruptcy of the democratic forces in Weimar was never clearer than in this Presidential election of 1932. Hindenburg was prevailed upon to run, although he was in his eighties and probably senile. Forces that needed him appealed to the old man's patriotism and vanity. The two elements, in any event, were indistinguishable parts of his character. The Social-Democrats, the largest party in the Reichstag, did not even put up a candidate. They hid behind the authoritarian Hindenburg in order to shield the proletariat from Hitler. The Communist candidate, Ernst Thaelmann, had no chance of winning. Chancellor Heinrich Bruening campaigned for Hindenburg, making effective speeches all over the country. Bruening thought that he was on the verge of great successes in the disarmament talks taking place in Switzerland. This could only strengthen his political position at home. Bruening felt that a resounding Hindenburg victory would dazzle the public and, in collaboration with his Interior Minister Groener, allow him to crack down on rowdy groups such as the SA. The camarilla around Hindenburg, consisting of his State Secretary, Meissner, his son Oskar, and his new favorite, the renegade Catholic Center politician Franz von Papen, saw its own interests at stake in preserving Hindenburg's Presidency. They feared the loss of political power for their class, and the expropriation of their lands and property. Hindenburg did not win a clear majority in the first round, and in the runoff he barely received 50 percent. This was more than enough for victory, however, though the fact that so many millions of Germans voted for Adolf Hitler was an ominous sign.

No document is more revealing of the rapidly alternating sense of hope and despair which animated the Nazi leadership in this year than Joseph Goebbels' published (1934) diary, *From the Kaiserhof to the Reich Chancellery.* The Kaiserhof Hotel was the headquarters of the Party in Berlin. By 1932 Goebbels had long since hitched his star to that of Hitler, and he was never to turn away from this course. Yet he was burdened by financial worries due to the high cost of political propaganda. Too many elections were being held in 1932. Goebbels also realized that unless the Party succeeded in seizing power within the near future, forces within it might break away from Hitler's leadership and attempt either violent revolution or collaboration with non-Nazi politicians such as Kurt von Schleicher and Franz von Papen.

6. Von Papen and the Bankruptcy of Reaction

In a monumental act of personal ingratitude and political stupidity, Hindenburg did Hitler a real favor by withdrawing Presidential support for Bruening's emergency decrees soon after his successful runoff for the Presidency. The camarilla around Hindenburg had been impressed by the Nazi showing in that runoff and by increased Nazi militancy on the streets. Bruening had responded to this violence and to his presumed victory in the Presidential election by outlawing the SA. Hindenburg was uneasy about this because, as the men around him whispered, the real threat was from the *left* and not from Hitler. The oily Franz von Papen, who flattered the old man's vanity better than any other individual, told the Reich President that if he were appointed Chancellor he could bring the Nazis into some kind of stable collaboration with the government. Thus, it would no longer have to govern by emergency decree.

In supporting the quasi dictatorship of Bruening, Hindenburg had ever more closely identified himself with the unpopular economic policies of his "hunger" Chancellor. If there was one thing that Hindenburg did not want, it was unpopularity or direct political responsibility. Hence he was relieved when von Papen told him that it was possible to form a new government which would have a broad base and a national mandate. One of von Papen's first acts as Chancellor was to withdraw Bruening's decree against the SA. He showed his militant antileftist spirit by using the Reichswehr under Defense Minister von Schleicher to disband the democratic Weimar coalition in Prussia on July 20, 1932. Von Papen, however, had the support of only about 10 percent of the deputies in the Reichstag, and there was no hope of collaboration with the Nazis so long as the old, unrepresentative 1930 Reichstag was in power.

In the new Reichstag elections, held at the end of July, the unpopularity of the von Papen-Hindenburg regime became clear. The Nazis gained well over a hundred seats, emerging as the largest party in the Weimar Republic. They were now the strongest single legal political force in Germany since the heyday of the Social-Democrats in 1919. The Communists also made gains, but the dynamics of the situation were such that for every vote that the Communists gained, two frightened German petit bourgeois or bourgeois fled to the Nazis. The parties of the center and the moderate left were the big losers in the elections of July, 1932. Von Papen's position continued to be difficult, though the Nazis, jockeying for power and digesting their great election gains, did "tolerate" him (*Politik der Tolerierung*) in the summer and early autumn. Von Papen's so-called Cabinet of Barons was the most reactionary government the Weimar Republic had ever known, though surprisingly, von Papen was more in favor of economic expansion through public expenditure than Dr. Bruening had been. The Nazis reaped the popularity accruing from these public works projects after Hitler came to power, when pump priming planned and approved by the von Papen government resulted in thousands of jobs.

With the winter approaching—always the worst time in terms of unemployment—von Papen became increasingly desperate. He could not put together a viable coalition in the Reichstag. The Social-Democrats, remembering what his government had done to them in Prussia, would have no part of him. The Communists were, of course, still in opposition. The Nazis, though they tolerated him for awhile because of the favors that he had done for them, began to feel the pressure from below for new elections or for some type of dramatic action. Von Papen, who had been nominally associated with the Center Party for some time, now beheld the unhappy spectacle of the Nazis and the Center collaborating in the Reichstag in electing Hermann Göring to its Presidency. With little support in the Reichstag, von Papen was in an impossible position. The real question was whether he would be able to dissolve the Reichstag before his enemies put through a motion of no confidence. In the confused jockeying which occurred in September, the only thing which clearly emerged was that new elections would be held in early November. Von Papen knew of the popular pressures to which the Nazis were being subjected by their following, and he felt he could only gain from new elections. How much further, after all, could their negativism and intransigence carry them? The Nazi coffers were almost empty due to the four major campaigns which had already taken place in 1932.

These elections of November 5, 1932 were somewhat of a setback for the Nazis. Their number of seats in the Reichstag dropped from 230 to 196, though they were still by far the largest party in that chamber. The Communists polled almost six million votes and now had 100 members in the Reichstag. The German Nationalists, whose relationship to the Nazis had been growing cooler during the later von Papen period, also made gains. None of this could really alter the chaotic and conspiratorial nature of late Weimar politics, but von Papen smugly viewed the "new" situation as a victory for his policy. Having rebuffed the Nazis at the polls, he now felt he could bring a chastened Nazi leadership, particularly Hitler, into a rightist majority coalition. True, the Nazis had lost votes, but von Papen was still unable to put together a viable coalition. His schemes and conspiracies, which had caused the national fever to rise ever higher through insanely demoralizing (and violent) election campaigns, had temporarily run their course. Von Papen resigned, owing to Hindenburg's reluctant pressure, on November 17, though the old man was still fond enough of his "young friend" to send him a portrait of himself with the inscription *Ich hat' einen Kameraden*, "I had a comrade."

7. Reich Chancellor Adolf Hitler

Von Papen's successor was Kurt von Schleicher, a political desk general who had been Minister of Defense in the von Papen government. In this capacity he, along with General von Rundstedt, had been directly responsible for the expulsion of the Social-Democratic coalition government from Prussia on July 20, 1932. Von Schleicher was full of schemes. He thought that he might be able to detach the "social" wing of the Nazi Party from Hitler's leadership. Thus, he hoped that he would be able to make a deal with Gregor Strasser. Unfortunately, Strasser was irresolute and went on a vacation to Italy, thus killing this scheme. Schleicher felt that he might be able to turn to the free trade unions and the Social-Democrats, but these were precisely the forces that had been most offended by his coup d'état of July 20. Though certain trade unionists would deal with him, the Social-Democrats were generally adamant in their refusal to collaborate. Schleicher prided himself on being the "social general," a man who would inspire confidence in both the nationalist and Socialist camps, but his dealings with "radical" elements only undercut his popularity with Hindenburg. The old man sharply changed his attitude toward Schleicher between Christmas 1932 and early January, 1933. The camarilla around Hindenburg was afraid that Schleicher, like Bruening before him, was too sympathetic to "Bolshevistic" radical reformist elements. There were rumors that Schleicher was behind the investigation of the alleged embezzlement of *Osthilfe* or eastern agrarian relief funds by great East Prussian landlords, among them the son of President von Hindenburg.

Von Papen schemed constantly from its inception early in December, 1932 to bring down the Schleicher government. The obvious prize was Hitler's National Socialist movement. Whichever rightist or "nationalist" politician could tame the Nazis and bring them into a respectable coalition regime with majority support in the Reichstag would have supreme power. What men like von Papen and Schleicher did not understand was that Hitler was determined to secure supreme power for himself. He would accept only the Chancellorship, not a vice-chancellorship in a government appointed by Hindenburg. Hitler had recently met with Hindenburg, on August 13, 1932. This meeting had aroused great expectations, and when Hitler failed to become Chancellor, his prestige in the Nazi *Bewegung* suffered a drop. Hitler, as

Goebbels noted in his diary, would never again undergo such a humiliation. This time it would be *va banque,* complete power or a major political crisis.

The elections in the small state of Lippe-Detmold, scheduled for mid-January, 1933, offered the Nazis a golden opportunity. They threw all their funds and energy into this electoral campaign in order to prove that they were not in decline, as the Reichstag elections of November, 1932 had seemed to indicate. The Nazis did very well in Lippe-Detmold (though not spectacularly so), and they flaunted this victory as renewed proof of the "irresistible" nature of the Nationalist Socialist movement. For rightist, nationalist politicians and leaders such as von Papen, Schleicher, and Hindenburg the question was more than ever not the destruction of the Nazi movement, but its incorporation into a rightist coalition. Von Papen felt he had the answer, and Hindenburg was always willing to listen to his "loyal, young friend." Von Papen argued that if Hitler were made Chancellor and he himself Vice-Chancellor in a cabinet in which only three or four members were Nazis, the nationalist movement for renewal of the *Volk* would take a great stride forward. The Nazis would obviously become more responsible with the acquisition of power. If von Papen, Hugenberg, and Hitler could agree on a coalition, it was conceivable that such an alliance would gain a majority in a newly elected Reichstag. With Hindenburg's friend von Papen in control of the Vice-Chancellorship, the ship of state would remain steady, though it would, of course, veer starward. The embarrassing investigations of the *Osthilfe* scandals would cease. The street violence, so typical of clashes between the Nazis and other paramilitary groups since 1930, might come to an end. Further, Paul von Hindenburg would no longer have to govern through unpopular emergency decrees. Ironically, one of the attractions for von Hindenburg of the appointment of Hitler as Chancellor would be that as leader of the largest party in the Reichstag he would restore a semblance of legality to the Weimar governing processes, over which he presided, thereby relegitimizing them and him. By late January, 1933 Schleicher was finished, though rumors swirled about regarding a supposed coup on his part, aimed at preventing von Papen's scheme from going through. This was nothing but gossip—unfortunately.

The Weimar Republic was conceived in despair and nurtured on the hope of social renewal. It died in the midst of demoralization and economic hopelessness when President von Hindenburg agreed to appoint as Chancellor a man who would bring about a "national revolution."

CHAPTER IV

Adolf Hitler Rules the Reich, 1933-1939

1. Into the Third Reich: "Coordination" and "Renewal"

THE German right generally greeted Hitler's appointment as Chancellor with glee. Some Catholic conservatives soon changed their minds, as did the rightist historian Oswald Spengler; others, such as the Nationalist leader and communications king, Alfred Hugenberg, were unceremoniously dumped in 1933 when they had served Hitler's purposes. The scheming Catholic aristocrat Franz von Papen did more than any other Hindenburg associate to bring Hitler to power (with himself as Vice-Chancellor), and he was almost murdered for his efforts on at least two later occasions. Ironically, von Papen was acquitted at Nürnberg in 1946. Millions of "good Germans" hailed this new age of a determined, authoritarian *Führer,* this "victory of one half of the nation over the other half," as the aged German historian Friedrich Meinecke phrased it in 1945. The Social-Democrats were demoralized owing to years of economic failure and political infighting with the Communists, and the latter showed by their passive behavior in 1933 that Stalin's strategy for the past five years had been criminally stupid. Hitler knew that his main immediate tasks were threefold: (1) restore the German economy, do this or go under; (2) give the nation a sense of community and direction, however false; and (3) achieve parity for German rearmament—the undoing of the *Diktat* of Versailles—without frightening the erstwhile and burdened Allies and their eastern "satellites" into intervention. In examining these problems it will be useful to consider the views of various historians who have come to grips with National Socialism.

Wolfgang Sauer, in posing the question: "National Socialism: Totalitarianism or Fascism?"[1] examines some of the interpretations which have been advanced regarding this force which came to power in 1933. The bulk of his article describes other historians' theories, occasionally criticizing them. Toward the end, Professor Sauer, building on the work of German social historians, advances an interesting thesis. He sees the crisis of German culture as representative of a gap between an embattled élite and the frustrated masses. One part of these masses formed their own sane subculture, Marxian Socialism. This, however, had clearly failed by 1933, for it was divided and impotent. Other segments of the masses, however, including elements of the middle and lower-middle classes, embraced what Sauer aptly calls barbarism. They responded to Hitler's appeal to the uprooted, and hence he succeeded.

By the evening of January 30, 1933 Germany was led by a Nazi Chancellor and a rightist, mainly non-Nazi cabinet. The right had intended to use Hitler's mass movement against the left, and in this at least the right was not to be deceived. What men like the Nationalist leader Alfred Hugenberg did not expect, however, was that they too would be without power by the autumn of 1933. Hitler needed the Nationalists in order to achieve a working majority in March in the newly elected Reichstag. He needed the terrorized deputies of parties such as the Center in order to carry out a dictatorial revision of the Weimar constitution later in the same month. Once these things were accomplished, Hitler had no further

---

[1] *American Historical Review,* LXXIII, 2 (December, 1967).

use for the non-Nazi right. He continued, however, to woo large masses of people with pictures of himself, alongside the revered von Hindenburg. Hitler was careful to associate himself with values and symbols dear to the traditionalist right, but he ruled through the NSDAP alone.

William Sheridan Allen has given us an imaginative recreation of the results of this Nazi seizure of power in a small town in north-central Germany.[2] This town, to which the author gives the pseudonym Thalburg, had a Nazi electoral majority even before 1933. In this it was a bit atypical. In other ways, however, Allen's portrait captures the results of Nazi "coordination" (Gleichschaltung) policies as they changed the atmosphere and social life of Thalburg, and countless other places like it. Desperate "little men" of all classes, fed up with economic collapse and the political stagnation of the Weimar Republic, greeted the advent of National Socialism with either enthusiasm or apathy. There was almost no outright resistance. The SPD was demoralized, and democracy had clearly been a failure. While some Thalburgers deplored the anti-Semitic excesses of the Party, they generally overlooked these in favor of the "positive" Nazi policies: enthusiasm, patriotism, a new sense of national life, collective work to overcome the Depression, and destruction of the "trouble-making" unions and parties.

Allen is successful in showing how the NSDAP atomized German society by forcing all autonomous groups into situations in which their membership related more to the state than to each other. A member of a hunting club, for example, was now a member of a National Socialist Hunting League, and he might be judged accordingly. Allen shows how personal opportunism led many to the Party (see the huge number of membership applications in March, 1933), while local Party leaders abused their powers in order to settle old scores.

---

[2] The Nazi Seizure of Power: The Experience of a Single German Town, 1930-1935 (Chicago, Quadrangle Books, 1965).

One significant point is that the NSDAP leadership, itself so colorful in terms of morality and personal codes of conduct, by no means disowned spontaneous brutality and even thievery on the part of *Gau-* and *Kreisleiter*. The NSDAP had to toe the line between this alliance of barbaric impulses and the equally important "bourgeois" call for a "revolution" based on law and order. Hitler knew this.

It is not difficult to appreciate why a large segment of the threatened *Mittelstand* (artisans, small businessmen, middling peasants) reacted positively in 1933 to Hitler and his policies. But in order to maintain his power in 1933, Hitler also needed the tacit support or at least the tolerance of more stable groups, such as the old German civil service, the army, and the diplomatic corps.

The men who staffed the Reich and Prussian civil service corps were generally conservative nationalists who had loyally served the republic while disliking the principles on which it was based and the circumstances in which it had arisen—the defeat of Germany and sporadic civil war. Hitler's entourage was noticeably lacking in men of managerial and administrative capacity, at least in 1933. He needed the careerist traditionalists as much as he despised them. But how did he win them over? For one thing, their jobs were at stake, and when it became clear that (except for the Jews, of course) there would be no major purge of the civil service, they heaved a sigh of relief. The Nazis had an administrative apparatus throughout the Reich before 1933 (organization by *Gau* and *Kreis*), and their aim was to parallel and control the state bureaucracy, not to destroy it.

The nationalism of the Nazis, combined with the favor which respected conservatives bestowed upon the new Chancellor, impressed the civil service and the diplomatic corps. Such men wanted to smash the "fetters" of Versailles, and if they thought in such long-range political terms, most of them probably imagined that Hitler, guided by von Papen, Hugenberg, and von Hindenburg would restore the German frontiers of 1914 without a major war. As an added bonus, Hitler might restore Imperial Germany's social structure. Yet by the end of 1934 Hindenburg was dead, Hugenberg and von Papen were politically comitose, and the DNVP (Nationalist Party) and the right-wing veterans' league (Stahlhelm) had been dissolved. Despite such unpleasantries, the governmental establishment felt that Hitler had done great things for the Reich. These civil servants and diplomats rationalized their roles even after 1933 by telling themselves that they were needed as a "moderating" influence. Thus, they rejoiced at Hitler's destruction of the "radical" leadership of the SA on June 30, 1934, though they found his methods a bit distasteful. . . . Men such as the aristocratic career diplomat Herbert von Dirksen continued to serve the Third Reich, and they desperately tried to convince themselves that there were elements of Wilhelminian continuity in Hitler's policies. Von Dirksen's memoirs[3] are quite frank on this point, and they are especially useful in explaining why these arrogant servants of the German state lent their talents to Hitler's regime.

Men such as Herbert von Dirksen were not theoreticians. Behind all of Hitler's ravings they found precious nuggets of traditional conservatism and old-time Bismarckian foreign policy aims. What men such as von Dirksen wanted to overlook was the Nazi destruction of the legacy of the *Rechtsstaat,* the state based upon justice, natural law, and widely accepted Western principles of equity and fair procedure. Yet as early as 1933 the Nazi legal theorist Carl Schmitt set forth a revolutionary Nazi concept in murky Teutonic prose *(The State, the Movement, and the Nation: The Three Arms of Political Unity)* when he argued that the liberal party-state had been replaced by the racial Führer-state. The state was no longer an arena for clashing political and economic interests, all of which were entitled to equity; it was now the emanation

---

[3] *Moscow, Tokyo, London: Twenty Years of German Foreign Policy* (Norman, Oklahoma, University of Oklahoma Press, 1952).

of the *Volk*, of the race as led by the Führer Adolf Hitler. All institutions, including von Dirksen's beloved diplomatic corps, would have to serve this new state—or be crushed. They served.

2. Youth and the Churches

Hitler knew that most German adults had serious reservations about this new paganism and the demoniac totalitarianism that he embodied. He was especially fervent when addressing the assembled youth at the annual Nürnberg Party rally in September, 1934. Hitler gloated over the way in which this youth belonged to the movement body and soul—"You are flesh of our flesh, and blood of our blood, and it cannot be otherwise!" Ever resentful of his social betters and of class distinctions which had humiliated him in the past, Hitler and Youth Leader von Schirach saw this youth as being "without class distinctions and without caste." In the serried ranks of the Hitler Youth they saw a Nazi *Volksgemeinschaft* in embryo, a folk community which would incarnate the ideals of the Party. This community would embrace the youth of the nation: "He who does not go through your comradely community will not belong to us!" Baldur von Schirach, a minor poet and Hitler Youth leader, described the aims of this organization in 1934 in his *The Hitler Youth: Idea and Form.*[4]

The German youth movement antedated von Schirach by a hundred and twenty years. It had always been nationalistic, with an increasingly racist and anti-Semitic tinge after 1890. This earlier German youth movement satisfied the yearnings of alienated young people by leading them back to the countryside, to the timeless ideas of comradely friendship and the erotic cult of community. The Hitler Youth thus built upon a venerable German tradition. Von Schirach, however, was careful to

---

[4] See George L. Mosse, *Nazi Culture* (New York, Grosset and Dunlap, 1966).

point out that the HJ (Hitler-Jugend) wanted no part of the apolitical sentimentality that marked the nature worship of this earlier phenomenon.

He did, however, parade the cult of the superiority of the countryside over the "morally corrosive dangers" of the great cities. This old rightist theme struck a responsive chord in many a German heart, but privately Hitler himself had been brutal regarding the prospects for the survival of small private agriculture in the eastern *Gaue*. He did not talk about the "idiocy of rural life," as had Marx in 1848, but he was just as deterministic in his assumption that world-power status implied great industries and cities above all else.

Similarly, von Schirach wrote that, "Every youth movement needs the spiritual cooperation of the parental home." What was more sacred to the German imagination in a time of crisis than the image of the stable, solid, bourgeois family? The Nazis knew that quite often they would be in a struggle with the parents or the Church of a given child for his or her body and soul. They preferred peaceful capitulation by the other side, so sweet words were spewed forth by the same Party which in 1920 guaranteed that it stood for a "positive (*i.e.*, Nazi) Christianity."

The Nazis wished to atomize existing institutions without destroying them. They wished to end the influence, for example, of a teacher over his pupils insofar as the teacher instilled a desire for free intellectual inquiry in the student. Nevertheless, they needed the teachers. The function of the teacher during this regime was to teach his specialty along with a correct appreciation for National Socialist doctrine. Von Schirach was very careful in dealing with this problem. The social egalitarianism of much of the Nazi movement made the teacher—presumably a "reactionary" of Aryan background who had survived the limited professional turnover of 1933—a natural object for the resentment of youth. Here was a petty authoritarian figure whose only source of authority was the tolerance of the regime. How could he dare interfere with the demands of the Hitler Youth upon the time of his students? No teacher should embarrass a Hitler Youth leader in front of his peers by disciplining him, and the teacher should not think of his status as automatically leading to a high position in the Hitler Youth organization, even if he had joined the Party in February or March of 1933. This type of intimidation "coordinated" the German teachers, most of whom had always been outspoken nationalists.

The Nazis came up against a touchier problem when dealing with the Evangelical and Catholic churches. The German people have always considered themselves thoroughly Christian, and with very rare exceptions those hailing Hitler in the 1930's did not see any inherent contradiction between this attitude and the teachings of the churches. Far from it. As in all nations, so in Germany, organized Christianity had long since come to terms with the modern nationalism that had so disturbed Pope Pius IX in 1864. German Protestants ever since Luther had been schooled in respect for the state as an "order stemming from God." The Catholics, given their bitter experience in the struggle with Bismarck in the 1870's, had more reason for suspicion. Yet their Center Party had reached an accommodation with the state long before World War I, and during the Weimar period it had participated in both the Weimar (Prussian) and Grand (Reich) Coalitions. Both of these were committed to the support of the liberal state. Von Papen had negotiated a concordat with Pope Pius XI on behalf of Prussia in 1932, and in the following year Hitler reached an agreement on behalf of the Reich. The presence of von Papen in the Hitler government as Vice-Chancellor quieted the fears of many Catholics. The Center voted for Hitler's Enabling Act in March, 1933. Most Protestants and most Catholics saw themselves first and foremost as Germans suffering under the disabilities imposed upon the Reich by the Treaty of Versailles and the Weimar system. In this sense religious affiliation is at best a weak guide to a study of their political attitudes in 1933.

Adolf Hitler despised Christianity. Like his Head of the Party Chancellery after 1941, Martin Bormann, Hitler saw Christianity as a Jewish offshoot immersed in an ethic of pity which destroyed the strong in order to perpetuate the weak. Furthermore, Hitler viewed the Christian religion as a supranational phenomenon that transcended the new "science" of the twentieth century—National Socialist racism. The NSDAP contained its radical anti-Christian wing, which was represented by Bormann, Goebbels, and Rosenberg. These men intended to extirpate German Christianity after the victorious conclusion of the Second World War. Hitler sympathized with this aim. He criticized Houston Stewart Chamberlain, one of the founders of racist theory, for his "Christian" sentiments. Hitler had been born a Catholic, but religion seems to have played a small role in his upbringing. Chancellor Bruening once made the incisive remark that Hitler came from an area of Austria that "had not seen any religion" for centuries. Be this as it may, Adolf Hitler respected the power of the Catholic Church—he, unlike Stalin, never would have asked, "And how many divisions does the Pope have?"—because he knew that it could turn important segments of world and German opinion against his regime in a time of crisis. For the Protestant churches he had little but contempt.

The Nazi Party had always been pagan in spirit. Its original program mumbled something about a Germanic, "positive" Christianity, but this was a meaningless electoral device. Hitler was capable of many such distortions. For example, he kept appealing to nationalistic Germans in the 1920's on the basis of an attack against the "slavery" of the Versailles Treaty. This led many Germans to feel that Hitler, possibly like the Nationalists or even Gustav Stresemann, merely wanted to return to the borders of 1914 and get back a few African colonies. Such was not the case. Hitler appealed to traditional German values a good part of the time, and he did not intend to undo his potential by foolish anti-Christian utterances. Writing in 1924, Hitler criticized the early Austrian pan-

German racialist Georg von Schoenerer for alienating the Catholic Austrian masses by his blatant Teutonic paganism. Adolf Hitler would make no such mistake. He wanted at least the tacit support of the churches while consolidating his regime, just as he needed the support of other traditional institutions in German society. By and large, Hitler received this support.

J. S. Conway's important study, *The Nazi Persecution of the Churches 1933-1945*,[5] has skillfully outlined the different stages of Nazi ecclesiastical politics. At first, as Conway shows, Hitler made promises to Rome, and encouraged clerics of differing confessions to attend the Nürnberg rallies. Of course, local actions by Gauleiters could always be an embarrassment, but they were not inspired by Hitler. A typical sermon preached by a Lutheran pastor on the Sunday following the Enabling Act of March 5, 1933 was called, "What a transformation through the Almighty's dispensation!" Was not Hitler, after all, a believer in God, a man who often referred to "divine Providence" (*die göttliche Vorsehung*) in his speeches? The Nazis looked askance at self-proclaimed atheists, preferring the neutral designation *Gottgläubige* (believer in God). Only a "Marxist," after all, would call himself an atheist.

In the early years of the Third Reich Hitler tried to lure the membership of the Protestant churches away from them by patronizing an Evangelical Reich Church headed by Reichsbischof Ludwig Mueller. Nazi propagandists argued that Hitlerism and Christianity were one. This experiment was a failure, and by 1935 another tack was decided upon. On July 16, 1935 a Ministry of Church Affairs was established under the leadership of Hans Kerrl. This attempt to manipulate the churches from above led to the rise of ecclesiastical and lay resistance, and Kerrl was no more successful than Ludwig Mueller's German Christian movement. High officials and organs of the Party continued to spread scurrilous

[5] (New York, Basic Books, 1968).

rumors about the churches and their personnel, and the paganism of men like Rosenberg and von Schirach was impatient with a state ministry that seemed to spend its time bargaining with the despised clerics. As the years passed, more churchmen understood the nihilist, pagan nature of the Third Reich, and it is not surprising that the Christian faith hardened the will of the opposition to Hitler after 1938. Yet it is a sad testimony to the spirit of our age that so few men protested the barbarisms of the early Nazi regime, particularly its anti-Semitism.

3. The Agony of the German Jews

It is impossible to understand this regime without examining the problem of anti-Semitism. Even A. J. P. Taylor, otherwise so anxious to play down any seriousness or consistency in Hitler's ideological views, admits that his anti-Semitism never wavered on the road to its ultimate destination. It is safe to say that a large portion of the German population harbored anti-Semitic sentiments in 1933, but this tells us little about the men who carried out Germany's Jewish policies after that date or about the historical and social processes which provided the framework for such policies.

In examining Hitler's formative years, we have briefly speculated upon the sources of his anti-Semitism. In the case of Vienna, this was a social and mental illness, the radicalism of the alienated and the misfits, the cunning of politicians and the income of pornographers. It had an even more deadly ingredient: scientific racism, claiming a base in the sciences of history and biology. The Austrian and German apocalyptic collapses of 1918, and the social chaos of the next few years gave a powerful impetus to this element, which had been in existence before 1914. To many people the Jew had now become the symbol of everything wrong with modernity, ranging from Bolshevism to finance capitalism, from the unfair competition of department stores to the Treaty of Versailles. Even in the abysmal conditions of 1932 Hitler may have come to power *despite* this anti-Semitism rather than because of it, but it remains true that large segments of the German *Mittelstand* possessed images of the Jew that made it easy for Hitler's words to manipulate latent symbols in the psyche of the masses.

As George Mosse has aptly remarked, when Hitler talked about Socialism, he meant only the expropriation of the Jews. Early in 1933 the Jews were thrown out of the teaching and civil service professions. On April 1, 1933 the Nazis began a nationwide boycott of Jewish businesses under the sadistic and paranoid slogan: "Germans, defend yourselves—Don't buy from Jews!" Hitler gloated as Goebbels described indignities visited upon Berlin's largely middle-class Jewish community. The Jews themselves were taken by surprise. Extremely patriotic, proud of their German heritage and their successful and creative assimilation into German life, they could not believe what was happening. One of their spiritual leaders, Rabbi Leo Baeck, understood it all too well and sadly commented that "The thousand-year history of German Jewry is over." Indeed it was. The Jews accounted for at most 1 percent of the German population at that time, and although they were prominent as professional men, merchants, large retailers, and middlemen they certainly had precious little control over the heart of the German economy—industry and its dependent banks. This April 1 boycott should have opened everyone's eyes, but some Jews were still convinced that World War service or some other contribution to the nation would ultimately save them. Many German Jews shared their Christian compatriots' contempt for the *Ostjuden* or more traditional Jews from the East. This did not help them. To Julius Streicher, pornographic editor of the *Stürmer*, a vicious lecher and lout who doubled as Gauleiter of Upper Franconia (until removed by Hitler, who was getting too many complaints), a Jew was a Jew. Streicher played a major role in this boycott. Unfavorable international publicity in the West made this the last concerted public anti-Semitic atrocity until 1938. What followed, however, was a long, drawn-out strangulation of the means of livelihood of the Jews in Germany. Nicholas Berdyaev, the famous Russian philosopher, early realized that this Nazi anti-Semitism was of a new variety. It was racial in nature even though it drew upon traditional folk and religious anti-Jewish hatreds. It viewed the victims as bacilli without souls, as morbid entities who poisoned the nation. The Nürnberg Laws of 1935 defined the Jew along racial lines, and some of the Jews still in the Reich breathed a sigh of relief. Now that the situation was legally clarified, "one could make do." Actually, the situation of the Jews grew more perilous than ever. Many of the wealthier Jews had already emigrated, in some cases using domestic bribery and foreign connections in order to take some of their property out with them. Three years of economic strangulation had impoverished the Jewish community, and few foreign countries, the United States included, did much to help them. Autarchy ruled in Europe, and national hatreds were growing in intensity. Anti-Semitism was everywhere a factor during the economic crises of the 1930's, so several hundred thousand Jews were still in the Reich in 1937. The official Reich policy was one of emigration without property. This was the situation of these *deutsche Staatsbürger jüdischen Glaubens* (German citizens of the Jewish persuasion), as the German Jews had once proudly called themselves. The Jews who did get out of Germany before 1940 became some of the greatest intellectual lights of England and America.

On the night of November 9, 1938 violent anti-Jewish riots, instigated by elements of the Nazi Party, occurred all over Germany. Synagogues were burned, and there was so much glass from their windows lying about the streets that this became infamous in history as "Crystal Night." One of the most illuminating and shameful documents of this period was the record of Hermann Göring's November 12 conference on the "Jewish problem." Point 7 states that the Jews themselves would pay for the damage to their own property! A one-billion-mark fine was to be levied on the Jewish community. And let us remember that this community was impoverished by five and a half years of depredations. Emigration was still the official Reich policy on the Jews, but it became more difficult of achievement. The cycle was a vicious one: The more impoverished the Jews became, the more impossible it was for them to get visas from other countries. Nazi policy was thus cynical to the extreme. It had the further charming element of assuming that the export of "hated" refugee Jews would be the best advertisement for the solid basis underlying its own persecution of the Jews.

A circular of the Foreign Ministry, dated January 25, 1939, speaks of emigration of the Jews as the goal, but looks with hostility upon the idea of a Jewish state in Palestine. Evidently no one told Adolf Eichmann this, for at his trial he claimed that during this early period of his concern over the Jewish question, he had studied some Zionist works and was interested in that solution. German concern for Axis interests in the Arab world, however, ruled out consistent support for such a solution. Three parallel events in this same month underlined the stark tragedy that was in the making. The British White Paper on the Mandate Territory of Palestine stated that Jewish emigration to Palestine would be limited to 75,000 more persons, and would end entirely by 1943. President Roosevelt showed an awareness of the dark economic position of the Jews in Poland, not knowing that his concern was prophetic: Within less than three years they would be in ghettos that were waiting centers for the death camps of Auschwitz and Treblinka. Finally, Adolf Hitler told the Reichstag that if the *Jews* unleashed another war, they would not survive it.

4. Adolf Hitler and German Capitalism: Clashing Views

Many observers sensed that such a European war was indeed approaching in 1939. On March 15, 1939 Hitler annexed Bohemia and Moravia and on September 1 he attacked Poland. What was the state of the German economy on the eve of this Second World War? This question leads us to an examination of several inter-related problems. These concern, in order: (1) the nature of German society after six "peaceful" years of Nazism; (2) the nature of the German economy—capitalist, Social-ist, or something new; (3) Hitler, the armed forces, and economic preparations for war; and (4) Himmler's police and SS empire on the eve of their great expansion.

Hitler had made his peace with German capitalism long before the famous meeting with the captains of industry and banking at the Düsseldorf Club in January, 1932. German industrial barons such as Fritz Thyssen and Hugo Stinnes were nationalists who believed in the tradi-tion of economic nationalism taught by Johann Gottfried Fichte and Friedrich List. They wanted to continue and consummate the cartelization and monopolistic amal-gamation of German industry, which had begun forty years earlier. Far from regressing during the days of Weimar, this concentration of the German economy from precious raw materials to finished consumer or capital product had actually accelerated through the 1920's. The industrialists feared the KPD (Communists) and the Social-Democrats, and they resented the strength of the free trade union movement. In Hitler some of them saw a man who would lead Germany back to parity in arma-ments, national dignity, economic recovery, and social "order." The former president of the Reichsbank, Hjal-mar H. G. Schacht, an opportunistic, vain banker of strong nationalist tendencies, met Hitler in 1931 through Göring and Thyssen. He was a useful figure in winning over the financial community, because he was a man of great prestige and few scruples.

All of this raises a fundamental interpretive problem. Many German industrialists and bankers welcomed Hitler and cooperated with him. After 1933 profits steadily climbed and unemployment disappeared, as did the trade unions and the "Marxists." Yet should this lead one to assume that these twilight capitalists (to borrow a concept from Werner Sombart) took over the Nazi movement in 1932, bought it out so to speak, and manipulated it thereafter for their own ends? This interpretation of National Socialism was quite popular in the age of the Third Reich, largely because it blended nicely with certain key Marxist presuppositions about the relationship between economics and politics. To Marxists, Fascism—and National Socialism was for them a variety of this phenomenon—meant the manipulation of alienated, frightened, lower-middle-class masses in an age of capitalist crisis. Using nationalist and racist slogans, Hitler preyed upon fears of proletarianization and used the Nazi movement to smash temporarily the wave of the future—Marxism In the case of Mussolini, this interpretation seems to make a bit more sense, for Fascism in Italy was inseparable in its earliest growth from the industrial revolutionary crisis which had existed in Italy in 1919-1920. Even for Italian Fascism, however, this simplistic deterministic view of the phenomenon overlooked peculiar psychic and historical factors. Such a theory is even more inadequate in the case of Germany, an advanced industrial society, and thus potentially a more barbarous one. Historians of National Socialism who have made use of fundamentally Marxian premises include Franz Neumann and George W. F. Hallgarten. Hallgarten wrote in 1969 that ". . . I find it regrettable that our historians too often refuse to deal with the type of problems under discussion in a manner that would enable them to provide a convincing answer to the explanations advanced by the Marxist-Leninist schools." Hallgarten was referring to the connection between big business and the rise of Hitler.

Ernst Nolte, a prominent German historian of Fascism, has advanced a totally different viewpoint: "Fascism is only an important subject of historiography if it was more than the tool of certain private interests, and this decisive point *cannot* be cleared by narrating the various relations between the party and some industrialists. In this sense 'the neglect of the economic angle' may be the precondition of writing the history of genuine fascist movements." A clearer contrast in viewpoints cannot be imagined. Nolte has viewed different Fascist movements as similar insofar as they represent a revolt against alienating factors in modern history—social, intellectual, political, and economic—that have furthered the "transcendental integration" of all being over and above the personal and historical rootedness that older institutions provided for the individual. Nolte's approach borrows elements from the Hegelian and idealist traditions. He views National Socialism in the light of a general European revolt against the supranational.

Ernst Nolte sees Fascism as a structurally integrated phenomenon, one which died in Germany and the world in 1945. For Hallgarten and Franz Neumann National Socialism represents the German national form of late capitalism. Because they interpret it in the light of economic phenomena, rather than in terms of the *Zeitgeist* and its breakup, they would be less certain that it ended forever in 1945. Perhaps the most famous work embodying a Marxist interpretation of the Nazi phenomenon is Franz Neumann's *Behemoth,* first published in 1942.[6] Neumann's interpretation is worthy of some consideration, for it is not the vulgar Marxism explicit in Stalin's (post-1941) statement that "Hitler, Goebbels, Ribbentrop, Himmler and the other rulers of present-day Germany are but watchdogs of the German bankers and place the latter's interests above all other interests." Such a statement was good propaganda but idiotic analysis—at least if Stalin had said "industrialists" the crudeness of the statement would have been less apparent.

Franz Neumann was convinced that only economic determinism can explain National Socialism. He referred to the German economy after 1933 as "totalitarian monopoly capitalism." Neumann argued that the aim of total cartelization and monopolization could not have

---

[6] (New York, Harper & Row, 1966).

been achieved by German industry under the Weimar Republic, even in 1932. This led some industrialists to Hitler before 1933, and most of them to him after that fateful date. Neumann makes a powerful case when he tries to show that the cabinets of Bruening, von Papen, and von Schleicher fostered this aim of German industry, and that, in a sense, such an aim had been clearly before its eyes since 1890. On the economic level, Neumann saw continuity between the Weimar era and National Socialism.

Neumann's great work has manifold weaknesses. Its continuity is questionable and it is largely monocausal; that is, it deduces all of National Socialism's policies after 1933 from German economics. Neumann was building upon Marx's concept of the accelerating concentration of capital in the age of the dissolution of traditional capitalism. In this sense, both Franz Neumann and David Schoenbaum,[7] a non-Marxist interpreter of Nazi society, agree that there was a gap between Nazi ideology and Nazi performance. Neumann showed that the Nazis, who had earlier made much of the threats posed by big capital and big labor to the *Mittelstand* or independent middle classes, sped up the decline of this group by their monopolization policies. A modern full employment and war economy demanded efficiency and coordination—bigness—not the small entrepreneur or the petit bourgeois artisan. Neumann's investigations departed from "vulgar Marxism" by their thoroughness and their comprehension of difficult economic data. If his book is poorly organized, this was at least in part due to the early date of its publication—1942. He was trying to say a great deal about a phenomenon which still existed, and particularly in the last part of his book, where he dealt with the German New Order in wartime Europe, he was breaking new ground.

Neumann pointed to important contradictions in Nazi

---

[7] *Hitler's Social Revolution: Class and Status in Nazi Germany 1933-1939* (New York, Doubleday, 1966).

ideology. He showed that the old Nazi and "radical conservative" attack on *raffendes Kapital* (rapacious capital) as opposed to *schaffendes Kapital* (creative capital) was spurious. The Third Reich did *not* in fact actually control profits, and it gave managers the free run of their concerns. More relevant was the fact that the bankers, supposedly representing the rapacious capital that an early Nazi crackpot economist named Gottfried Feder associated with *Zinsknechtschaft* or "interest slavery," had by 1933 long since lost control of German industrial capitalism. The great concerns of 1933 usually generated their own capital, and in attacking the bankers the Nazis had been flogging a dying horse.

Franz Neumann makes one important point which may have unknowingly undermined his own thesis. After 1933 the NSDAP became an important business concern. Before that it had owned little more than the Franz Eher Verlag (the Party press), but after the seizure of power it developed various business interests. Among these were the Hermann Göring Stahlwerke (steelworks) and the different projects of the Deutsche Arbeitsfront (DAF, run by Dr. Robert Ley). Like Bertolt Brecht *(The Resistible Rise of Arturo Ui)*, Neumann viewed National Socialist Germany as a gangster capitalist state, one in which any entity needed its own economic freedom in order to survive. Hence the businesses of the Party. Yet if this was the case, does it not undermine the idea that the Party was the mere tool of big industry? How could the Party be this and simultaneously threaten, say, the steel industry? Perhaps if we understand the Party as a combination of nihilistic, atavistic ideology and of a desire for plunder and power, the point about Party combines will make more sense. Or does the Party turn from a puppet of business in 1933 to a monster devouring even its masters by 1942? These questions are suggested by Neumann's study; they are not answered in his book.

Franz Neumann tells us much about capitalism during the Nazi period. David Schoenbaum *(Hitler's Social Revolution)* asks important questions about the German people. In 1944 Carl Goerdeler, former Mayor of Leipzig and a major anti-Nazi conspirator, admitted that National Socialism had "democratized" Germany to the extent of creating a community based on mutual aid in times of crisis. The important contemporary West German sociologist, Ralf Dahrendorf, has pointed to the Hitler regime as a time of breakdown for old class distinctions and provincial particularisms.[8] Hence, in its own perverse and at times unintended manner, it was a *modernizing* factor. Building on insights such as these, Schoenbaum's study asks questions about status and social mobility during the Nazi period. He is dealing with ideology and attitudes as well as with quantifiably measurable sociological factors, and in this sense his study is a useful complement and antidote to Neumann's economic-deterministic approach.

Schoenbaum, following the work of political scientists such as Laswell and Lerner *(World Revolutionary Elites)*, argues that the NSDAP élite represented a relatively young group, a "mobilization of disaffection." In a time of crisis and frustration, the young saw more upward mobility and meaning in the Party than they did in society as a whole. Even during the Third Reich, there was some new social mobility in the economy, the army, and the civil service, which together are the heart of any modern state. On this basis, Schoenbaum attacks Neumann as accurate in a limited but misleading way. In the study of society during the Third Reich one must assume complexity in motives and attitudes rather than a single pattern of economic causation. A single-cause theory hinders rather than furthers the pursuit of truth. Classes and social mobility did alter between 1930 and 1940, but more importantly, so did attitudes and expectations. The antiurban, antimodern ideology that many Nazis carried over into the 1930's clashed with the modern industrial nature and needs of the Greater German Reich, but this does not mean that this ideology was without effect upon

---

[8] *Society and Democracy in Germany* (New York, Doubleday, 1967).

the consciousness of the nation. The old élites reasserted leadership in organizations such as the Hitler Youth after 1935, but they in turn were altered by their role within the "revolutionary" Party.

Schoenbaum makes an interesting argument about the new nature of politics in Nazi Germany. Formerly, a certain social rank implied a certain political attitude or party. Now politics was desocialized, that is, every social group (except the Jews) could associate with the one legal Party and take from its ideology the bias or interest that justified that social group's participation in the life of the Third Reich. And while class lines remained, each class could look on with glee while the Nazis coordinated or destroyed one of its enemies. Yet class lines remained strong in 1945, for Fascism has never succeeded in overcoming the essential contradictions of a modern or quasi-modern society. This addendum represents an extension of one of Schoenbaum's conclusions.

The very groups to whose antimodern tendencies the Nazis so stridently appealed before 1933 continued to weaken after that date. The tradition of autarchic theory gave way, as Neumann observed, to the idea of the world as the exploitation base for the Greater German Reich and its enormous economic needs. Urbanization made new advances, and we might note that totalitarianism, so lacking in the atavistic self-image of the disoriented social groups that flocked to the Nazis, was in itself the greatest proof of the Nazi union of archaic values and technological modernity. Hitler himself once commented to Rauschning that it was hopeless to try to save a peasantry in decline. He was less open about this point in his electoral appeals to East Prussia in 1932. This totalitarianism was the negation of creative spontaneity, and the asocialization implicit in high crime rates was the converse side of the often hypnotic sense of community that the Nazis injected into the German social bloodstream.

5. Hitler's Conquest of the Wehrmacht

From German society we move back to its leader, Adolf Hitler, and see him on the eve of World War II. There is no question about his opinion of war: It was a vital and creative human activity. It was especially apt for Germans, because their best elements were heriocally Nordic and their geographic and demographic situation dictated certain needs that only a successful war could satisfy. At times the Führer could grow quite lyrical about art and peace, but he sensed that his own creativity would be mirrored in the diplomatic and military creation of a millennial national organism. Western historians have long been fond of depicting the difference between the conservative, hierarchical tradition of Prussia and the wilder, more romantic, racial and geopolitical musings of Adolf Hitler. Harold Laski saw Hitler as a failed pipe dreamer late in 1932, and the British historian A. J. P. Taylor tends to view his racial and geopolitical theories as the typical rightist visions of a semiliterate Central European bohemian. Yet it would be a mistake to go too far in this direction. We need not fall into the opposite trap and view Hitler (as did Churchill during the war) as but the latest incident in "Prussian" militarism. Yet Hitler's militarism fed upon the Prussian tradition of sacrifice, military posture, and war even as it devoured that tradition in 1944. Hitler hated the aristocratic pretensions of some of his generals, but he needed their officer corps. As we have seen, this was also true of the diplomatic corps, even after von Ribbentrop became Foreign Minister in February, 1938. It will be useful to investigate the relationship between Hitler and his human, economico-technological instruments of war.

The work of Sir John Wheeler-Bennett is a good starting place for a discussion of this topic. Sir John showed in 1953 (*Nemesis of Power*)[9] how and why the German officer corps rallied to Hitler in 1933. Ambition and

[9] (New York, St. Martin's Press, 1954).

social hostility to the republic played their role, but two famous illustrations from the year 1933 are even more revealing. One is the photograph of Hitler reverently shaking hands with President (and Field Marshal) von Hindenburg at Frederick the Great's Potsdam Garrison Church on March 21, 1933. To the officer corps of the Reichswehr, this signified the reconciliation of two Germanies, that of the Prussian tradition and that of the nationalistic (but democratic) masses. "The old Field Marshal and the young Chancellor. . . ." The second example is a poster that shows Hindenburg and Hitler side by side, with the caption, "The Field Marshal and the Corporal: Fight with Us for Peace and Parity." Hitler never alluded to his World War rank except when it suited a demagogic purpose. He knew that men like Generals von Brauchitsch and Halder sneered at the "Bohemian corporal."

One of Hitler's prime aims, considering his view of the state as an armed voice of the *Volk* in international affairs, was total control of the armed forces, of the Wehrmacht. He replaced the dead Hindenburg as Commander in Chief of the armed forces in the summer of 1934. Hitler demonstrated his own contempt for the social being of the German officer corps when he almost simultaneously disgraced and dismissed Field Marshal von Blomberg, the Minister of War, and General von Fritsch, Commander in Chief of the army, in 1938. Other ambitions and prejudices entered into these cases, but Hitler seized upon them to overthrow traditional control of the Wehrmacht. Hitler took over the War Ministry, reorganized it, and subjected its functions to his personal control or that of his lackey, General Wilhelm Keitel. The army, under von Brauchitsch, precariously maintained some of its esprit and independence, but even that largely disappeared by 1942. What is perhaps most amazing in all this is not the Nazi "coordination" of yet another traditional institution, but the ease with which Hitler took a proud but functionally apolitical body and used its demoralization and ambition for his own ends. Hitler thus exerted a perverted form of "civilian" control over the armed forces. Some older officers may have accepted this control as grudgingly as they had that of the Weimar Republic, but many newer and younger officers had boundless faith in Hitler. Colonel von Stauffenberg was politicized by what he came to see as Hitler's assault upon military honor and rational policy. Even if this unusual officer had killed the Führer at Rastenburg on July 20, 1944, the time for a reassertion of the Prussian military idea had long since passed.

Despite Hitler's concern to control the armed forces, and despite all of the Nazi Party's attempts to militarize and discipline the entire German nation, there remains a legitimate historical problem regarding the commitment of the government and the Party to a war economy before 1939. Although his use of certain statistics has been questioned, Mr. Burton Klein[10] has made a strong case for the argument that Hitler and Göring (head of the Four-Year Plan after 1936) did not commit Germany to relatively large-scale rearmament until 1938, years after the "myth" of German total rearmament had been born in the West and in Germany itself. Klein's statistics suggest that autarchy was no more a reality in 1939 than it had been in 1930.

6. Heinrich Himmler and Internal Security

As soon as the Nazis came to power they began to build up a new, centralized police force. In part, they worked with older elements in the Prussian and Reich ministries of the interior. There was a juridical problem in that the German Reich was not a unitary organism before 1933. The police of the *Länder* or states, of which Prussia was by far the largest, were under the control of interior ministers and police presidents who resented any Reich

[10] *Germany's Economic Preparation for War* (Cambridge, Cambridge University Press, 1957).

encroachment upon their prerogatives. Mr. Gerald Reitlinger[11] has argued that Hitler wanted an internal
militarized force at the exclusive disposal of himself and
of the Party. If this assumption regarding the growth of
the SS is correct, then Hitler expected a major war at
some time, for Reitlinger argued that Hitler saw the SS
as a reliable Party force in a time of potential internal
crisis. As Hitler often put it, there would never again be
a 1918, a German capitulation. Defeatist forces and sub-
versive elements would be ruthlessly dealt with, but for
this one had to have a centralized police force answerable
to Adolf Hitler and his trusted lieutenants. Was Hitler
planning a war, then, as early as 1934 and 1935?

In one sense, we cannot understand the Third Reich
unless we disassociate brutality from efficiency. One does
not always lead to or symbolize the other. In effect, the
confused Nazi administrative machine consisted of a
series of *rival fiefdoms,* all of them run by prominent Party
personages desperately trying to uphold their positions
within the NSDAP state. In this way, *governmental* positions did not necessarily connote real power. Joachim
von Ribbentrop was much in the news after 1938, but
he had little power. Rudolf Hess seemed close to Hitler
but his power base within the Party bureaucracy slipped
badly after 1938. Martin Bormann was little known to the
German public, but he consolidated his hold on the powerful Party Chancellery, with its access to Hitler, even
before Hess's position seemed to have weakened. Göring
built up his strength through the Prussian police and the
Geheime Staatspolizei (Secret State Police or Gestapo),
but after 1936 any real strength that he had rested upon
his economic power as Commissioner for the Four-Year
Plan and his command of the Luftwaffe. Heinrich
Himmler built his empire upon the police, particularly
after 1934. These men, and many others, disputed their
rivals' claims and endlessly plotted to enlarge their own
empires. Alliances were formed and dissolved. It is

[11] *The SS: Alibi of a Nation* (London, Heinemann Educational Books, 1956).

difficult to assume that Hitler was unaware of these struggles. Indeed, they probably pleased him, *for division meant that he was final unquestioned arbiter of the Reich's destiny*. In addition, such confusion, disguised under a plethora of impressive and status-laden titles, approximated his own style of life. Hitler made much of the fact that he took ultimate responsibility for his appointees' actions. He did not always say that he had also assumed ultimate power. He did not have to.

Heinrich Himmler built his own power on the basis of control of the German police. The SS had started before Himmler as an élite bodyguard for Hitler. After 1934 it grew rapidly, but certainly not as an independent army or élite Nazi alternative to the regular army. Himmler played a crucial role in the extermination of the supposedly dissident and "revolutionary" leadership of the mass paramilitary SA on June 30, 1934. The SA, an enormous group, had frightened the army, because it appeared that it might become the nucleus of a people's army on the French revolutionary model (1793), one that would replace the narrow Prussianism of Potsdam with the egalitarian Nazi fervor of the streets (1931). This indeed was the dream of Ernst Röhm, head of the SA. Hitler needed the support of the army in order to assume Hindenburg's military and symbolic prerogatives when the old man (or the "old idiot" as Hitler called him behind his back) died, as he finally did on August 2, 1934. Therefore, Röhm, a potential rival and current embarrassment, the possible leader of a radical "Second Revolution," was murdered along with other victims on June 30. Himmler, Hitler's *treuer Heinrich* (loyal Heinrich), showed his loyalty on this Night of the Long Knives.

Hitler did not have cause to doubt this loyalty until the last month of the Second World War. This is what accounted for Himmler's phenomenal rise, not his Nordic, romantic, racial visions. Hitler, in any case, had little but a bemused shrug of the shoulders for the latter. Himmler made use of the sinister talents of Reinhard Heydrich, future head of the ubiquitous Reich Security

Main Office (RSHA), for the purpose of compiling confidential information on Party and non-Party individuals —not excluding Adolf Hitler himself—as early as 1931. Himmler's power was thus based upon his police, intelligence, and SS network. By 1943 Himmler had long since displaced Göring as the second most powerful individual in Hitler's Europe.

The Gestapo was the Prussian creation of Hermann Göring, soon loosely subject to Wilhelm Frick, Reich Minister of the Interior. Early in 1934 Himmler got control of this organization. By 1936 he had himself appointed Chef der Deutschen Polizei (Chief of the German Police). Yet despite the expansion of the German police during this period, even the dread Gestapo was until 1936 in some legal manner subject to higher civil authorities within the Reich. This was not the case after 1936, even *de jure*. But Himmler's fiefdom consisted of far more than the police. He built the SS into an élite organization that controlled the concentration camps (the Totenkopfverbände or death's-head battalions), provided special guards of honor for Hitler (Leibstandarte Adolf Hitler), and had an auxiliary force ready for any internal contingency (the Verfügungstruppen or all-purpose troops). Himmler seems to have dreamed from a quite early date of turning the past-mentioned into the heart of a new élite army, one uncorrupted by the prejudices against National Socialist ideology that typified the Wehrmacht. In this his ambitions transcended those of Hitler, who at the time had no desire to see a "new SA" develop, even under Himmler. The rapid buildup of such a force would have antagonized the army, an abrasion which Hitler could ill afford during this period. Unlike Stalin, Hitler never tried to purge or decimate the German officer corps as a whole. He lopped off individuals and seized the top of the apparatus; he never challenged the army as the major armed force of the nation in international conflict.

7. Alan Bullock on Hitler: A Brief Critique

Adolf Hitler, the man at the center of this Third Reich, thought of himself as a political genius who would carve out adequate *Lebensraum* for the German *Volk*. Alan Bullock, a British historian, has approached Hitler from a political angle, and before embarking on a study of Hitler's prewar foreign policy, it may be useful to summarize Bullock's approach, and to criticize it. Bullock's biography of Hitler is the most detailed and famous of the many Hitler biographies that have appeared since 1932. As the subtitle of his book indicates *(Hitler: A Study in Tyranny)*,[12] Bullock has borrowed the ancient Aristotelian concept of tyranny and applied it to Hitler. A tyrant, according to Aristotle, was a ruler who abused his powers. But let us go from Bullock back to Aristotle and use the Greek philosopher's full definition: "This tyranny is just that arbitrary power of an individual which is responsible to no one, and governs all alike, whether equals or better, with a view to its own advantage, not to that of its subjects, and therefore against their will." Except for this last phrase, Aristotle's definition seems surprisingly modern, and Bullock successfully applies it to Hitler. We may also surmise that Machiavelli has influenced Bullock in his approach to the phenomenon of Adolf Hitler.

Alan Bullock argues that "the only principle of Nazism was power and domination for its own sake. . . ." In this observation his point of departure is the empirical, liberal British tradition, one which sees statesmanship as service to broad areas of the national community within certain restraining administrative and ethical safeguards. Bullock tends to isolate the Nazis from their environment (his book is most dated and weak on the crucial period before 1932), and the economic causal problems that Neumann wrestled with, however unsuccessfully, play no role in his writing. Bullock tends to make Hitler the motor force in the entire German experience after 1933, and in this he

---

[12] (New York, Doubleday, 1953).

may be right, but we have had the obligation to ask certain questions: (1) How did the moral and economic collapse of Germany prepare the German nation for Hitler? (2) How did the Nazis relate to the economic demands of certain of their sponsors? and (3) Is the rather formalistic Aristotelian concept of power and tyranny adequate to explain this unique man and his movement? Bullock does not satisfactorily answer these questions; indeed, he seldom if ever asks them. We have discussed the first question in Chapter III and the second question in this chapter, so let us look at the third problem, however briefly.

Bullock's portrait of Hitler as will and idea is a good one. All of the elements of Hitler's personality and world view are described. Yet we are left puzzled. How could this self-conscious, insecure, resentful man mobilize such vulgar ideas and overturn the world with them? This is where the organic totality of history is lacking in Bullock's presentation. In order to understand Hitler's demonic personality in terms of its effects, one has to see how he interacted with the social, economic, and psychic needs of the German nation. A description of his uncanny ability to spot what his audiences wanted does not provide enough of an explanation. Every good political orator in history has had this sense, and even some who are forgotten. Is it not equally important to reverse the procedure and ask whether Hitler's audiences did not also sense and approve what *Hitler wanted?* If this is indeed the case, then Bullock cannot fully explain Hitler because he omits any psychological and sociological study of the dialectical interaction between idea and reality, between the man and his nation. After all, from what we know, Hitler was a man who only took on meaning and wholeness in war and then in politics. What does this say about the German nation? Did the nation sense this inexorable tragedy, and did it see itself reflected in the demon of Adolf Hitler?

GERMANY AND EUROPE
1919–1937

Miles
0   100   200

Legend:
- Lost by Germany 1919
- Saar: League of Nations control 1919-1935
- Demilitarized Rhineland 1919-1936
- Austria-Hungary until 1918
- Plebiscite Areas
- Former territory of Imperial Russia

NORWAY

SWEDEN

FINLAND

Oslo

Helsinki   Leningrad

Stockholm

ESTONIA

DENMARK

Riga   LATVIA

Copenhagen   Memel   LITHUANIA

Baltic Sea   Vilna   Minsk

North Sea   Danzig Free City

Kiel   EAST PRUSSIA

U. S. S. R.

HOLLAND

BELGIUM   Berlin   Poznan   POLAND

Aachen   Bonn   Weimar   Saxony   Warsaw
Coblenz

Mainz   Breslau

Saar   Alsace-Lorraine

FRANCE   GERMANY   Prague   Cracow   Lvov

Bavaria   Munich   CZECHOSLOVAKIA   Bessarabia

SWITZERLAND   Vienna   AUSTRIA   Budapest   Transylvania   Cluj

Trent   Graz   HUNGARY   RUMANIA

ITALY   Slovenia   Trieste   Bucharest

Croatia   YUGOSLAVIA   Belgrade   Serbia
Sarajevo
Adriatic Sea   Bosnia   BULGARIA
Montenegro   Macedonia   Sofia
ALBANIA   GREECE   TURKEY

Germany and Europe, 1919-1937

CHAPTER V

Adolf Hitler Creates Greater Germany, 1933-1939

1. The Work of Gustav Stresemann

ADOLF HITLER'S foreign policy concepts were revolutionary in nature; he viewed the German nation as the tool which would enable him to bring them to fulfillment. Despite the revolutionary nature of his foreign policy, however, the "Führer" did not operate in a historical vacuum. The spirit of his foreign policy differed greatly from that of the foreign ministers of the Weimar Republic, but Hitler's "peaceful" accomplishments in foreign policy before 1939 in part represented the achievement of certain aims dear to a great Weimar foreign minister such as Gustav Stresemann. Too often, historians have examined Hitler's foreign policy without prior analysis of the accomplishments of Stresemann and his colleagues in undoing major aspects of the Allied peace settlements or *Diktat* of 1919. Thus, our first task must be an analysis of the foreign policy of Gustav Stresemann. This leads to an evaluation of Germany's position in Europe and the world on the eve of Hitler's appointment as Chancellor. We will then analyze Hitler's foreign policy concepts as of 1933. Finally, we move on to an interpretive study of Hitler's "peaceful" creation of the Greater German Reich before the Second World War.

Gustav Stresemann was the most significant Foreign

Minister of the Weimar Republic. He dominated German foreign policy between 1923 and his death on October 3, 1929. Stresemann was a member of the German Peoples Party (DVP), a right-of-center group which enjoyed the support of many industrialists and bankers. He had been associated with the National Liberal Party before 1918, and his credentials as an outspoken nationalist could not be questioned. Stresemann belonged to that group of realistic individuals who did not love the Weimar Republic, but who accepted it as a viable and necessary entity at this particular time in German history. Like most Germans, Stresemann loathed the Treaty of Versailles and the limitations which it placed upon German ambitions and power. Yet at the same time, Stresemann also deplored the disastrous effects which the Great War had had upon Europe's young humanity and culture. He sincerely believed in a Franco-German rapprochement, and hoped that in gaining the friendship of former enemies such as France, Belgium, and Italy, Germany would, in the long run, drastically lessen the reparations burden and perhaps undo some of the other discriminatory clauses of the Treaty of Versailles. Gustav Stresemann was the principal German force behind the Locarno Agreement of 1925. The "Spirit of Locarno," for which Aristide Briand worked in France, was based upon Stresemann's pledge that Germany would never seek to alter the territorial status quo in Western Europe. Thus, in a calmer and freer atmosphere than that which had prevailed at Versailles in 1919, Germany recognized that she had forever lost Alsace-Lorraine to France, and Eupen and Malmédy to Belgium.

Stresemann undoubtedly felt that this era of good fellowship would further other, more ambiguous German foreign policy aims. German nationalist opinion might curse the Treaty of Versailles and express hatred for the "hereditary enemy" France, but these feelings were mild compared to the contempt in which most Germans held their newly independent neighbors to the east, the Czechs and the Poles. Stresemann resolutely opposed the idea of an "Eastern Locarno," that is, an agreement between Poland, Germany, and Czechoslovakia regarding the preservation of the eastern territorial status quo. Although Stresemann stated that Germany would not use military force in attempting to undo the results of the years 1918-1919—the years in which the Czech-German and Polish-German frontiers had been carved out—he believed that in the long run it was the task of German diplomacy to isolate Poland and keep the question of the German minorities in the Eastern European countries before the attention of an increasingly sympathetic liberal world opinion. In reaching a *modus vivendi* with the French, Stresemann felt that he was furthering such foreign policy aims in the East. France and Poland had been military allies since 1920, and Stresemann correctly believed that in pacifying French public opinion by diffusing some of its anti-German tendencies, he was contributing to the isolation of Poland. Neither Stresemann nor his successors (including Adolf Hitler) would ever agree to an Eastern Locarno. The French and the Russians considered such a plan as late as 1934, and Adolf Hitler and his subservient Foreign Minister Konstantin von Neurath undermined this Eastern Locarno plan in the same subtle manner as had Stresemann. While constantly renewing his pledges of peaceful intentions, Hitler made it clear that German diplomats should have nothing to do with such a scheme.

There was a widespread desire for Franco-German cooperation among people in the two countries in the 1920's. Pacifist propaganda was very strong, for the memory of over three and a half million dead Frenchmen and Germans haunted both nations. Stresemann furthered this spirit of reconciliation, but the nationalist German public looked on his undoubted diplomatic gains for Germany with a sullen lack of comprehension in a mood of hostile ingratitude. By 1930 the last French troops had been withdrawn from the Rhineland, and Germany ceased paying reparations by 1932. The worldwide capitalist economic depression had led President Herbert

Hoover of the United States to put a moratorium in 1931 upon the repayment of war loans to the United States by Britain and France. Although America had always insisted that there was no legal connection between Allied war debts and German reparations to the Allies, this Hoover moratorium had a dominolike effect. Britain and France stopped paying their war debts to the United States, while Germany "temporarily" stopped paying reparations. This was an informal agreement, but it turned out to be permanent. In 1932 the representatives of the German government at the disarmament talks in Switzerland gained the *de facto* recognition of the principle of prospective equal rights for Germany in the area of armaments. But this concession was a theoretical recognition, one which did not alter Germany's weakness and unpreparedness, and Weimar leaders gained little domestic political capital from it. All of these gains, which came after Stresemann's death, represented the fulfillment of his work. They rested in part upon reconciliation with Germany's former enemies, in part upon a clever undoing of the consequences of the Treaty of Versailles.

By 1932 the German public was so demoralized and so caught up in the economic and political crisis of the regime that such diplomatic gains could not shore up the faltering Weimar Republic. In speaking of Stresemann during the Second World War Adolf Hitler, in his "table talk," acknowledged that Stresemann was "not the worst" of his predecessors, but that "he had made the mistake of selling a nation into slavery" in order to achieve a few piecemeal gains. This was probably the attitude of a majority of vociferous German nationalists in the 1920's. In 1929-1930, for example, the German government, following Stresemann's policies, negotiated the Young Plan with the Allies. This plan further clarified and lightened the German reparations burden. German acceptance of the plan, however, was the signal for gigantic agitation on the part of the Nationalists and the Nazis against the "continuing enslavement" of the German nation. In an era of growing mass hysteria, Stresemann's patient but effective diplomacy did not have the impact which its successes merited. Ultimately, it only further undermined the resolution of the Allies and increased the sense of guilt that Western liberals felt concerning their early indictment of Germany as the sole aggressor in the World War. Stresemann's work strengthened the position of Germany in the world, but it was Adolf Hitler who reaped the harvest, not the more moderate German forces which had supported Stresemann.

2. A Pariahs' Alliance: Germany and Russia

A vital pillar of Weimar foreign policy rested upon Germany's relations with the Soviet Union. In 1922 Foreign Minister Walther Rathenau met his Soviet opposite, Chicherin, in Rapallo, Italy. They inaugurated a decade of Soviet-Weimar diplomatic, military, and economic collaboration. In the eyes of men like Rathenau, Stresemann, and the Commander in Chief of the army, General Hans von Seeckt, collaboration with Soviet Russia, though it might be ideologically offensive, had overwhelming advantages. The German army would send instructors to train the young Red Army, and would in return be able to practice with modern weapons forbidden to the Reichswehr by the Treaty of Versailles. The two pariahs of European diplomacy would be able to collaborate and thereby overcome their isolation. Poland was their common enemy, and Poland was sandwiched in between the two past and future colossuses. Poland and the Red Army had been at war between 1919 and 1921. By the Treaty of Riga of 1921 Poland received a great deal of Ukrainian and White Russian territory, though not so much as she would have liked. The Soviet Union resented the reactionary Polish regime, particularly after the seizure of power by Marshal Pilsudski in 1926, while Weimar public opinion was violently anti-Polish. Poland, like Czechoslovakia, was a product of the hated era of the Treaty of Versailles. Both states were allied with

France, and both had large German minorities, though in the 1920's the Germans concentrated more upon the plight of the German ethnic minority in Poland than in Czechoslovakia. This was due to two factors: (1) The Poles proved themselves more intolerant and chauvinistic than the Czechs, and (2) Poland bordered on the Soviet Union, an ally of the Weimar Republic, thus making it more susceptible to pressure and isolation.

After the signing of the Locarno Pact in 1925 Germany joined the League of Nations as a great power. This was the supreme symbol of reconciliation among former enemies. In this same year, 1926, however, the Germans negotiated the Treaty of Berlin with the U.S.S.R., thereby indicating that they continued to place great value upon Soviet friendship and economic collaboration, and would not jeopardize these in order to buy reconciliation with the West. Von Seeckt had expressed a common Prussian attitude in a memorandum which he wrote in the early 1920's. It contained the pregnant phrase "Poland must disappear." This was an attitude inherited from the Prussian tradition, and men like von Seeckt, though they might abhor Bolshevism, felt it was natural to collaborate with the Russian state in order to further an anti-Polish policy.

In any evaluation of Weimar foreign policy, two factors stand out. The successes of that policy in undoing the results of the First World War are quite clear, but equally significant is the hostility with which German nationalist public opinion looked upon the work of men such as Rathenau, Stresemann, and Bruening. On the eve of Hitler's appointment as Chancellor, Germany was no longer paying reparations. She had secret illegal adjuncts to the Reichswehr in existence all over the country. Germany had persuaded the French to withdraw their occupation troops from the Rhineland. She had entered the League of Nations as a great power. She had gained the friendship of Soviet Russia, and had used Soviet territory for experimentation with some of the latest weapons. Germany had lulled French and British public opinion into thinking that by 1929 a "new Germany," to use Philipp Scheidemann's phrase, had come into being. These were major, even gigantic accomplishments. It was Adolf Hitler, however, who was to reap their harvest.

3. Adolf Hitler: Race, Space, and German Power

Adolf Hitler's grandiose foreign policy and geopolitical concepts were there for all the world to behold well before 1933. Hitler had enjoyed a brief period of notoriety in the foreign press during the time of his trial for high treason in 1924. After that, he disappeared from the pages of the world press, reemerging only in 1930-1933.

Hitler's concept of the outside world was provincial and dogmatic. He viewed the world largely in terms of the European great powers, a tendency which was already becoming anachronistic in the 1930's. Hitler's knowledge of the world was largely based upon what he had learned in Vienna about the "eternal conflict" between Teuton and Slav. It was composed of German attitudes that were widespread before and during the First World War, when the "perfidy" of England and the "hereditary enmity" of France became staples of the nationalist lexicon. By the end of 1926 Hitler had published the second volume of *Mein Kampf*, which contained a fairly detailed outline of his foreign policy concepts. In 1928 he suppressed the publication of a sequel to the second part of *Mein Kampf*, a book which was only published fifteen years after Hitler's death as *Hitler's Second Book*.

Hitler suppressed the book because a leading issue for all German nationalists in 1928 was the question of the "oppressed" German minority in the Italian South Tyrol. Since an alliance with Italy was a major part of Hitler's foreign policy, he did not feel that it was politic to jeopardize a potential friendship with Mussolini over a few hundred thousand Germans in northern Italy. He could not say this in print, so he suppressed the book. Here we have an example of Hitler temporarily suppressing a deeply held conviction because of pragmatic political considerations. In the two years after his accession to power, Hitler showed the same degree of caution, never abandoning his fundamental ideas, but putting them less to the fore than had been the case in the past and would be the case in the future.

There are other sources for Hitler's foreign policy ideas during this period besides his own writings. He unburdened himself of his view of foreign policy in great detail to his Nazi collaborator from the Free City of Danzig, Hermann Rauschning. Rauschning later broke with Hitler and published his conversations in a series of books with properly ominous titles such as *The Revolution of Nihilism* and *The Voice of Destruction*. Hitler felt that the inconsistent policy of Germany before 1914 had been based upon a series of mistaken premises. The Führer argued that Germany's "eternal" geographical and demographic position dictated her needs and aims in the area of foreign policy. Germany needed *Lebensraum* or "living space" for her teeming millions. The popularity of a novel by Hans Grimm, *Volk ohne Raum (Nation Without Space)*, published in 1926, indicates that this theme found a responsive echo in the hearts of many Germans. But Grimm's book had been about the German's fate in the world, the German as colonizer, while Hitler felt that it had been a *mistake* for Germany to get into a conflict with England over maritime and colonial questions.

Adolf Hitler viewed an alliance with Great Britain as a natural adjunct to any healthy German foreign policy. Thus, Britain would dominate the seas and her colonial empire would be "guaranteed" by Germany while the Reich would achieve hegemony on the continent of Europe. Hitler had no understanding of the fact that since the sixteenth century Britain had been anxious to prevent any single great power from dominating the shores opposite her secure little island. She even showed great reluctance in the face of *French* diplomatic hegemony in Europe in the 1920's. Hitler overlooked this, for he felt that "racial affinity" and a "rational" division of Europe's and the world's resources would appeal to the Conservative leaders of Great Britain. Hitler always sought an alliance with Great Britain, the last attempt possibly having been Rudolf Hess's flight to Scotland in May, 1941. Hitler also said he would not begin a war which would force Germany into the position of having to fight on two fronts, as had happened in 1914.

Hitler was convinced that France was morally, politically, and militarily rotten. As he had told Rauschning years before 1940, he would "maneuver France out of the Maginot Line without losing a single man. How I will do so is my secret." If Hitler could neutralize Britain or turn her into an ally of the Reich, the constellation of powers which had doomed Germany in 1918 would never again come into being. Hitler would not antagonize Britain over German colonial demands, though for reasons of prestige he intended to demand the restoration of certain of Germany's colonies, lost after 1914. Hitler had a renewed flurry of interest in colonies in 1940 and 1941, but that was a relatively minor, inconsistent episode. Hitler profoundly desired an alliance with Britain; he was so naive, however, about British history and attitudes that he easily fell prey in this quest to the wiles of a mediocre confidence man like Joachim von Ribbentrop. Ribbentrop, an "international businessman" who had dealt in wines and champagnes, was a pompous, oily, pedestrian individual; an opportunist who had only joined the Nazi Party in 1932, just in time to peform important services for Hitler as a go-between in negotiations leading to the Hitler Chancellorship. Ribbentrop, who spoke fluent English, was later rewarded by the Ambassadorship to the Court of St. James's. He told Hitler what Hitler wanted to hear. Hitler assumed that Ribbentrop, with his supposed contacts with the British aristocracy and ruling class, was in a position to get Hitler's "peaceful" attitudes across and build a foundation for a future alliance. In speaking of Ribbentrop's work to a critical Hermann Göring, Hitler would say, "Yes, but Ribbentrop knows Lord So-and-So," to which Göring would reply, "Yes, but Lord So-and-So knows Ribbentrop!" If alliance with Great Britain was one fundamental aspect of Hitler's foreign policy, a military pact with Fascist Italy was another. Hitler assumed that it was only because of the ramshackle Habsburg monarchy that Germany became involved in war with Italy in 1915. He did not intend to repeat that mistake. Hitler sincerely admired Mussolini until the end. He saw in the Duce the herald of Fascism, a man who had taught many Europeans to appreciate the leadership principle. He would not jeopardize an alliance with Italy over a ridiculous issue such as the fate of the Germans in the South Tyrol. So far as Hitler was concerned, Italy's natural destiny lay in the Mediterranean and the adjacent lands of the Maghreb and East Africa. Since these lands were in the hands of the French or the British, Hitler felt that there were no interests dividing Germany from Italy. In Hitler's ideal model, therefore, Britain would rule the high seas and would receive a German guarantee of her colonial possessions. Italy would dominate much of the Mediterranean littoral and would reach an agreement with Great Britain over the few sources of possible abrasion between the two countries in East Africa, while the Reich would be the dominant power north of the Alps and east of the Rhine.

The realization of both German and Italian ambitions, Hitler knew, implied the destruction of France as a great power. Hitler, like most Germans, assumed (in part correctly) that France had always been the enemy of German national aspirations, no matter how justified or rational these might be. Hitler knew that France was the principal military and diplomatic guarantor of the anti-German successor states in East-Central Europe, particularly Poland and Czechoslovakia. In order to destroy the

Versailles system, he would have drastically to curtail French power. Hitler had little doubt that a military conflict would be necessary in order to accomplish this task. In his desire to destroy French power, Hitler was following in the footsteps of the despised men of 1914. In September of that year Chancellor Bethmann-Hollweg wrote in a memorandum that France would have to be destroyed as a great power. This was the single aim which Hitler pursued in his French policy between 1936 and 1944. Once France was relatively isolated, Hitler knew he could deal with Poland and Czechoslovakia.

The Versailles system was not merely built upon the armaments limitation clauses of the Treaty of Versailles. It was a system encompassing a series of diplomatic alliances aimed against Hungary, Germany, and the Soviet Union. The inventor and protector of these alliances was nationalist France. Hitler knew, however, that he could not afford to act prematurely. Thus, one of his earliest interviews in 1933 was given to a sympathetic French journalist. Hitler spoke movingly of his experience in the trenches of northern France in the World War; of how he, as a common soldier, abhorred war and would do his best to see that war never again occurred. He skillfully played the demagogic anti-Communist, going so far as to speak of Germany's role as a defender of Western Christian [sic] Civilization. France, in the midst of ever-deepening economic and political crises, was receptive to such words. The last serious attempt made by France to strengthen her military and diplomatic position in Eastern Europe occurred in 1933-1934. Once the author of these diplomatic attempts, Louis Barthou, was assassinated in Marseilles in 1934, the French turned inward upon themselves, ultimately abandoning their Eastern allies to their fate. Britain, which had been suspicious of French hegemony in Eastern Europe after 1919, did little to encourage the French to keep up the Versailles system. France's construction of the Maginot Line after 1930 was a warning to her allies about the strategy which she intended to pursue in case of a new war. Hitler thus lulled some Frenchmen into a false sense of security, while proceeding to tear down the foundations of that security in Eastern Europe. "Peace and Parity," this was Hitler's theme in 1933. He indicated that Germany merely wanted practical equality in her right to rearm, that she wished to undo some of the more onerous clauses of the Treaty of Versailles through bilateral negotiations with the concerned parties. In the 1920's there had been a growing sense of guilt among liberals in the West regarding the Treaty of Versailles and its branding of Germany the aggressor of 1914. Revisionist historians such as Sidney Bradshaw Fay, making use of the newly published German diplomatic documents of 1871-1914, argued that Germany had been no more guilty than any other great power. Thus, when Hitler argued for peace and parity he struck a responsive chord in the foreign policy circles of Britain and America. As late as September, 1934 Hitler was playing the same tune. Thus, in one of the mammoth and well-publicized sessions of the Nürnberg rally, Rudolf Hess turned to Hitler and said, "You were for us the guarantee of victory; you are now for us the guarantee of peace!" Yet in June, 1934, in his first meeting with Mussolini, Hitler had secretly proposed a joint attack upon France, whereupon Mussolini confided to his intimates that he had just met a "mad monk"! Such a proposal, however, which Hitler knew was absurd and would be rejected by Mussolini, may have been psychological in intent, for it showed Hitler's boundless confidence both in the Third Reich and in Mussolini's Italy. Hitler was on the verge of a major coup, the murder of Ernst Röhm and the "radical" leadership of the SA, and he wanted Mussolini's support in any crisis which could occur. According to Otto Strasser, Mussolini was in part the author of this purge, for in the spirit of collegiality he had urged Hitler to get rid of radical troublemakers such as Röhm. Thus, Hitler's plan for an attack on France may have been the calculated, high-strung, probing appeal of an indecisive neurotic on the verge of a major decision.

4. 1933-1937: Burying Versailles

Not a single power withdrew its representative from Germany because of Hitler's accession to the Chancellorship. The Soviet Union did not even break off relations after the Nazi destruction of the KPD after February 28. Perhaps Stalin, like Ernst Thaelmann, actually believed that a Hitler Chancellorship would accentuate the "contradictions" in German capitalist society, making more inevitable and proximate a victory of the Communists. German Communists, after all, had a slogan in 1932-1933: "After Hitler, us!" At this point, Hitler indicated that he wanted peace with everybody. Even the anti-Semitic excesses of the boycott of April 1-4 were not repeated, largely because of their disastrous effect upon international opinion. Instead, Hitler concentrated upon constructive actions such as a Reich concordat with Rome. In 1932 Franz von Papen had negotiated a concordat on behalf of the state of Prussia. Von Papen's presence in the cabinet as Vice-Chancellor quieted the fears of many German and foreign Catholics regarding the nature of the National Socialist regime. The concordat with Rome on July 22, 1933 boosted the prestige of National Socialist Germany; indeed, it represented the first international act of recognition of the legitimacy of the new regime. Hitler had a grudging respect for the Catholic Church, and he must have been aware of the way in which the Italian Fascist regime had been strengthened by Mussolini's historic Lateran Pact with the Papacy in 1929. Even Hitler's destruction of the Catholic Center Party in June did not obliterate the positive aspects of this pact from the viewpoint of the Nazi regime or from that of Rome. Von Papen, after all, remained in the Cabinet, and he was a prominent Catholic layman who had once been associated with the Center Party itself.

When Hitler came to power he was afraid that the Poles might launch a preventive war against Germany. East Prussia had been isolated from the Reich since 1919, cut off by the so-called Polish Corridor, which gave Poland the access to the sea that Woodrow Wilson had promised her early in 1918. If Marshal Pilsudski decided upon such a venture—and there is some evidence that he thought of it at various times in 1933—was it not possible that even the demoralized French might join in? Against such an attack Germany would have few defenses. Certain Poles, by the way, had interesting but by no means coherent attitudes towards the Nazi regime. An intelligent Polish diplomat such as Josef Lipski actually believed that Hitler wanted *better* Polish-German relations over the long run. Lipski was afraid of the old German Nationalists (DNVP) with their Prussian, anti-Polish attitudes. He was more afraid of Hugenberg than of Hitler. Hitler was effusive in his expression of friendship toward the Polish people in 1933 and 1934, and the Poles, ever fearful of the Soviet Union and mistrustful of France's new isolationism, proved susceptible to Nazi blandishments.

In October, 1933 Hitler made his first dramatic diplomatic move. Claiming that the League of Nations was a creature of the Versailles system and was a body in which Germany could not achieve the armaments parity to which she was entitled, Hitler took the Reich out of the League. A plebiscite soon thereafter showed the German people expressing confidence in the foreign policy of the new regime. This move frightened Polish governmental and public opinion. Hitler had to allay Polish fears. Still playing his anti-Russian, anti-Communist card, and anxious to pacify Polish opinion, Hitler signed a ten-year nonaggression pact with Pilsudski in January, 1934. This bilateralism was a major aspect of early Nazi foreign policy. Hitler was afraid of any joint Franco-Soviet pressure on Central and Eastern Europe, pressure which might force Germany to accede to an "Eastern Locarno" pact, which would forever guarantee the status quo in that area. By signing this pact with Poland, Hitler effectively killed any such French or Soviet plan, for Poland showed herself willing to deal with the Reich bilaterally, with a minimum of consultation with her Western ally.

While Hitler's ethnic hatred for the Poles was not nearly so great as his contempt for the Czechs, in the long run he did not see room for a great Polish state in European politics, though as late as October, 1939 Hitler was willing to tolerate a satellite: occupied Poland within the German sphere of influence. Germany's relations with Poland between 1934 and early 1939 were generally quite good. Hermann Göring attended Pilsudski's funeral in Cracow in 1935 as Hitler's personal representative, and he often made hunting trips to the great forests of Poland. Anti-Communism was a stronger factor in the Polish ruling class than was fear of Germany, for as a Polish saying went, "With the Germans we lose our freedom, with the Russians we lose our souls." Hitler played upon this attitude in order to isolate and manipulate Poland, and at various times he initiated vague but grandiose discussions aimed at a possible Polish-German alliance, one which would dismember the Soviet Union and give even larger areas of the Ukraine and White Russia to Poland. The Poles continued to maintain correct if not friendly relations with the Soviet Union, but they were less fearful of, and more attracted to the National Socialist regime than should have been the case.

The German diplomatic corps did not show any hesitation in serving Hitler. Most of the German diplomats were career men with strong nationalist convictions. There were very few Jews or "part-Jews" among them. Men of stature, such as Herbert von Dirksen, convinced themselves that by staying in their posts they were serving as a moderating influence upon the regime. This is the same conservative apologia which was used by men such as Franz von Papen and Alfred Hugenberg. The very fact that foreign nations continued to deal with the same German diplomats was a factor in mollifying foreign diplomatic opinion about the new regime. No one doubted after October, 1933 that Hitler was acting as his own Foreign Minister, but the presence of Baron Konstantin von Neurath in that post until 1938 had a soothing effect upon world opinion. Neurath did not make German foreign policy, nor was he an important factor in its execution, rather his presence served to prove that the Nazi regime was made up of "reasonable" men, men whose very presence proved that Hitler's early fulminations and writings, above all *Mein Kampf*, were mere campaign oratory. Despite this superficial harmony, however, serious conflicts raged within the German Foreign Ministry between 1933 and 1938.

Reichsleiter Alfred Rosenberg, the important Nazi theoretician, had foreign policy ambitions, indeed, he wished to become Foreign Minister. However, this dour, tactless, pedestrian individual clearly lacked the qualities for such a task, and Hitler knew this. In 1933, on a trial diplomatic mission to Great Britain, he gravely offended British opinion by laying a wreath with a swastika on the tomb of the Unknown Soldier. Hitler had fobbed off Rosenberg's foreign policy ambitions by making him head of the Nazi Party Foreign Policy Office (APA). In this office he had purely advisory functions, and he would not receive a state position until 1941.

Joachim von Ribbentrop's relationship to the Foreign Office was even more ambiguous. Between 1933 and 1936, he was a sort of spy and go-between for certain officials in the Foreign Ministry and the highest Nazi authorities in the Reich. He headed an unofficial group known as the Ribbentrop Bureau (Dienststelle Ribbentrop or Ribbentrop Büro). The function of this Nazi bureau was to undercut the conservatism and sense of traditional élitism embedded in career diplomats in the Foreign Office. In 1936 Ribbentrop was appointed Ambassador Plenipotentiary to Great Britain. Finally, in February, 1938, as Hitler was on the eve of the creation of the Greater German Reich, Ribbentrop replaced von Neurath as Foreign Minister. In this capacity Ribbentrop was exceedingly pompous to the outside world, while being almost uniformly servile in the presence of Hitler. He did not make German foreign policy, though his recently acquired hatred for Great Britain may have influenced Hitler in certain unrealistic directions after 1938.

Building upon the work of Stresemann and Brüning, Hitler took further steps to undo the Versailles system after 1933. By September, 1934 the Saar became an important political rallying cry in this work of revision: The industrial Saar basin had been placed under League of Nations control for a period of fifteen years. There was to be a plebiscite there early in 1935. At the Nürnberg rallies in September, 1934 demands for the reincorporation of the Saar into the Reich were ubiquitous. The population of the Saar was German-speaking, and in 1935 the inhabitants of the district voted overwhelmingly for reunion with the Reich. This was an aspect of the peaceful, legal revision of the Treaty of Versailles. The reincorporation of the Saar into the Reich was particularly gratifying to the Nazis because many sharp-tongued German political emigrés of the left had used it as a base for propaganda attacks against the Third Reich. That was not the first time that Hitler used the Nürnberg rallies to further the aims of his foreign policy. The impressive rallies represented the gathering together of hundreds of thousands of storm troopers, army troops, and party functionaries every September. Many foreign observers would be present, and they would certainly be impressed by the discipline and enthusiasm of the assembled Germans. Thus, the rallies were an excellent backdrop for portentous foreign policy announcements. In September, 1938 Hitler used the Nürnberg rally to launch vituperative fulminations against Beneš and the "oppressive," unyielding Czech government.

In his work of undoing the Treaty of Versailles and

the Versailles system Hitler had the overwhelming support of the German people. In 1934-1935 he inaugurated the air force or Luftwaffe, an arm forbidden to Germany under the Treaty of Versailles, although Germany had been experimenting with airplanes and gliders in Russia since 1923. Hitler appointed Hermann Göring head of the Luftwaffe, largely because of his prestige as a former head of the Richthofen Squadron. This appointment ultimately proved to be a disaster, but by 1940 Hitler could only marvel at the manner in which this major weapon of modern war had built up, as he put it, "out of nothing." The gala public inauguration of the Luftwaffe was made even more festive by the composer Richard Strauss, who contributed an anthem for the new force.

Hitler wished to demonstrate to Great Britain that his program of rearmament and revision was in no way directed against that power. He also wished to further decapitate the crumbling Franco-British alliance, an alliance which had been falling into disrepair almost since the day of the armistice in 1918. In 1935 the British, acting behind the back of their French ally, concluded a naval pact with the Führer. This pact pledged Germany to limit construction of surface war vessels to no more than 35 percent of the existing British fleet, while granting parity to the Reich in U-boat construction. Hitler was probably sincere in this commitment. Indeed, the reconstruction of the German navy between 1933 and 1940 was much less impressive than similar work in the army and the Luftwaffe, and Germany did not even build at the rate permitted under the 1935 pact. As part of his plan for an alliance with England Hitler did not wish to frighten or challenge England, as had Wilhelm II and Grand Admiral Tirpitz between 1898 and 1914.

The French were shocked that the British had reached this accommodation with Germany without consulting their ally. Such an action on the part of Great Britain further confused an already hapless French public opinion. There was greater sympathy in Great Britain for German revisionist aspirations than there was in France, and Britain, in the grip of a terrible depression, was riddled with pacifism and hostility to rearmament. The British right was impressed by Hitler's destruction of the "Bolshevik menace" in Germany, and even Winston Churchill, otherwise so prescient in matters concerning Hitler, reflected this point of view. Hitler and Ribbentrop believed that King Edward VIII was solidly pro-German, that he would, upon his accession, lead England into Hitler's fervently desired Anglo-German alliance. Whatever the merits of this viewpoint, Edward abdicated in 1936 and Hitler, who had planned personally to attend Edward's coronation, was furious and indicated that he would merely send an official representative to the coronation of George VI.

Under one of the more onerous clauses of the Treaty of Versailles, German troops were not permitted west and immediately east of the Rhine, that is, they were forbidden in the purely German Rhineland. The Germans, ever self-pitying, were rankled by this clause. They did not realize that a Frenchman, Marshal Foch, had in 1919 seriously proposed the annexation by France of the Rhineland, which would have made the Rhine France's eastern frontier. In 1923 French authorities in the Ruhr had patronized Rhenish separatist movements, though by 1930 the last French troops had withdrawn from the Rhineland. This evacuation went almost unnoticed in the Reich. All this meant little to German public opinion, which was still galled by the fact that German troops could not freely move about on a part of German territory. In March, 1936 Hitler launched his most daring political and military move to date: He ordered German troops into the Rhineland. The German army was still relatively small. Although Hitler had violated the Treaty of Versailles in 1935 by proclaiming the resumption of universal military service, the German army at this point was no match for its French adversary. The French, led by weak leaders such as Sarraut and Flandin, and demoralized by the increasing polarization of domestic political opinion, did nothing except protest the German move. The British, true to the policy which they had inaugurated in 1935, and unhappy about France's recently ratified Soviet treaty, indicated to the French that Britain would do nothing to support any French countermove. The French seized upon this in order to corroborate their own policy of doing nothing. Such was to be the case until 1939, when it was too late. If the French had offered resistance to the German forces Hitler would have been obliged to withdraw his troops, for they were under orders to withdraw if the French counterattacked. He might have suffered a major propaganda setback, and even a crisis of his regime. Perhaps at that point certain of his generals would have moved against him for his adventurism and his failure. There is little point, however, in such speculation. The move into the Rhineland was a major propaganda victory for the Nazi regime. Priests sprinkled the entering German troops with holy water, and young girls garlanded them with flowers. Bit by bit, Hitler was destroying what was left of the Treaty of Versailles. He had inaugurated the Luftwaffe, he had proclaimed universal military training, he had reincorporated the Saar, and now he had remilitarized the Rhineland.

In looking back upon the first five years of his regime, Hitler viewed such successes merely as the prelude to much greater world-historical tasks. To a select assemblage of military officers and his Foreign Minister on November 5, 1937, Hitler indicated that in undoing the Treaty of Versailles, Germany was preparing for her logical mission to the east. Austria would have to be "reincorporated" into the Reich, Czechoslovakia and Poland smashed, living space won for the German people to the east. The Hossbach Memorandum, which recapitulates this meeting, has been challenged by A. J. P. Taylor as an historical document. Perhaps it is but a rough approximation of what was said at the meeting, yet the words ring so true and are so consistent with everything which Hitler said (and did) about foreign policy before and after November 5, 1937, that it seems somewhat petty to question the sense of the document. This meeting further provoked men such as General Ludwig Beck, Chief of the General Staff, into thinking about active resistance to Hitler's adventurism. There is, however, no record of serious opposition to Hitler's monologue at the meeting itself.

Within a few months of this meeting, Hitler, taking advantage of information presented to him by Himmler and Göring, had forced the dismissal of his Defense Minister, von Blomberg, and the Commander in Chief of the army, von Fritsch. When in this same year, 1938, the popular General Beck resigned as a way of showing his disenchantment with the adventurism of the regime, Hitler replaced him with the first Bavarian Catholic to head the German General Staff, Franz Halder, who occupied the post until late in 1942. In dismissing von Blomberg and von Fritsch, who had been enthusiastic servants of the new regime, Hitler reorganized the military structure of the Reich. He created a High Command of the Army (OKH), a High Command of the Armed Forces (OKW), a High Command of the Luftwaffe, and a High Command of the Navy. He abolished the Defense Ministry and made General Wilhelm Keitel, a natural-born lackey, head of the High Command of the Armed Forces. This position, despite its resounding title, was not concerned with the making or serious coordination of military policy, but rather with the transmission of Hitler's orders to the other services. The reordering of the structure of the German armed forces gave real meaning to the title which Hitler had had since the death of von Hindenburg: Supreme Commander of the Armed Forces. Knowing that he was on the eve of major political and military moves, Hitler wanted an army which was pliable. It seems incredible that the revolting manner in which von Blomberg and von Fritsch were disgraced did not provoke more opposition among the German officer corps. Yet "patriotism," opportunism, and fear go far towards explaining the lack of such serious opposition until 1943-1944.

5. Hitler and Austria, 1933-1938

Hitler had a special feeling for Austria. He loved the Austrian countryside, and he constantly reminded listeners of the fact that his mother, a simple Austrian peasant woman who "would cut a poor figure among our society ladies of today," had "produced a son" for Germany. Yet Adolf Hitler never forgot the shame and misery of his years in Vienna. Now he needed Austria in order to outflank Czechoslovakia and establish a common frontier with his future ally, Mussolini. In doing this he would destroy Austria and avenge himself upon Vienna.

The present Austria was the creation of the Treaty of St. Germain. It consisted of about six million German-speaking persons, and in the eyes of foreigners it amounted to little more than Vienna and its suburbs. Metternich once said that "Europe ends at the Ringstrasse" (in Vienna), but be this as it may, the Austrians of the 1920's yearned for the days in which Vienna had been the city to which many peoples of the great multinational Habsburg empire had looked as the cultural and commercial center of Mitteleuropa. Austrians looked back nostalgically to the days of the Emperor Franz Joseph, overlooking the fact that the destruction of the Habsburg monarchy had largely been due to the manner in which Vienna had steered Austria-Hungary into the German orbit between 1879 and 1914. Austria by itself was not an economically viable state in these years. In 1914 over half of the industry in the Habsburg monarchy had been located in Bohemia and Moravia, now in Czechoslovakia. In the 1920's and 1930's economically troubled Europe went through a period of autarchy, that is, economic nationalism and high tariffs. Austria, which produced little in the way of industrial goods, was at the mercy of her neighbors. She was dependent, for example, upon Germany for a good part of her vital tourist trade, and when the Nazis wished to put pressure upon Vienna (1934-1936) they merely had to make the cost of an exit visa prohibitive for German citizens.

Austria was torn by many conflicts. Most Austrians had wanted to join the Weimar Republic in 1918-1919. The very name of the new Austria, "Deutsch-Osterreich" or German-Austria, reflected this yearning. If Austria could not be the center of a great multinational empire on the Danube, let it at least be an autonomous province of the German Republic. The Allies, however, forbade such an *Anschluss* or union with Germany. In 1931, when both Austria and Germany were in desperate economic straits, they tried to negotiate a customs union, the Schober-Curtius pact. This too was voided, largely due to French pressure. Such a shortsighted attitude on the part of the Allies harmed the cause of Austrian autonomy, for which even in 1938 there was considerable support inside the Austrian state. Austria was an ill-balanced state; people referred to it at this time as a *Wasserkopf* (waterhead), or a small body ill-supporting an enormous head. This referred to the fact that fully one-third of Austria's citizens lived in Vienna or its suburbs.

Despite its small size Austria was not a politically harmonious state. By 1933 it had a growing National Socialist contingent. The other important political parties were the conservatives or the Christian-Socials, led by Monsignor Seipel and later by Engelbert Dollfuss, the Nationalists (the old Pan-Germans), and the Social-Democrats. The onset of the Depression in Central Europe reinforced radical and authoritarian currents in little Austria. Thus, the Austrian state under Seipel and Dollfuss moved in the direction of a sort of clerical corporativism, one which emphasized the Catholic, corporative, independent nature of the Austrian state. Dollfuss warned his largely provincial supporters that Austria was threatened by "foreign ideas," whether of a National Socialist or Marxist nature. By 1933 Dollfuss had largely junked Austria's democratic constitution. He had formed a broad "Patriotic Front," which borrowed its ideology from Mussolini, the Vatican, Austrian anti-Semitism, and anti-Viennese provincialism.

The Austrian Social-Democrats had produced some of the most significant Marxist theorists of the century, men such as Rudolf Hilferding and Otto Bauer. By 1934 the left wing of the Social-Democrats in Vienna was goaded into a desperate revolt by the authoritarian, provocative measures of the Dollfuss regime. The conservative press of the West cheered while Dollfuss' forces murderously suppressed the workers' revolt in the Karl Marx housing project of Vienna in February, 1934. This was to be a short-lived victory for Dollfuss and his Patriotic Front. In July some Austrian Nazis murdered Dollfuss in the anticipation of a rapid *Anschluss* with Nazi Germany. The Christian-Socials had been the enemy of *Anschluss* ever since Hitler's accession to power in January, 1933, and Dollfuss had correctly viewed the Nazis as a pagan force alien to the truest Austrian traditions. In a grotesque act, typical of their subhuman nature, the Austrian Nazis not only murdered Dollfuss, they let him bleed to death on a couch in his office without the benefit of either medical aid or clergy.

Everyone assumed, probably correctly, that the Germans had instigated the coup. Mussolini, still nominally friendly to Italy's former allies of the World War, rushed troops to the Brenner Pass. Hitler, fearing a confrontation with Mussolini, denied any responsibility for the assassination of Dollfuss. Relations between Germany and Austria continued to be disastrous, however, for Hitler's hatred of Austrian provincialism and Catholicism was boundless, and he felt with a special passion the desire to bring German-Austria back into the Reich as the *Ostmark* or the East March. As long as Mussolini opposed this plan, however, Hitler would have some difficulty in achieving his aim. Germany was not rearmed by 1934, and Hitler had no desire to jeopardize a future alliance with Mussolini. As late as 1935 Mussolini showed concern over German rearmament, and it was only in 1936-1938 that Hitler won over Mussolini as an ally.

The assassination of Dollfuss shocked opinion in Austria and the world. Kurt von Schuschnigg, Dollfuss' successor, pledged to continue the policies of the martyred leader. When Dollfuss lay in state, thousands of people came to Vienna to pay their last respects to him. Schuschnigg was a schoolmasterly, authoritarian type who had little of Dollfuss' earnest, yokel-like charisma. He did reach a tentative *modus vivendi* with the Germans in 1936, but Schuschnigg knew that Austrian independence ultimately depended upon the goodwill of Mussolini and Allied determination. Mussolini had been particularly furious because of the presence of Dollfuss' family in Italy at the time of his assassination. Schuschnigg tried to put together an Austrian coalition which would defend Austrian independence against the Nazis. Austria's economic plight remained disastrous, however, and the Nazis made many recruits in the provinces. Schuschnigg (the Schleicher of Austria) could not very well turn to the trade unions or to the Social-Democrats for support, for he had backed Dollfuss in crushing those forces in February, 1934. Since Austria possessed only a small, if loyal army, Schuschnigg was largely dependent upon the Heimwehr under Prince Stahremberg. This was largely a rural militia, somewhat similar to the German Freikorps. It first arose after the war as a response to Yugoslav challenges in the regions of Carinthia and Carniola, but by the 1930's it had grown into a powerful striking force. It had been weaned on struggles with the Socialist paramilitary Schutzbund, which it helped crush in 1934. The Heimwehr was conservative, rural, monarchist, and Catholic in its ideology, and there was no question about its loyalty to the independent, clerico-Fascist Austrian state. Schuschnigg had the support of the Catholic Church in Austria, the

Vatican, the Heimwehr, the tiny Austrian army, and the Patriotic Front. The anti-Semitism of the Christian-Social Patriotic Front movement antagonized the large Jewish minority in Vienna, but the Jews certainly preferred Schuschnigg to Hitler. All of these forces, however, were increasingly minuscule as compared with growing German might in the mid-1930's. By 1938 Germany was almost a great power again in the military sense. Although the Western Allies probably exaggerated her strength, Germany's military superiority over little Austria was evident. Schuschnigg's domestic political position was not catastrophic in 1938, but he had to have the support of a great power if Austria was to maintain her independence. This great power could only be Mussolini's Italy, since the French had shown at the time of the Rhineland crisis in 1936 that they would not even act in the defense of their own interests.

Hitler was particularly venomous when it came to the Austrian arguments that Austria had an independent tradition of her own. He summoned Chancellor Schuschnigg to Berchtesgaden for a discussion in February, 1938. Schuschnigg has left a detailed account of this nightmare in his memoirs. Hitler, flanked by a forbidding General Keitel in order to impress Schuschnigg with the seriousness of the situation, raved on about how the history of Austria had been one long "betrayal" of Germany. Hitler worked himself up into a rage, and when Schuschnigg pointed out that artists such as Beethoven had found in Austria a pleasant, creative environment, Hitler roared back, "Beethoven was a German from the Rhineland!" This meeting did not produce the result which Hitler desired. In March, Schuschnigg defiantly indicated that he would hold a plebiscite on the question of Austrian independence. Hitler had tried to give the world the impression that the vast majority of the Austrians, except perhaps for the Jews and the Communists, desired the incorporation of Austria into the Reich. Schuschnigg believed otherwise; and if threatened he planned to test his beliefs in a referendum, for he could no longer be sure of the unconditional support of Benito Mussolini.

Mussolini had in 1935 at Stresa joined Italy's former allies of the World War in protesting Germany's resumption of conscription. Late in 1935, however, Mussolini embarked upon his great imperialist adventure. He attacked Ethiopia, and the League of Nations, largely due to British pressure, voted economic sanctions against Italy. Although the French and the British secretly agreed to undermine those sanctions by a pusillanimous but ultimately repudiated agreement with Mussolini (the Hoare-Laval Pact), Mussolini still had qualms early in 1936 that his Italian East African Empire might crumble before the blows of Allied economic power. Although the Hoare-Laval plan was abandoned, the British and French governments went out of their way to appease Mussolini after Italy had conquered most of Ethiopia. They did not enforce crucial sanctions, for if oil imports via the Suez Canal had been denied to Italian industry, Mussolini would not have been able to continue the war. Though the Allies were forced to renounce the Hoare-Laval Pact because of the scandal created before the eyes of an aggrieved world opinion, they appeased Mussolini just the same, and there were no effective sanctions.

Through this difficult period Adolf Hitler stood aloof from the League and the Allies, recognizing Mussolini's conquest, and encouraging the Italians. Dissension among Germany's World War enemies could only help Germany. Mussolini was grateful for Hitler's friendship, and he came to Berlin in 1937. His visit there was the firm foundation upon which the "brutal friendship" between Hitler and Mussolini was built, though it had something of a comic opera about it. Mussolini spoke at the *Maifeld* outside of Berlin to a cheering crowd of thousands of Germans. He spoke in German, but since the rain drenched his notes, the words that came out of his mouth were barely comprehensible. During this same visit, Mussolini seems to have been surprised and shocked by the extent of German military strength. He put aside whatever qualms he may have had, however, and remembered only German diplomatic support during the Ethiopian crisis of 1936. In 1937 Italy joined the Anti-Comintern Pact, an ideological piece of nonsense which the Nazis and the Japanese had concocted in 1936. This was the formal inauguration of the Italian-German Axis, which only became real in a treaty sense in May, 1939.

When Hitler irrevocably determined to incorporate Austria into the Reich in March, 1938, Austria could no longer rely upon its Italian protector. Adolf Hitler had made it clear that the fate of the German minority in the Italian South Tyrol was of no great consequence to him. The *Volksdeutsche* there could be resettled in the Reich. Hitler would not jeopardize an Italian alliance over them. This was, after all, the reason why he had suppressed his book on foreign policy in 1928. Mussolini had been worried about the South Tyrol, but it now seemed as if there was more agitation in still independent Austria over the fate of the Germans there than there was in the Reich itself. Such was the power of a modern dictator to still protests. Mussolini made a fatal blunder in March, 1938, for in order to realize his growing imperialist ambitions he would now have to march in step with Nazi Germany. The Duce did not realize that, given Germany's greater military discipline and economic power, such an alliance could only wind up as humiliating bondage for the Italians. By 1942 this was clear to Mussolini, but by then it was too late, for he had made his choice in 1936-1937.

When Hitler learned of Schuschnigg's plan for an Austrian plebiscite, he went into a long rage. He expected that Austria would yield its independence on the altar of German power and common German patriotic sentiment. Schuschnigg was now appealing to the Austrian people, who would undoubtedly support him in his quest for Austrian independence. At this juncture Britain and France gave Austria almost no support. Mussolini turned a cold shoulder to Schuschnigg's questions concerning Italian support. While most of the Heimwehr and the Austrian army were prepared to take on the Austrian

Nazis and even the German Wehrmacht in the defense of Austrian independence, using the mountains and rivers of Austria as natural defense points, Schuschnigg lost his nerve. He believed that it would be wrong to "spill German blood in a civil war." Schuschnigg did not think ahead to the scores of thousands of Austrians who would fall victim to the Gestapo in a few hours if he yielded to the Germans. This was his failure as a statesman. Schuschnigg reluctantly agreed, under German pressure, to withdraw his plan for a plebiscite. President Wilhelm Miklas finally caved in and appointed an Austrian Nazi, Artur Seyss-Inquart, in Schuschnigg's place. Seyss-Inquart, negotiating with Göring, arranged by telephone for the peaceful transfer of German troops to Austria.

On March 14, 1938 Hitler made his triumphal entry into Vienna, the city of the enchantments and traumas of his youth. Every major building was festooned with swastikas, including St. Stephen's Cathedral. As Karl Dietrich Bracher has put it, nowhere in Central Europe did Hitler ever get so hysterical a welcome as in Vienna. He solemnly visited the graves of his parents near Linz, and then proceeded to turn Austria into a conquered province of the Reich. The Gestapo ran riot in Vienna, and the Austrian SA took its toll. Many Jews committed suicide, while thousands of others, in a pathetic gesture, lined up outside the Polish Embassy for visas. From Hitler's viewpoint German Austria was back where it belonged: in the Reich. The Allies protested this violation of the treaties of Versailles and St. Germain. Hitler ignored their protestations, and reaffirmed his desire for European peace. To Mussolini, however, he was more effusive. He ordered his ambassador in Rome to tell the Duce that he would never forget what Mussolini had done for him by not defending Austrian independence. The Nazi Austrian Legion perpetrated savage excesses in Vienna. Nazi officials from Germany were appointed to key posts in the *Ostmark,* and within a few years even the enthusiastic Austrians of 1938 were grumbling about

German "efficiency," German conscription, German wars, and German defeats.

There were many reasons for the generally favorable Austrian reaction to *Anschluss,* and these do not contradict less obvious or overt enthusiasm before *Anschluss.* Austria did not seem to be a viable state. Cardinal Innitzer of Vienna, the most powerful figure among the Austrian clergy, urged the Austrians to vote yes in the Austro-German plebiscite which followed *Anschluss.* Even Karl Renner, a prominent Socialist, saw "Socialist" elements in the realization of *Anschluss,* while anticlerical agrarian liberals saw in Nazi domination a counterpoise to the hated authority of the Catholic Church. Mussolini graciously accepted a common frontier with the powerful Reich as if it was actually in Italy's interest. Hitler had now outflanked Czechoslovakia, and had gone a long way towards the geographical realization of that Greater German Reich dreamed of by liberal nationalists in 1848.

6. Spain, Munich, and the Collapse of the Versailles System

Hitler's attitude towards Mussolini's invasion of Ethiopia, the Anti-Comintern Pact, Mussolini's acceptance of *Anschluss*, and parallel German-Italian intervention in the Spanish Civil War were milestones on the road to Mussolini's loss of political independence to his German ally. In 1936 a group of Spanish military leaders, among them Francisco Franco, launched an uprising from Spanish Morocco against a progressive Spanish republican front which had just won a hotly contested electoral victory. Mussolini saw an ideological affinity between Italian Fascism and the Spanish rebels. He also wished to augment Italian power in the western Mediterranean at the expense of both Spain and Britain. By 1937 Mussolini had made major troop commitments to the Spanish Nationalist cause.

At first, German policy had been more cautious and Machiavellian. Soon, however, Hitler agreed to sell arms to the Spanish rebels and dispatched the famous Condor Legion of the Luftwaffe to Spain. Hitler used Spain as a convenient testing ground for the new weapons of the Wehrmacht. The barbaric bombardment and destruction of the Basque town of Guernica in 1937, typical of the murderous methods and intentions of the Nazi regime, were immortalized in a famous Picasso painting. Italy and Germany cynically took part in the International Nonintervention Committee discussions on Spain, all the while flouting it. The rise of a new Fascist power on France's southern flank could only further weaken the hapless Third Republic and aid the anti-French schemes of Hitler and Mussolini. France, caught up in its own political and economic crisis, not to speak of a real crisis of morale, did not do after 1936 what it should have done to aid the Spanish Republic. By the spring of 1939 Franco had made a triumphant entrance into Madrid. The Axis powers had contributed further to the isolation of France. The Germans had tested new weapons, using live targets, while the Italians, as was usually to be the case, got little except an expanded national debt and many dead out of their commitment to Franco. The value of Mussolini's troops in Spain was doubtful in any event, and Franco refused to turn any Mediterranean islands over to the Italians after his victory.

Adolf Hitler hated the Czechs more than he did any other non-Jewish nationality. He had grown up in Vienna at a time when the national struggle between the Czechs and the Germans for parity or hegemony in Bohemia and Moravia was at its height. The Czech state was democratic, Czech-dominated, an indirect product of the armistice of 1918 and the Treaty of Versailles. It was a cornerstone of the French alliance system in East-Central Europe. For all of these reasons, Hitler felt an irrational, unbounded hatred for the state of Thomáš Masaryk and Eduard Beneš. In the Middle Ages Bohemia and Moravia had been part of the German Holy Roman Empire, but like most

German nationalists Hitler overlooked the fact that a great Moravian kingdom had existed before the coronation of Otto the Great as the first Holy Roman Emperor. After *Anschluss*, Hitler and the Nazis suddenly discovered that the Czechs were making life unbearable for the three-million-plus Germans living in the Czech state. Nazi influence among Czech Germans had increased after 1933. The leader of the Sudeten German party, Konrad Henlein, was a subservient tool of Berlin. *Anschluss* meant that Czech territory was surrounded by the Germans on three sides, and that German agitators and political broadcasts could easily infiltrate Czech territory. Most of the Germans in the Czech state lived in the outlying areas of Bohemia, a region loosely known as the Sudetenland. By themselves they would probably never have made a move against the Czech state, though many of them were susceptible to the blandishments of Nazi propaganda.

This first Czechoslovak Republic was undoubtedly a unitary Czech national state, though the Germans had full representation in the Prague parliament and could scarcely be oppressed in the sense that the Germans were in the South Tyrol in Mussolini's Fascist Italy. But the Germans were not the only nationality problem confronting the Czechs in 1938. The Slovaks, though speaking a dialect of the Czech language, inhabited a remote and backward eastern part of the Czech state. Certain Slovak political leaders were interested in political autonomy, or even independence, willing to exchange satellite status within a Greater German Reich for their present role as second-rate citizens in the Czech Republic. The Carpatho-Ukraine, located at the very eastern tip of Czechoslovakia, was made up of several nationalities and was an extremely backward region. Here, too, Nazi agents were active. There was a substantial Hungarian minority in southern Slovakia, while the Teschen district, bordering on Silesia, contained a large Polish minority. Thus, in any attempt to disrupt the Czech state, Nazi diplomacy, if skillful, might be able to rely upon the passivity of Mussolini, the active intervention of Poland and Hun-

The Establishment of the Greater German Reich 1935-1939

Legend:

- GERMANY 1933
- Gained by Plebiscite 1935
- Remilitarized 1936
- Annexed 1938
- Annexed 1939
- Protectorate established 1939

Map labels:

North Sea

Baltic Sea

HOLLAND

BELGIUM

LUX

FRANCE

SWITZERLAND

ITALY

Hamburg

Berlin

G E R M A N Y

Cologne

Frankfurt

RHINELAND

SAAR

Leipzig

Breslau

Munich

Berchtesgaden

Eger

Bohemia

C Z E C H O S L O V A K I A

Moravia

Vienna

AUSTRIA

Bratislava (Pressburg)

Ruthenia

Memel

Königsberg

Danzig

LITHUANIA

Vilna

Poznan (Posen)

Warsaw

P O L A N D

Lublin

Cracow

GERMAN SATELLITE
MARCH 15, 1939

HUNGARY

Budapest

RUMANIA

Miles

0   100

gary, and the alliance of Slovak autonomist and separatist leaders.

By the autumn of 1938 the once vaunted French alliance system in Eastern Europe was in shambles. In 1935, responding to aggressive Nazi rearmament, the U.S.S.R. and Czechoslovakia and France and the Soviet Union signed mutual security agreements. The Franco-Soviet treaty was more vague than was France's older commitment to Czechoslovakia. In 1938 the Soviet Union was ready to aid Czechoslovakia against the Nazis if France honored her commitment to the Czechs. Since Czechoslovakia, however, had no common frontier with the Soviet Union, the Soviets would have to receive permission for the Red Army to cross Polish or Rumanian territory in order to come to the aid of Czechoslovakia. Both Poland and Rumania were still nominally French allies, but they had reactionary anti-Soviet regimes, which perhaps even with the greatest French pressure would not have acceded to such a Soviet request. Czechoslovakia was the heart of the French-inspired "Little Entente," which consisted, in addition, of Yugoslavia and Rumania, but this Little Entente was aimed, first of all, at Hungary's revisionist aspirations, not at either Germany or the Soviet Union. This is all the three small powers had in common. France had viewed the purpose of the Little Entente more broadly, but the opinion of its three members was more important in a crisis. It might be adequate for its anti-Hungarian task, but hardly for any containment of Germany and/or Russia. Poland was France's main anti-German ally in Eastern Europe, but the Polish regime of Colonel Beck and his colleagues was increasingly dubious about French strength and the French commitment to Poland. Poland's predatory designs on part of Czechoslovakia further crippled the possibility of any strong anti-German cooperation from that quarter.

Since 1933 Nazi Germany had done everything in its power to disrupt this French alliance system in Eastern Europe. The Germans had signed a nonaggression pact with Poland. They encouraged frontier troubles between

Poland and Lithuania. They went out of their way to pay homage to Marshal Pilsudski after his death in 1935. They emphasized the anti-Communism of both the Warsaw and Berlin regimes. Nazi anti-Semitism had strong admirers in the Polish government, especially after 1935. Now, in 1938, Germany pointed out to the Poles that "legitimate" Polish territorial interests in Czechoslovakia could be protected if common action were undertaken against the oppressive Czech state. Through a series of economic measures increasing German trade and investment in Southeastern Europe, Germany managed to weaken the Allied hold upon the foreign policies of Little Entente states such as Rumania and Yugoslavia. By late 1938 the Germans had more or less destroyed the Little Entente, another creation of the Versailles system.

Hitler put his Wehrmacht and many construction workers feverishly to work on the construction of the "Siegfried Line" in western Germany, for in the event of war between Germany and Czechoslovakia Hitler wanted a strong defensive line in the West. Yet this line was still extremely weak by the time of the Czech capitulation in October, 1938, and the Czech army was well trained and armed, ready to fight. There was no evidence, even during the time of the Munich Conference, of major Sudeten German subversion in the Sudetenland. It was only a forty-five-minute flight from Czech airfields to vulnerable German cities such as Leipzig and Dresden. The Czech fortifications in the Sudetenland had cost a fortune, and appeared to be effective. A major German military figure such as Colonel-General Ludwig Beck, head of the General Staff of the army, fearing that a conflict with Czechoslovakia would mean war with France and the Soviet Union and the end of Germany, resigned. German generals grew restless. Hitler, however, was determined to destroy the Czech state and thereby solve the question of the German minority in Czechoslovakia.

Hitler's hatred for Beneš knew no bounds. At the Nürnberg rally of September, 1938 he screamed threats and imprecations at Beneš for the "atrocities" inflicted by the Czechs upon the Germans in the Sudetenland. He flattered the Poles and Hungarians, his possible allies against the Czechs, by comparing their "thousand-year-old cultures" and histories to the "meaningless" existence of the upstart Czechs. Hitler would tell the Allies that his demands on Czechoslovakia were just and represented the "last territorial demands" which he would make in Europe. A British commission under Lord Runciman, which went to Czechoslovakia in the summer, reported back sympathetically on "just" German aspirations there. Britain had scarcely begun her rearmament program, and Prime Minister Neville Chamberlain was a man of pacifist inclinations who could not understand why Britain should get involved in a war over a minor nationalities squabble concerning a "faraway people," of whom he knew nothing. Hitler, displaying incredible nerve, assumed that neither the British nor the French would fight in 1938, that both democracies were internally rotten and lacking in backbone. Certainly, the state of German rearmament in late 1938 was not such as to enable the Reich simultaneously to fight England, France, Czechoslovakia, and the Soviet Union, or even any two of those powers. A few German generals grumbled, and there were even conspiracies to overthrow Hitler.

Konrad Henlein, acting on the orders of Ribbentrop, constantly stepped up Sudeten German demands so as to make them unacceptable to the Czech government. Hitler wanted at least the Sudetenland, with its massive fortifications. The French talked of mobilization, while Neville Chamberlain began to panic. Mussolini, who knew that Italy was totally unprepared for any major conflict, wished both to gain the prestige of having preserved the peace and prove himself Hitler's loyal ally. Hitler and Ribbentrop put increasing pressure on the Hungarians, the Poles, and the Slovaks so that they would play their role in the destruction of the Czech democracy. The Soviet Union indicated that it would honor its commitment to Czechoslovakia if France did the same. Given the military and geographic facts of life, this seems to have been a reasonable demand, especially since the French alliance with Czechoslovakia far antedated that of the Soviets and the Czechs. Hitler indicated to his generals that war was in sight, that it would begin by October 1 at the latest.

Mussolini was disconcerted when the first Chamberlain visit to Germany did not produce any results. He had no quarrel with the Czechs, and the German demands seemed too extreme. By the middle of September Chamberlain was negotiating with the Germans as the tacit representative of England, France, and even Czechoslovakia. The Czechs were kept in the dark, and such was to be their fate even during the Munich conference. The Soviet Union was not taken seriously nor was it consulted. At this point Hitler's attitude was fairly clear. He would be willing to receive the Sudetenland (as a minimum) without a war, but the thought of a war was not abhorrent to him, rather it excited him. Mussolini intervened and suggested the convening of a four-power conference, one involving Italy, Germany, France, and England. Chamberlain and Daladier, the French Premier, readily agreed, and on September 29 the four heads of government met in Munich. Two powers, which had more than a peripheral interest in the situation—Czechoslovakia and the Soviet Union—were not invited. They waited anxiously in the antechamber, so to speak. Chamberlain won some minor concessions, but this Munich conference represented the high point of the disastrous policy of appeasement being pursued by France and Great Britain. The Sudetenland, with its fortifications intact, was to be handed over to the Germans within ten days. The Western Allies were to guarantee the new Czech frontiers, and they would be joined in this guarantee by Germany and Italy as soon as all minorities problems between the Czechs and the Poles and the Czechs and the Hungarians had been resolved.

This was the Czech tragedy, but it was also to prove the tragedy of France. Chamberlain went back to Great Britain and told a cheering crowd at the airport that he had won "peace in our time." Mussolini breathed a sigh of relief. He appeared to be a strong man, and yet was the peacemaker of Europe. Italy would not be prematurely involved in a European war. Daladier returned to Paris, and when his plane was landing he looked out of the window and saw an enormous crowd. He expected that it was there to lynch him. Instead, when he emerged from the plane he was greeted by tremendous cheers. Such was the state of public opinion in France and Britain. Hitler said in 1939 that Britain and France would not fight: "I saw those worms at Munich." The Soviet Union now began to rethink its policy of collective security with the West. Stalin had no desire to be trapped in a war with Nazi Germany, one in which the Western Allies sat on the sidelines while dishonoring their commitments to states like Czechoslovakia and the Soviet Union. . . . But the situation was most tragic for the Czechs. A viable democracy soon became a truncated, hyphenated state (Czecho-Slovakia).

Despite his bloodless and almost total victory at Munich, Adolf Hitler seemed disappointed that he had not had an opportunity to invade Czechoslovakia. The post-Munich Czech state had a short-lived history. Its government became more rightist and authoritarian, trying in vain to appease Nazi Germany by alignment with German foreign policy. Thus, this government of Josef Beran denounced the Czech-Soviet mutual assistance pact. The Hungarians took part of southern Slovakia, while the Poles absorbed the Teschen district. Slovakia received more autonomy, though certain Slovak separatists and local German leaders were still dissatisfied with the remaining ties to the Prague regime. Hitler's concept of Greater Germany was an historical one as well as a racial one, and he was not content merely to absorb three million Sudeten Germans into the Reich. Bohemia and Moravia, despite their overwhelming Czech majorities, must also be "reunited" with the Reich. Before and after Munich Hitler had often said, "We want no Czechs." He had impressed Chamberlain with the tone of pathos in which he described his aspiration that all *Germans* should be united in one national state. In March of 1939, however, Hitler decided finally to destroy Czecho-Slovakia.

Ribbentrop put intolerable pressure upon Monsignor Josef Tiso and other Slovak nationalist leaders, for they were to aid in the final dismemberment of the Czech state, while the Slovak-despising Magyars impatiently put in a claim for the Carpatho-Ukraine. On March 15 German troops entered Bohemia and Moravia. Slovakia became an autonomous German protectorate, while German troops entered western Slovakia. Hitler had declared that the Czechs "had been up to their old tricks," that is, they had been pursuing an anti-German course and feverishly rearming. These, of course, were lies, as had been Hitler's earlier statement that he "wanted no Czechs." The demoralized Allies, who would not fight for a strong Czechoslovakia, certainly would not make a move in behalf of this pathetic Prague regime. They lodged protests. Neville Chamberlain, indeed, was furious, for Hitler had made him look like a fool. Nevertheless, nothing was done. Hitler promised world opinion that the cultural and social future of the Czech people was safe in the hands of its new German masters. Perhaps because of the way in which they had been betrayed by their erstwhile allies, the Czechs proved the most docile people for the Germans to rule. As late as March, 1944 Hitler congratulated the puppet Czech head of state, Emil Hácha, for the loyal way in which the Czech people had behaved after the "historic reabsorption" of Bohemia and Moravia into the Reich. . . .

Mussolini was furious over Hitler's move. As usual, he had received no advance notice. The Duce decided to clutch at several straws in order to regain the prestige which he had lost by Hitler's violation of the Munich agreement, over which he had presided. Mussolini indicated that he was going to attack and occupy Albania, in which Italy had had strong interests for a half century, and Hitler gave his approval. It was at this point that Mussolini and his Foreign Minister, Galeazzo Ciano, along with several Italian ambassadors, began their long series of desperate, fumbling attempts to create a countervailing block to the new, revolutionary German power in Europe. Mussolini was impressed by German might, and like a jackal he wished to pick up the crumbs that might fall from the German table. Yet he knew that his policy of alliance with Germany was reducing Italy's ability to maneuver independently. The Duce now took some solace in the rather minor fact that Hungary and Poland had a common frontier because of the Hungarian absorption of the Carpatho-Ukraine. Presumably these two states, along with Slovakia, might provide some sort of balance in East-Central Europe, a limitation upon further German moves (!). Such an idea, of course, was ludicrous. Mussolini recognized this when he signed the so-called Pact of Steel with Hitler in May. This pact had all the earmarks of an offensive military alliance. As far as world opinion was concerned, the two dictators now seemed unbeatable. Mussolini had easily conquered Albania. Hitler had taken Bohemia and Moravia, and soon thereafter the Memelland from Lithuania. Franco's Fascist forces, aided by the Germans and Italians, had just triumphed in Spain. America was still pursuing a fundamentally isolationist policy, and Roosevelt's occasional forays into pro-Allied internationalism were probably far ahead of American public opinion.

The essence of Adolf Hitler's foreign policy in these years was the creation of a strongly centralized Greater German Reich. This, however, was not the ultimate aim of his foreign policy. He needed the creation of such a Reich so that a German state would exist which would have the power to carve out the necessary living space for the German people in the East, that is, in Russia. Hitler's image of the Greater German Reich in the East included Austria, Bohemia, Moravia—and parts of Poland. Early in 1939, however, Colonel Beck, Marshal Smigly-Rydz, and other Polish leaders regarded themselves as being in Germany's good graces. They had a nonaggression pact with the Reich; they had taken part in the dismemberment of Czechoslovakia. More sensible men would have understood that with the collapse of the French system of alliances in East-Central Europe, Poland's security had been irrevocably undermined. The tragedy of the Versailles system in these years was a story without a villain. The French, tormented by internal difficulties, neglected their alliances in the East. The Poles, relying upon bilateral agreements with Germany, tried to maintain a precarious neutrality. This, in turn, reinforced the growing French sense of isolation and security behind the incomplete Maginot Line. Munich had shown that France would sell out her strongest Central European ally, and the Poles all too readily drew certain conclusions from this French action. Unfortunately, so did the Soviet Union. While Poland cooperated with the Reich in the destruction of Czechoslovakia and tried to maintain a precarious neutrality between Germany and the U.S.S.R., Stalin, at some point after September, 1938 decided to consider a reorientation of Soviet foreign policy.

7. The Polish Crisis and a Diplomatic Revolution

Soon after Hitler absorbed Bohemia and Moravia he began to talk about the rights of the Germans in the city of Danzig. Danzig was a Free City under a League of Nations High Commissioner. It had an overwhelmingly German majority, but it was vital to Poland's position as a Baltic power. In the spring and summer of 1939 the Nazis began to talk about the return of Danzig to the Reich, and about an extraterritorial connection through the Polish Corridor linking East Prussia with the rest of the Reich. This should have neither shocked nor surprised the Poles. They themselves had raised the issue of self-determination for the Polish minority in Czechoslovakia at the time of Munich. Certainly, Hitler's passionate demands for the reincorporation of all East-Central

European Germans in the Reich was consistent with his policy over the past year.

Adolf Hitler had broken his word, given at Munich, by seizing Bohemia and Moravia. Even the Chamberlain Conservatives in Britain and Daladier in France were now disturbed by Hitler's new pressures on Poland. Britain reacted excitedly by offering guarantees to Poland, Greece, and Rumania, while in the Soviet Union a major ministerial change took place. V. M. Molotov replaced Maxim Litvinov as Foreign Minister on May 3. Litvinov, a Jew, had been associated with the Soviet policy of collective security against Fascism, while Molotov, it was believed, would more neutrally reflect any changes in Stalin's line. Stalin was now omitting customary anti-National Socialist comments from his speeches. By late May the Nazis were picking up these feelers. When the German ambassador to Moscow, Schulenburg, relayed the sense of a change in Soviet policy to Ribbentrop, the pompous dullard was slow in picking up the nuances. Hitler, however, was quite clear by the end of May about the significance of what was happening. In racial terms, certain Nazi leaders speculated that Stalin, the "nationalist Russian," was veering away from the "Jewish internationalist policy" symbolized by Litvinov.

Hitler realized that the Soviet Union might be interested in more than an economic agreement with the Reich; it might want a full-fledged political alliance. Hitler's moves, after all, were now being made closer to the frontiers of the Soviet Union. Would the Soviet Union, ignored at Munich, be forced by the Western powers into a single-handed struggle against a Nazi-dominated East-Central Europe? These were probably some of the questions going through Stalin's mind. He knew that the Polish regime was conservative and violently anti-Russian, and the same was true of King Carol's in Rumania. Yet if these nations would not agree to the passage of Soviet troops so that they might engage Nazi forces, what would be the value of the Soviet Union's existing ties with the

West? Even after guaranteeing Poland, Greece, and Rumania, the Chamberlain government showed no interest in a military pact with the Soviet Union. We do not know if Stalin, by late May, had made up his mind to sign a nonaggression pact with the Nazis, thereby paving the way for the partition of Poland. We do know that Stalin had no intention of getting involved in a struggle against Nazi Germany on behalf of a reactionary Polish state, while the Western democracies looked on as smirking neutrals.

In early December, 1938 Ribbentrop had made a state visit to Paris, where he and French Foreign Minister Georges Bonnet had signed a friendship pact, pledging mutual consultation on matters of common interest. This Franco-German rapprochement, coming so soon after Munich, only furthered Stalin's fears regarding the aims of the West. Reactionary circles in England (Lothian and Halifax) had spoken of their acceptance of the fact that Hitler might turn eastward and satisfy himself at the expense of the Soviet Union. It may be too much to assume that Stalin suspected that the real motive behind the British guarantee to Poland was to make Poland negotiate in a flexible manner (à la the Czechs) with the Reich. But Stalin was a suspicious man, and any coolheaded appreciation of Neville Chamberlain's foreign policy leads one to assume that by guaranteeing Poland's existence against aggression, Chamberlain was readying her for concessions to the Reich.

A man who would not fight for Czechoslovakia would scarcely fight over a *German* city named Danzig or an extraterritorial railroad through the Polish Corridor. He might, however, fight over the *existence* of an ally in East-Central Europe. This was the meaning for Chamberlain of the British guarantee to Poland. The only problem was that the Poles interpreted the guarantee quite differently. Although they tried to accommodate themselves to the presence of a newly powerful German neighbor after 1933, the Poles were at heart reckless patriots pursuing a shortsighted policy. The fact is that they did not intend to yield on any question, least of all one concerning Polish rights over the Corridor. Beck took the British guarantee as encouraging Polish intransigence. The British made the mistake of not immediately coupling their guarantee with (1) an Anglo-Russian pact, and (2) pressure upon the difficult Poles for the negotiation of a military alliance with the Soviet Union. This oversight, for which the British and French halfheartedly tried to make up later in the year, proved fatal.

As the Polish crisis heated up in the summer of 1939, angry voices were raised among the British opposition. Men of as diverse backgrounds as Winston Churchill and David Lloyd George argued that British support for Poland was useless unless a military alliance was concluded with the Soviet Union. Had Stalin made up his mind to sign a pact with the Reich by the end of May? Was he insincere in inviting British and French delegations with plenipotentiary negotiating powers to the U.S.S.R. in the summer of 1939? Until Western scholars are able freely to use the Soviet archives, this question remains without a sure answer. Early in August, 1939 the British and French sent delegations to the Soviet Union. They took their time in reaching Leningrad, indicating to the sensitive Soviets that they were neither serious nor fully empowered to negotiate a military pact. The French seemed to be more serious than the British but the recent memoirs of a participant, Colonel André Beaufre, leave one in doubt as to the general sincerity of Allied intentions. The British delegates not only were unable to make military commitments, they indicated that British capabilities on the continent of Europe upon the outbreak of hostilities with Germany would be minuscule compared with those of 1914. The French were still looking over their shoulder at the British, afraid to commit themselves, not realizing that at this point it was crucial that they draw the Soviet Union into a military alliance, even at the risk of offending British sensibilities. The Allies wanted a pact without teeth, a gigantic bluff that would make Adolf Hitler more rational. The fact that

Voroshilov, a high-ranking Soviet military figure, negotiated with the Allied delegations would seem to indicate that Stalin was still interested in what the West had to offer.

Britain and France put only belated and feeble pressure on Poland to compel that power to permit the Red Army access to its territory in the event Germany attacked Poland. The reactionary rulers of Poland were so anti-Russian and anti-Communist that even at this hour they did not realize that the main danger to Polish freedom, and indeed to the existence of the Polish people, came from the West, not from the East. Certain officials, such as the French ambassador to Warsaw, indicated to their respective Allied governments that the Polish army was overrated, that Poland alone was a relatively useless ally for the West. What they did not (and could not) indicate to the Poles was that the Western powers were a relatively useless ally to Poland, and that the only country which could really render substantial assistance to the Poles in the event of an attack by the Reich was the despised Soviet Union.

When it was clear that the Franco-British-Soviet negotiations were getting nowhere, Stalin and Molotov adjourned them on August 17, soon inviting Reich Foreign Minister Ribbentrop to Moscow. In a matter of hours on August 23-24, Ribbentrop, soon to be hailed by his Führer as a "second Bismarck," had negotiated a Nonaggression Pact with the Soviet Union. This was signed on August 24, and it provided for ten years of peace between the two powers. Secretly, the pact recognized German interests in western Poland, Vilna, and Lithuania, and Soviet interests in eastern Poland, Finland, Latvia, Estonia, and Bessarabia (in Rumania). In some ways the pact was reminiscent of the division of Eastern Europe by Napoleon and Czar Alexander I at Tilsit in 1807.

The 1939 pact was the prelude to the fourth partition of Poland. It also represented the great moment of Ribbentrop's diplomatic career, but even here he did not play an original role, for he was merely carrying out his master's wishes. Ribbentrop supposedly said that he felt when he was with Stalin and Molotov in the Kremlin it was as if he was with "old Party comrades." This was a rather disingenuous statement, for Ribbentrop was anything but an "old fighter" in the Party, having only joined the NSDAP in 1932. He tried to calm Stalin's fears regarding the anti-Communist past of the Nazi Party by saying that "even the Berliners, who are noted for their wit, were asking the question, 'Oh, the Anti-Comintern Pact—hasn't Stalin joined it yet?' " It is possible that this old champagne salesman had a few too many vodkas in the Kremlin that day. The conclusion of the pact showed the shortsightedness of the British, the stupidity of the Poles, and the cowardice of the French. The French looked to Chamberlain, while Chamberlain tried to look in the opposite direction whenever there was a foreign crisis. The Poles were intransigent, as usual, feeling that it was more important to safeguard their honor than to preserve their nation.

8. The Outbreak of War

The leaders of these three nations were misled by a strong current in world opinion during the spring of 1939. Revulsion at Germany's violation of the Munich accords had led President Franklin Roosevelt to ask Nazi Germany to guarantee the security of a number of countries. While Hitler ridiculed Roosevelt's list before an amused Reichstag, there is no question but that many people in the West still thought that it was now inevitable that the U.S.S.R., Poland, Britain, France, and America would ultimately use their superior forces against the Reich in order to prevent further Hitlerite aggression. This haphazard smugness was one of the factors underlying the disasters of Western diplomacy in that fateful

August of 1939. Another such factor was Western anti-Communism and the feeling that the Red Army, having been purged of so many of its officers by Stalin in 1937-1938, was no longer a respectable fighting force. These miscalculations and emotions cost the West dearly during that last summer of peace.

The tragedy of Poland during World War II leads us to consider an unpopular hypothesis: Should the Poles have diplomatically capitulated to the Reich before the Hitler-Stalin Pact? If the Poles had yielded the Polish Corridor, Danzig, and certain areas along the East Prussian and Upper Silesian frontiers to the Reich, Poland might have been reduced to a German satellite, perhaps useful as a springboard for a future attack against the Soviet Union, but the horrors visited upon the Polish people between 1939 and 1944 might well have been mitigated. The Czech example may be of value here. When he returned to Prague after the war, Eduard Beneš looked down at the ancient city, the only capital in Central Europe which had not been reduced to rubble, and said that Prague was still Prague because of the peaceful capitulation of the Czechs in 1938-1939.

The British and the French realized late in August that they might have to go to war against Hitler. They finally did so reluctantly, but offered no aid to their ally in Eastern Europe. The Poles themselves were inflexible to the very end. The British, it must be remembered, had seen their guarantee to Poland as an encouragement to Beck to negotiate the Corridor and Danzig questions with the Germans in a flexible manner. The Poles were adamant about allowing Soviet troops on Polish soil, and the British and French had precious little leverage with the Soviet Union in their feeble negotiations during August, 1939. While ostensibly standing firm at the side of their Polish ally, the British and the French clutched at every straw, hoping against hope that another Munich might emerge from the Danzig crisis.

When the Germans indicated on August 29 that they

would receive a Polish plenipotentiary, the British put pressure on the Poles to cooperate. Actually the German offer was forced and insincere, and when on August 31 Ambassador Lipski indicated that he did not have plenipotentiary powers Ribbentrop treated him curtly and then dismissed him. A Swedish businessman, Birger Dahlerus, trying to act as an intermediary between the British and high Reich personalities such as Hermann Göring, did his best to avert hostilities in these last days of peace. Indeed, Göring quite possibly was anxious to avoid war with Britain and France. He loved power and the plunder which it brought him, and he intended to enjoy both. Whether or not Göring was operating on his own initiative in these last days of peace is not known, but he gave the impression to foreigners that he was the spokesman for peace in Hitler's entourage.

Mussolini made it clear to the Germans that he did not feel obligated to march by their side under the terms of the Pact of Steel. Italy was not ready for war, and besides, Mussolini was looking forward to a great international exposition to be held in Italy in 1942. He felt that this exposition would tremendously boost the prestige of his regime. Further, Mussolini looked back to the days of Munich as a time of tremendous prestige for the Duce as European peacemaker. He was not at all averse to repeating that role, especially since it coincided with the material interests of Fascist Italy. Hitler, however, was bent upon war. Confronted by Polish intransigence over the question of Danzig and an extraterritorial connection between East Prussia and the Reich, Hitler had upped his demands. He privately declared that the entire Polish-German frontier, an indirect product of the hated Treaty of Versailles, would have to be drastically altered in favor of Germany and the German ethnic principle. Hitler wanted war; he wanted to smash Poland. He had always stated that he would never begin a war in order to restore the "limited" frontiers of 1914. Though Hitler would soon involve Germany in what was theoretically a two-front war, he felt that he had mitigated its dangers by the Ribbentrop-Molotov pact. In 1939 Hitler saw beyond his limited demands upon Poland, and once having finished the construction of the Greater German Reich by annexations of Polish territory, Hitler would prepare to carve out "living space" for the German people in the East. He wanted war with Poland by September 1, at the very latest. Hitler told his generals this, and as far as Mussolini's would-be peacemaker role went, Hitler confided, "I hope some *Schweinehund* does not try to mediate."

Hitler was convinced that a local Polish-German conflict need not become a general European war. He did not believe that the men of Munich would fight for Poland when they had abandoned Czechoslovakia. Hitler did not appreciate the fact that the age of European hegemony had passed. A European power such as Germany could *create* an incident which might lead to a world war, but it was in no position to *determine* events once such an incident had occurred. Following the advice of his stupid and now violently anti-British Foreign Minister, von Ribbentrop, Hitler did not believe that England would declare war. He had a good enough grasp of the military and psychological realities of the western front to realize that he need not fear any immediate action by the French, even if France by herself did declare war upon Germany. After manufacturing incidents on the Polish-German frontier, Hitler began hostilities against the Poles on September 1. On September 3 the British informed Hitler that the peace could only be saved if German troops withdrew from Polish territory and negotiations over the issues at hand followed. Otherwise, Britain was in a state of war with Germany. When Hitler received this statement, he was somewhat angered and perplexed. He talked to Ribbentrop and plaintively asked, now what? Joachim von Ribbentrop could only predict that within a short time a similar note would probably arrive from the French. This was one of his few accurate predictions.

Hitler did not knowingly unleash the Second World

War on September 1, 1939. What, indeed, were his aims
at that point? Hitler intended to crush Poland, annex
areas in which there were German majorities or
minorities, perhaps allowing the continued existence of
a rump Polish state in order to placate Western opinion.
Having rounded out the Greater German Reich, Hitler
would work ever harder to consummate his dream of an
alliance with the world's greatest maritime power, Great
Britain. Having done this, thereby isolating France,
Hitler would probably launch an attack upon the French
Third Republic, destroying France as a great power. Or
perhaps he would destroy France first, if it took this to
bring the British to their senses. Hitler, like most Germans, felt that France was the inveterate enemy of German hegemony in Central and East-Central Europe. She
would have to be dealt with. Having England as an ally
and Soviet Russia as a neutral friend, Hitler would be
supreme upon the Continent. Taking advantage of his
alliance with the conservative British ruling class, Hitler
then planned to launch a lightning attack upon the Soviet
Union. This is the way his mind was working in early September, 1939.

The declaration of war by Great Britain, which was
quite predictable, should have jarred Hitler out of these
fantasies. Hitler had not rearmed Germany in such a way
as to provide for a long, drawn-out war. Yet with Britain
as a belligerent, historical precedent suggested that this
was exactly the type of war it would be. Deep down Hitler
probably sensed this, but he did not draw the proper
strategic and economic-military consequences from the
British declaration. He still believed that once Poland was
defeated, Britain would come to her senses. He continued
to state this belief openly as late as July 19, 1940. Indeed,
Rudolf Hess's flight to Scotland on May 10, 1941 *may*
have been Hitler's last such message to the British.

Franco greets Hitler at Hendaye, October, 1940.

To pity or to grieve: Marshal Pétain seconds before greeting Hitler at Montoire, October, 1940.

Göring amuses Hitler, October, 1940.

German photograph showing French African troops captured in 1940: "France the Poisoner of Europe."

Hitler receives a skeptical ally in June, 1942: Finnish Marshal Mannerheim.

Hitler receives Marshal Antonescu of Rumania, 1942. Interpreter Schmidt in the middle.

Hitler tries to contain his emotions: The funeral
of Dr. Fritz Todt, February, 1942.

Foreign Minister Tuka of Slovakia Signs
the Tripartite Pact, 1940.

Hitler and Marshal Antonescu Discuss the Military Situation
in the East, 1942.

Arab Nationalists in North Africa surrounding portraits of two of their heroes in 1942.

They never met again: Mussolini's farewell to Hitler, July, 1944.

A rare view of Heinrich Himmler late in 1944: Appeal to the People's Militia for total resistance.

State, Party, and Wehrmacht are one: *Volkssturm* rally in 1944.

"We will never capitulate." People's Militia (*Volksturm*) marching through Berlin on a gloomy day late in 1944.

A shaky, puffy-faced, but smiling Hitler moments after visiting victims of the July 20 assassination attempt.

A grim Doktor Goebbels gives the oath to men of the *Volkssturm,* late 1944.

French Fascist collaborator Marcel Déat speaks at a rally of "Europe United Against Bolshevism," 1944.

"I am not ashamed to thank Adolf Hitler. . . ." French Fascist Philippe Henriot speaking in Berlin, 1944. Henriot was assassinated by French patriots soon after his return to France.

The Russian turncoat, General Vlasov, addressing his "Liberation Committee" late in 1944.

Keitel and Doenitz at a common event in 1944: The state funeral of a high-ranking officer.

Belgian Rexist leader Degrelle (circled). "If I had a son, I would want him to be like Degrelle."—Adolf Hitler.

The best years of his life: Albert Speer inspecting a factory during the war.

A grim conference: Göring, Doenitz, Keitel, and Hitler. A rare photograph of Hitler holding eyeglasses.

CHAPTER VI

Adolf Hitler at War,
1939-1942

1. From Poland to Norway:
Indecisive Struggles, 1939-1940

HITLER knew that the Polish army, despite generally high morale, was no match for the German Wehrmacht. Poland's open plains and long frontiers were ideal for German military operations. The Germans used screaming, low-flying Stuka dive bombers to wreck Polish logistics and terrorize the civilian population. German tanks darted far ahead of the infantry and artillery, cutting up the enemy's lines, isolating pockets of troops, making resistance based upon an elastic defense totally impossible. At first the Poles tried to defend the entire stretch of their western frontier. This only played into the hands of the new German techniques of warfare. Some of these techniques were borrowed from foreign writers such as Colonel De Gaulle of France and Captain Basil Liddell Hart of Great Britain. The French made a few feeble military demonstrations along their frontier with Germany, but they hastily withdrew from German territory when it was clear that the Poles had been irrevocably smashed.

On September 17 the Soviets, alarmed at the rapid German advance, attacked Poland from the east in order to guarantee that Polish eastern Galicia and White Russia would fall to the U.S.S.R. as stipulated in secret clauses of the Ribbentrop-Molotov pact. There were certain details which still needed to be worked out. After the Poles were defeated, the Germans readily agreed that Lithuania would fall to the Soviet rather than the German sphere of influence, in order that the Germans might gain a bit more territory in Poland than had been stipulated in the original agreement. After this fourth partition of Poland, German and Soviet troops faced each other along several hundred miles of frontier. Their behavior was polite and correct. Nazi-Soviet relations were generally cordial in the year that commenced with the Ribbentrop-Molotov pact and ended with the Battle of Britain in the late summer and autumn of 1940. The Germans adopted a hands-off attitude when Soviet Russia attacked Finland late in 1939. At the same time, the Nazis were cool to Japanese pressures for an anti-Soviet alliance. The Japanese had suffered a major defeat at the hands of the Red Army in August of 1939, and they looked askance at the rapprochement then taking place between their Anti-Comintern ally and Stalin's Russia. Indeed, a major factor in Japan's decision not to expand westward and northward into Soviet Asia was the knowledge that Germany and Russia were now tacit allies in Europe.

Trade between Germany and Russia was important to both countries. It continued right down to June 22, 1941. The Germans generally exported finished industrial products, which Russia exchanged for raw materials and foodstuffs. At one point it looked as if the Germans would have to hand over a warship bearing the patriotic name *Deutschland* to the Soviets as part of their trade agreement, and although this embarrassing situation never occurred, the Germans hurriedly changed the name of the ship to a less eye-catching *Lützow*. Stalin was delighted with the pact with the Germans, at least until the autumn of 1940. He had bought time for feverish Soviet military preparations, and in the process he had undone certain of the anti-Russian results of the Versailles Era. After the end of the Polish campaign Stalin went out of his way to show his sympathy for the Germans, declaring that it was due to British and French machinations that the war now continued. Stalin had long since resolved to meet Japanese anti-Soviet military demonstrations in the Far East with force if need be. Thus, he was grateful that his European flank was now neutralized by the Ribbentrop-Molotov pact.

Hitler had not expected the Allies to declare war on Germany after his attack upon Poland. Once the Polish campaign had ended in a stunning German victory, Hitler waited for peace feelers from Britain and France. In October he indicated that he was willing to guarantee the status quo in the West, that is, the possession of Alsace-Lorraine by France, if the Allies would recognize German hegemony in East-Central Europe. He was even willing to go so far as to allow a rump Polish state to exist, thereby saving Western face and setting up the backdrop for another Munich-type conference. It appears from the military records available that the Allies had missed a major opportunity during the Polish campaign. Hitler's West Wall or Siegfried Line was only partially constructed and was not defended by the best German troops or the newest equipment. This was an opportunity for the French which would never recur.

Hitler felt that he would be able to knock France out of the war with a single, overpowering blow, thereby setting the stage for a renewal of his offers of alliance to a more "rational" Great Britain. The French sat in their Maginot Line, bored to death as this "phony war" or *drôle de guerre* continued into 1940. The Germans blared disintegrative pacifist propaganda at the French over loudspeakers, while the French *poilus* answered by loud boos and ridicule. Indeed, the French people had been somewhat relieved when war broke out in 1939. At least this would not be another nerve-racking false alarm followed by euphoria and disappointment, such as the Munich to Prague period (1938-1939) had represented. Yet by 1940 France was internally rotten. It was a nation divided against itself in many ways. Years before, Hitler had indicated that he would maneuver the French army out of the Maginot Line "without losing a single man." His original plan for an attack upon the West in 1939 was merely a variant upon the ill-fated Schlieffen Plan of 1914. Early in 1940 Hitler hit upon an alternative plan. It was developed late in 1939 by a brilliant officer, Erich von Manstein.

Most German generals were conservative in outlook. They did not want to attempt an attack on France, feeling that the losses incurred by the Germans would be proportionate to those which they had suffered during the agonizing siege of Verdun in 1916. The French sat in their Maginot Line convinced that the British blockade would ultimately starve the Germans out. The French even had a Ministry of the Blockade, thus showing their propagandistic faith in that tool of war. The Allies, horrified like all Europeans by the bloodletting of World War I, intended to avoid such catastrophes as that symbolized by the blood spilled in the infamous Flanders Fields. They would wait, wait, and continue to wait. They would isolate the Germans diplomatically, and finally starve them out. Unfortunately, this plan did not have much of a future early in 1940. Soviet Russia was in a sense an ally of the Germans. The Germans dominated East-Central Europe and had strong economic interests in the Balkans. Italy was a nonbelligerent pursuing a pro-German course. All this meant that the German position was stronger than that enjoyed by the Central Powers at a similar stage of the First World War. While the Allies waited, Hitler seized upon Manstein's plan and decided to implement it as soon as the weather permitted. There were several delays, but the plan was ultimately put into effect on May 10, 1940, with devastating results for the Allies.

Manstein had argued that the Ardennes, a thickly wooded and mountainous area in southern Belgium, Luxembourg, and around Sedan at a crucial crossing of the Meuse River, should be the focal point of the German attack. In 1934 Marshal Pétain had echoed one of the tenets of conservative military theory when he argued that the Ardennes were impassible to modern tanks. Manstein's plan called for a crossing of the Meuse in the Sedan area. German armor would then have a strong element of surprise on its side, for the Germans could move to outflank the Maginot Line to the south, head west for Paris, or could race for the Channel, thereby cutting off the Allied forces in Belgium. Since the Germans knew that the Allies assumed that the Germans would use a variant of their 1914 plan, they would race into Belgium to meet the Wehrmacht as far away from the frontiers of France as possible. German armor could then reach the Channel, cutting off the Allied forces in Belgium, which would contain the cream of the Allied armies. The Manstein plan was daring but dangerous: The armor would run far ahead of the infantry, and there would be a long, exposed left flank against which a resolute enemy might react. Hitler himself was nervous about the possibility of Allied counterattacks, but historians generally agree that the failure of the French to destroy the German forces west of the Meuse by May 17 cost them the war. Under the Manstein plan Belgian neutrality would once again be violated, but to the German *realpolitisch* tradition this was hardly a major concern.

The Allies were desperate for good news and cheap victories during this depressing winter of 1939-1940. This led their citizens to look to sea exploits by the Allied navies. The scuttling of the German pocket battleship *Graf Spee* off the coast of Uruguay in December, 1939 was hailed as a major victory by the Allied press. At this point the German navy was fairly weak, both in terms of submarines and of surface vessels. The Allies undoubtedly controlled the high seas. This, of course, was the basis of their feeling that Germany would ultimately be defeated by an Allied blockade. Yet there was a certain irony in this. Italy had an extremely long and exposed coastline. If Italy had joined Germany in September,

1939 the Allies might have achieved a major psychological and political boost by successful attacks upon the Italian peninsula. That would have demonstrated the clear-cut superiority of Allied naval power, and might have kept nervous neutrals in a pro-Allied stance. Italy pursued a pro-German course of "nonbelligerency," and in this way Mussolini deprived the British and the French of a major morale-boosting opportunity.

The men ruling England and France were probably more anti-Bolshevik than they were anti-Nazi. When the Soviet Union, with Hitler's tacit consent, attacked Finland late in 1939, General Maxime Weygand seriously suggested that the French consider a naval attack on the Soviet port of Odessa on the Black Sea. The British and the French prepared a major military buildup in order to help Finland. An important personality such as Harold Macmillan spent a good deal of time in Finland in order to smooth the way for massive Allied aid. The Allies were much more energetic in pursuing possible ways of aiding Finland against Russia than they had been in considering how to aid Poland against Germany. Norway was neutral but oriented towards Great Britain, and Norwegian public opinion was 100 percent pro-Finnish in Finland's war with Soviet Russia. When Finland finally capitulated and signed the Treaty of Moscow with Russia in March, 1940, Allied plans to aid Finland had to come to a halt. This Finnish war with Russia had an important side effect, however.

As plans for the abortive expeditionary force to Finland progressed, the British put heavy pressure upon Norway to cooperate with the Allies militarily and diplomatically. Even after the Soviet-Finnish armistice the British were considering the mining of Norwegian territorial waters in order to prevent crucial Swedish iron ore from reaching the Reich. To forestall such a move, Hitler launched a lightning attack upon Norway and Denmark on April 9, 1940. The Norwegian traitor Vidkun Quisling performed some minor services for the Germans during the month-long campaign that followed. His name, along with terms such as "blitzkrieg" and "GI," was a major linguistic heritage of the Second World War. The successful German attack upon Norway was particularly humiliating for the British. Although the German surface fleet suffered heavy losses in the April campaign, the Germans had good reason to be satisfied with its results. By May it was clear that the British position in Norway was hopeless. The Germans could now establish naval and air bases on the well-protected Norwegian coast. They would be able to attack Britain and British commerce from these bases. The successful German attack upon Norway and the failure of British counterattacks led to the downfall of the Chamberlain government, with many Tories deserting the Government's cause on the historic night of May 9-10. Winston Churchill, a fervent anti-Communist who had been warning the West about Hitler for a number of years, became Prime Minister of a coalition or "national" cabinet. He had not yet taken up residence at 10 Downing Street when the Germans launched their long-awaited offensive on the western front.

2. The Fall of France

The German attack on the Low Countries showed that modern war had added new dimensions to its terrors and techniques. Dive bombers tore up roads and canals, while fighters strafed panicked columns of military refugees. People believed that "fifth columnists" (a term arising from the siege of Madrid during the Spanish Civil War) were sabotaging the Allies and spreading false rumors among the civilian population of Belgium, Holland, and northern France. Nazi tanks tore through enemy lines and sowed panic and confusion in their rear support areas. The French and British responded by moving a large number of troops into Belgium, but Belgian neutrality, proclaimed in 1936, had made joint planning and preparations impossible. The Germans had the initiative, and they had still other surprises in store for the Allies. German armed forces broke through the Ardennes at Sedan and moved rapidly toward the Channel. This breakthrough meant that a large number of French divisions encamped in the Maginot Line were cut off from the rest of the French war effort. In Belgium the Germans made good use of their knowledge of silent, low-flying gliders, a type of aircraft with which they had experimented in Russia in the 1920's. Such gliders made possible the capture of a great Belgian fortress such as Eben Emael. By late May the Germans had cut off the British, French, and Belgians from the rest of France, and it was only owing to the stalwart efforts of the British navy and civilian population that so much of the British Expeditionary Force and some of its Allied soldiers (without equipment) were successfully evacuated at Dunkirk.

Historians have long speculated over why Hitler did not make more of an attempt to prevent the British from escaping at Dunkirk. There are several possible explanations. As early as mid-May Hitler had been somewhat frightened by his own success, and he began to wonder whether or not the Germans should be more cautious about permitting their tanks to run so many miles ahead of their infantry and artillery. This tactic, of course, had largely been responsible for German successes in Poland, and now in Belgium and Holland. Hitler feared a counterattack on his southern armored flank. Hermann Göring reinforced Hitler's caution when he told him that the Luftwaffe would be able to mop up any British troops who attempted to escape from the Continent. It also might be dangerous and impolitic for army generals to have the sole glory of destroying British power. Perhaps the German troops were held back because of a subconscious motive: Hitler's desire to come to terms with the British rather than destroy them. At any rate, the British Expeditionary Force did escape and it would provide the nucleus of the British army that landed on the continent of Europe on June 6, 1944. At this point the Germans paid little attention to the Maginot Line. In the few areas where they had probed it since the beginning of the war it showed that it was quite effective against conventional types of direct frontal assault. It may even be said to have won a "tactical victory" in this war, though the irony of this judgment is implicit in its articulation.

The British withdrawal at Dunkirk made the French feel more isolated than ever. There was growing French bitterness toward France's ally. General Weygand, a peppery, outspoken old man who had been Foch's Chief of Staff in the First World War, now became Commander of all French armies, while the aged Marshal Pétain, the hero of Verdun, entered the government as Vice-Premier. These men could not stem the German tide, which now crashed in upon the heart of France itself. Weygand tried to regroup his now badly outnumbered forces early in June for an effective defensive action along the Somme. In his diary Count Ciano gleefully noted that this French resistance had stiffened and become "almost heroic." These were passing moments, however. The French, though not lacking in certain types of modern equipment, were poorly led and demoralized. They now added hatred for Great Britain to the list of their other demoralizing tendencies. French conservatives began to fear that a prolongation of the war with Germany would lead to a Communist uprising, since, after all, everybody knew that the Communists were "in league" with the Nazis since the Ribbentrop-Molotov pact.

On June 10 Mussolini declared war upon the Allies. For months he had been telling Hitler that Italy would enter the war as soon as the German army had struck a major blow against the Allies. The Duce did not want to be left out of the peace talks and the division of spoils which would presumably follow an Allied defeat. Hitler's attitude toward Mussolini's policy in the first half of 1940 is quite interesting from a psychological viewpoint. Hitler had no undue illusions about Italian military might or potential, yet he seems to have been sincere in urging Mussolini to enter the war. He never trusted the Italian royal house or its attitude toward Fascism. In this, of course, Hitler proved quite prescient. Hitler constantly told Mussolini that Fascism would rise or fall with the success or failure of German armed might. He hated the thought that the Italian leadership or even Mussolini might be playing a duplicitous game, that is, veering towards pro-Allied neutrality or perhaps even hostility on the Allied side if things went badly for Germany. Hitler was morbidly suspicious, and it was only when Italy was in the same boat as Germany that his suspicions would temporarily die down.

The Allies were even more unrealistic than the Germans in their appreciation of Mussolini. Almost until his entry into the war French and British politicians felt that Italy could be detached from Germany. After all, this had been successfully done once before, in 1915. King George VI even suggested that he write a letter to King Victor Emmanuel begging Italy to stay out of the war. A French politician such as Pierre Laval was convinced until his dying day that if he had been Prime Minister in this situation, Italy would never have entered the war on Germany's side. As we have suggested, however, it would have been better from the viewpoint of the Allies for Italy to have been in the war in 1939. They might have then opened up a front against the Axis, and caused the Germans to divert major forces to this southern or Mediterranean theater. This is indeed what happened between 1940 and 1945. Hitler wound up his life cursing his alliance with the Italians and referring to his "brutal friendship" with Mussolini, one which had cost him the war. The Italian effort against France was quite limited. The French had no difficulty containing Italian thrusts into the French Alps between June 10 and June 25, 1940.

The French Cabinet was now presided over by Paul Reynaud. Reynaud, unlike the leading French military and political lights of the late 1930's, had realized that the Maginot Line would be an inadequate French response in the forthcoming war. Reynaud believed in Colonel De Gaulle's prophecies concerning armored warfare and the paramount role of the offensive in any future war. In June, 1940, however, Reynaud did not have enough confidence in himself or in France to lead the French Cabinet to the position which its majority probably favored: continuation of the war, even if this meant waging it from French North Africa. Indeed, this was a possibility the Germans greatly feared even after the defeat of the French in metropolitan France. Reynaud's will collapsed, largely due to the influence of his mistress, and the defeatists and conservatives had their way. France decided to conclude an armistice with the Germans, though on March 28 she had solemnly promised the British that she would never make peace alone.

French bitterness and defeatism, exacerbated by anti-British sentiments before and after Dunkirk, gave old men like Pétain and Weygand the upper hand. These men, demoralized and twisted by their desire to preserve the existing social structure and exterminate forces for progressive social change, feared that a continuation of the war would mean that French Communist leader Maurice Thorez "would be installed in the Elysées Palace." Indeed, there were rumors current in France in late June that he was already there, protected by a solemn cordon of German troops! The new French leadership under Pétain, who emerged as the last Premier of the Third Republic, decided to ask the Germans about armistice terms. The French were bitter when the Germans indicated that it would not be possible to sign an armistice with Germany alone. Even though the French troops in the Alps had contained the Italians after their dastardly stab in the back on June 10, an armistice would have to take effect simultaneously between France and Germany and France and Italy. It was also clear, however, that Mussolini had to follow Hitler in this matter, as in all others.

The collapse of France represented Hitler's greatest ecstasy since his appointment as Chancellor over seven long years earlier. Hitler was incapable of creating or organizing upon the basis of good will. He was congenitally unable to forgive his enemies. A subconscious sense of inferiority, inadequacy, of fear—these were at the root of Hitler's outward struttings and martial aura. In this, as in so many other respects, Hitler was merely a caricature of deep-seated emotions and tendencies present in the very bosom of the German nation. Hitler could not create or organize Europe. Thus, as an Italian diplomat wrote in 1943, "All of Europe is in revolt against the German attempt at hegemony, conducted with such bestiality." Hitler's policy toward France, which in the beginning seemed lenient, was an excellent example of this self-defeating brutality based upon psychological compensation.

There is no better description available of Hitler's mood at the time of the fall of France than journalist William L. Shirer's eyewitness account. Shirer saw Hitler enter a little clearing in the forest of Compiègne where the German armistice terms were to be read to a depressed French delegation. Hitler had personally insisted that the armistice be signed in the same railway coach where the November 11, 1918 armistice ending the First World War had been signed. Thus, Hitler would humiliate the French and wipe out the stain of the German capitulation. General Keitel read the preamble of the German terms to the French delegation. There occurred in this preamble the phrase which Hitler used again and again throughout the war: "This war, which has been forced upon us. . . ." Hitler's feeling was that the French had followed the British into the war, but that unless they atoned for this anti-German misdeed they, being the defeated Allied power, would have to pay the *entire* cost of the war. This was a form of blackmail with which he threatened the leadership of France for four years. But let us listen to Shirer:

Through my glasses I saw the Führer stop, glance at the monument, observe the Reich flags with their big swastikas in the center. Then he strode slowly towards us, towards the little clearing in the woods. I observed his face. It was grave, solemn, yet brimming with revenge. There was also in it, as in his springy step, a note of the triumphant conqueror, the defier of the world. There was something else, difficult to describe, in his expression, a sort of scornful, inner joy at being present at this great reversal of fate—a reversal he himself had wrought. . . .

Hitler reads it [the French monument commemorating the Armistice of November 11, 1918] and Goering reads it. They all read it, standing there in the June sun and the silence. I look for the expression on Hitler's face. I am but fifty yards from him and see him through my glasses as though he were directly in front of me. I have seen that face many times at the great moments of his life. But today! It is afire with scorn, anger, hate, revenge, triumph. He steps off the monument and contrives to make even this gesture a masterpiece of contempt. He glances back at it, contemptuous, angry—angry, you almost feel, because he cannot wipe out the awful, provoking lettering with one sweep of his high Prussian boot. He glances slowly around the clearing, and now, as his eyes meet ours, you grasp the depth of his hatred. But there is triumph there too—revengeful, triumphant hate. Suddenly, as though his face were not giving quite complete expression to his feelings, he throws his whole body into harmony with his mood. He swiftly snaps his hands on his hips, arches his shoulders, plants his feet wide apart. It is a magnificent gesture of defiance, of burning contempt for this place now and all that it has stood for in the twenty-two years since it witnessed the humbling of the German Empire. . . .

Hitler and his aides stride down the avenue towards the Alsace-Lorraine monument, where their cars are waiting. As they pass the guard of honour, the German band strikes up the two national anthems, *Deutschland, Deutschland über Alles* and the *Horst Wessel* song. The whole ceremony in which Hitler has reached a new pinnacle in his meteoric career and Germany avenged the 1918 defeat is over in a quarter of an hour.

This indeed was Adolf Hitler.

With the fall of France Hitler was at the very height of his prestige if not of his power. It was at about this time that Keitel turned to him and said, "My Führer, you are the greatest field captain of all time." On July 19 Hitler promoted Keitel to the highest German military rank, that of General Field Marshal. From this time onward Hitler seems to have believed in his military infallibility. The German press hailed him as the *Grösster Feldherr aller Zeiten*, the "greatest field captain of all time." By 1944-1945, when things were not going so well, the Berliners, who are noted for their wit, were abbreviating the first letters of these German words and referring to the Führer rather disrespectfully as *"Gröfaz,"* a word with no meaning but with slightly ridiculous overtones.

Mussolini expected that the defeat of France meant that Nice and Savoy, Corsica and Tunis, and perhaps parts of Algeria and Morocco would all fall to Italy. Hitler's armistice terms with France, however, were relatively "mild" considering the French military disaster. French military authorities, led by the venerable Marshal Pétain, assured the population that the terms contained nothing dishonorable and that "Our banner remains without a stain." Hitler was afraid that the French navy might go over to the British, or that the French government might continue the war from North Africa if the terms were too harsh. Hence, the armistice provided that the Germans would occupy three-fifths of France, including its Channel and Atlantic coasts, while the rest of the country would remain unoccupied. The French government would have administrative power over the entire nation. In reality, the terms were somewhat harsher than this, for another motive of Hitler was the further decimation of French morale and the sowing of confusion in the French populace through the division of powers implied in this partition of the nation. Hitler had no intention, on the other hand, of driving France back into England's arms by giving Mussolini what he wanted.

Hitler held several daggers at the throat of the French. If the French government and Marshal Pétain, soon to be situated at Vichy, did not cooperate with the Germans in both the economic and the political areas, the Germans might set up a rival French government in Paris headed by Fascists such as Marcel Déat or Jacques Doriot. If the Vichy French did not collaborate with the Germans, the Germans might hand their colonies over to the Italians or make a deal with the British which would mean that the French alone would pay the costs of the Second World War. Hitler did not understand the power of generosity, though he was capable of cheap histrionic gestures which had no real emotional or political meaning, such as meeting Marshal Pétain at Montoire on October 24, 1940, or returning the ashes of the son of Napoleon to the Invalides on December 15, 1940.

3. Hitler's Failure over Britain: Causes and Consequences

In the weeks after the fall of France, Hitler waited in vain for a conciliatory word from Great Britain. He had always been sincere in his willingness to pacify the British Empire by "guaranteeing" it. Certainly, Germany might want some compensation for the colonies taken from her during the First World War, but she wished above all else to have friendly relations with Great Britain. Hitler knew that this was a "rational" plan. Didn't the British understand that they had been beaten? How could Churchill be so "irrational"? Hitler believed that Churchill was guided by hatred of Germany, not by "reason." On July 19, Hitler presided over a victory session of the Greater German Reichstag. In addition to promoting various German generals who had distinguished themselves in the recent campaign, Hitler launched a peace feeler to Great Britain. By July 22 it was clear that Churchill and Halifax had rejected the German offer. Churchill saw Hitler as evil incarnate, and the British no longer had any confidence in his promises. Hitler had no desire to invade Great Britain, and his motives were military as well as racial, political, and sentimental: "On the land I am a hero. On the sea I am a coward." The German navy was vastly inferior to that of Great Britain. Hitler was afraid of the propaganda disaster which an unsuccessful attack upon the British Isles would represent. Thus, Hitler's preparations for "Operation Sea Lion" or the invasion of Great Britain were desultory in character and were ultimately postponed until some vague point in 1941.

Hitler thought he might be able to bring the British to their senses by air attacks. At first, the Luftwaffe tried to gain mastery of the air over Great Britain by destroying RAF ground installations and radar stations. In the long run (by November 1?) the Germans might have been able to achieve this goal, though in the year after Munich the British had produced quantities of the Spitfire fighter, which had a faster climbing rate than most of the available German fighters. Göring, alarmed by the rate of attrition being suffered by his fighters, promised Hitler that Luftwaffe day bombing attacks on British cities, especially upon London, would so wreck British morale that the British would be ready for peace with Germany. Hitler was infuriated by minor British attacks upon German cities, and he agreed to this switch in strategy. The Spitfires of the RAF Fighter Command made such saturation bombing seem less costly to the

Germans than far-flung, ill-coordinated fighter battles over southern and central England. Although the British suffered greatly in 1940-1941 due to Luftwaffe attacks on British cities, the RAF remained in strategic control of the skies over the Channel and Great Britain. In this situation strategic control refers to the fact that they were more than equal to the task of (1) preventing their own destruction, and (2) preventing any putative land attack upon Great Britain.

Even before the Battle of Britain had begun in earnest, Hitler had indicated that the British only held out because they ultimately expected the Soviet Union and the United States to enter the war. Hitler tended to underestimate the United States. He did not believe that such a "racial agglomerate" would be capable of acting as a great power militarily or economically. He claimed that he had seen American troops in the First World War, and that they had acted like "scared rabbits." In earlier times Hitler had shown some respect for the economic accomplishments of the United States. In 1940, egged on by men such as Göring and Ribbentrop, Hitler ignored or never saw the reports of his own officials in Washington. These reports indicated that the American potential was not negligible. In 1940 Hitler tended to ignore the United States as a factor in the European war. He did not ignore the Soviet Union, however.

While Hitler and Göring were struggling with the RAF, the Soviet Union was acting aggressively in Eastern Europe. It was making demands upon Rumania and the Baltic states, and there was talk of renewed pressure upon Finland with its vital nickel deposits at Petsamo. By the end of July Hitler felt that the destruction of the Soviet Union would accomplish two goals which were otherwise unachievable: (1) It would force the British to agree to an alliance with Germany, and (2) a defeat of the Soviet Union would guarantee the future of the German people by providing it with vital living space in the Ukraine and other parts of European Russia. There were certain characters in Hitler's court who felt that this attack upon Russia should follow, not precede, the subjugation of Great Britain. Admiral Raeder, having a sailor's viewpoint, felt that Hitler should explore further possibilities in waging war against Great Britain—such as an attack upon Gibraltar or an extension of the Dönitz U-boat program. Ribbentrop, blinded by his hatred of the British, thought in terms of putting together a European coalition against Great Britain. This coalition would include Germany, Italy, Spain, Vichy France, and perhaps even the Soviet Union. It would be modeled on Napoleon's Continental System of 1810, but presumably would be more effective. Raeder's viewpoint did not carry much weight with the Führer because of the fact that the German navy, on the surface and under the sea, did not control the waters around Great Britain.

Ribbentrop failed in his quest for a continental blockade because of Russian expansionist pressures in Eastern Europe and Franco's stubborn unwillingness to join the Axis before the defeat of Great Britain had become more obvious. In this Franco showed himself far more clever than Mussolini. Mussolini indicated that he would go to war against the Allies as soon as France had been defeated. Franco, understanding that a nation with an exposed coastline did not dally lightly with the British Empire, would not make his move until British power had been broken. By the end of October Great Britain was winning the battle for the skies over England. It was also evident that Franco was for the time being uninterested in joining the Axis in this military effort against the British.

4. Trouble in the Balkans and North Africa

The Soviet Union forced Rumania to disgorge Bessarabia and northern Bukovina on June 30. Hitler had presided over the further dismemberment of Rumania at the Second Vienna Award of August 30, by which Rumania lost northern Transylvania to Hungary. Rumania, an Allied state in the First World War, thus paid dearly for her earlier ties with the West. After the fall of France the Soviet Union had made gains at the expense of Rumania, and had absorbed Latvia, Lithuania, and Estonia. Hitler was now concerned about possible Soviet designs upon Bulgaria, which had long-standing ties of friendship with the Russian people. After the Second Vienna Award Germany guaranteed what remained of Rumania. In effect this meant that Germany had turned Rumania into an economic and military satellite. German troops began to pour into Rumania in October, 1940. That upset Mussolini almost as much as it did Stalin. The Rumanians, however, did not care much about the Duce at this point. They blamed Mussolini for their losses to the Magyars, for since 1927 Mussolini had shown himself to be a friend of Hungarian revisionism.

The Germans were concerned about further Soviet moves in the Balkans, for the Rumanian oil supply was vital to the Nazi war effort. Conversely, the Rumanians knew that they had nowhere else to turn for their security but to Berlin. They had converted themselves into a German satellite. German interests in the Balkans, which until 1940 had been repeatedly defined by Hitler as strictly economic, now took a political and military turn. The German presence in Rumania could only antagonize the Soviet Union.

Mussolini, humiliated by the totally German victory over France and by German diplomatic successes in the Balkans, decided to "pay Hitler back in his own coin." That is, he would attack a neutral nation *without warning and without telling Hitler*. Mussolini was deathly afraid of a Franco-German rapprochement. On October 22 Hitler had met Vice-Premier Laval, and two days later had had a well-publicized talk with Marshal Pétain, the French Head of State. Four days thereafter, as Hitler was on his way back to Berlin, the Duce ordered Italian troops in

Albania to attack Greece. This would show Hitler that Italy was vitally interested in the Balkans, that it was not a German satellite, and that it was waging a "parallel war" of its own against Britain and her Mediterranean satellite. Hitler was in a rage over Mussolini's attack upon Greece, for such a war played no part in his calculations. Mussolini's action could only upset the situation in the Balkans and perhaps involve the Soviet Union and Britain. Such an involvement would obviously take an anti-German direction. At this point, Hitler had little confidence in Italian military abilities. He would have preferred that the Italians create a true empire in North Africa, destroying the British positions in western Egypt and along the vital Suez Canal.

Mussolini was irritated and impatient, and he wanted to regain the initiative. He invaded Greece only a few days after Hitler had met Franco and Pétain. Mussolini was afraid that an alliance between Germany, Spain, and Vichy France would leave the Italians out in the cold. This was a major reason for his attack upon the Greeks, but the Italian invasion proved to be a disaster for the Duce. The Greeks fought heroically, even driving the Italians back into Albania by early December. Mussolini and Ciano were afraid they might have to call upon the Germans to mediate. The war between Greece and Italy dragged on into 1941. The British saw an opportunity for intervention against the Axis, and they landed forces in Greece. This, in turn, put terrible pressure upon Yugoslavia. If Yugoslavia joined the British and the Greeks, the Axis position in the Balkans (including the German position in oil-rich Rumania) would be threatened. This is precisely the situation which Hitler had wished to avoid. Now, however, he would have to deal with it.

The Yugoslav Regent, Prince Paul, was sympathetic to the Axis. In March, 1941 he agreed to join the Tripartite Pact and aid the Axis indirectly (and perhaps directly) in its war against Greece and Britain in the Balkans. Soviet and British pressure upon Belgrade, combined with the

British presence in Greece, led to a coup which overthrew Paul at the end of March. A new government headed by Dušan Simović was formed, one which represented a repudiation of Yugoslavia's recent adherence to the Tripartite Pact. Hitler felt he had been humiliated by the Yugoslavs, for the Yugoslav turnabout represented a deterioration of the Axis position in the Balkans. He resolved to smash the Yugoslav state once and for all in early April.

Since December, 1940 the Führer had been engaged in desperate and feverish preparations for his attack upon the Soviet Union. Operation Barbarossa had been fully outlined in Directive No. 21, dated December 18, 1940. Hitler wanted a tranquil Balkan Peninsula on his southern flank during this campaign. In this he showed that he was pursuing a single aim, the destruction of the Soviet Union. This was consistent with his authorship of the Tripartite Pact between Italy, Germany, and Japan, which had been signed in Berlin on September 27, 1940. The Germans viewed the Tripartite Pact as a device to frighten the United States and keep it out of the Second World War. The Japanese felt it might be useful because, given good German relations with Moscow, the Germans might act as intermediaries between Japan and the Soviet Union. Ever since the fall of Holland and France the Japanese navy and senior civilian politicians had been more interested in good relations with the Soviet Union. They now saw opportunities for expansion southward into areas rich in oil, tin, and rubber, into regions such as Dutch Indonesia and French Indochina. The forces which would oppose such an expansion would be Great Britain and the United States, not the U.S.S.R.

The United States had shown itself increasingly hostile to Japanese moves in the southwest Pacific since June, 1940. The Japanese felt that the Tripartite Pact would be a warning to the United States to stay out of any conflict which might break out between Japan and Vichy France, Japan and Great Britain, or Japan and the government in exile of Holland over Japanese expansion into

Asian areas formerly dominated by these European powers. It is ironic that the Japanese, now interested in good
relations with the Soviet Union so as to guard their north-
western flank, felt that the Germans might be "honest
brokers" in such a Japanese-Soviet rapprochement. *Hitler*,
of course, never told his allies anything of his plans. For
him the Tripartite Pact was a guarantee that: (1) The
United States would stay out of the European war, and
(2) if America foolishly did enter the war on the side of
Great Britain, it would have to fight a two-ocean war
because of the Japanese. Hitler believed that the United
States would not undertake such a risk. The triumph of
Roosevelt (over the equally anti-German internationalist
Wendell Willkie) a few weeks later should have warned
the Führer that he had misunderstood American determination. At the time of the Tripartite Pact Hitler was
considering his attack upon the Soviet Union. He saw the
pact as advantageous because it might guarantee American neutrality in the event of a Soviet-German war.

Mussolini's invasion of Greece and subsequent military
blundering had upset a major aspect of Hitler's plans. By
April, 1941 Hitler had to assume that German pacifica-
tion of Greece and Yugoslavia was the only answer to
what was happening on his southern flank. Mussolini's
attack upon Greece and its implied claim to Italian
hegemony in the eastern Mediterranean was not merely
a challenge to Great Britain, it was also Mussolini's way
of asserting Italian importance in the new Europe which
Hitler, not Mussolini, was creating. By October 28 it
appeared to Mussolini and Ciano that a stalemate
between Germany and England might be in the making.
Since Hitler had shown himself reluctant to crush France
completely and turn her colonial empire over to the
Italians and the Spaniards, any possible rapprochement
between Germany and France could only bode ill for the
Italian position in Hitler's New Order. If Italy was not
strong at the time of the peace conference—and this
meant being in a position to challenge the British at Suez
and on the high seas—then Italian interests would be sac-

rificed by Hitler. Thus, the Greek adventure was the logi-cal extension of Mussolini's "parallel war": It was most obviously aimed against Britain and her long-time friend Greece, but it was also a declaration of independence from the Führer. This, of course, was ironic, because Hitler ultimately had to be called in in order to save the disastrous Italian position, thereby further reducing Mus-solini's power and prestige.

By the end of 1940 the British Eighth Army under General Wavell had driven the Italians far westward into the deserts of Libya, and it was obvious that the Duce would not make a triumphant entry into Cairo. While Hitler meditated upon ways of saving the Italian army in Albania and Greece, thus guaranteeing the German position in oil-rich Rumania, he was faced with the prob-lem of what to do about renewed British strength in North Africa. The result was the commitment early in 1941 of Erwin Rommel and the Afrika Korps to Mus-solini's sinking fortunes in North Africa. If the British had not intervened in Greece early in 1941, it is possible that Hitler would have mediated the dispute between the Greeks and Mussolini. Indeed, a humiliated Mussolini would have had little choice but to accept such mediation, as he had realized early in December. Such mediation might have spared the Greek people the horrors of three and a half years of Axis occupation. The British presence in Greece was relatively ineffective, as the results of the German Blitzkrieg in April and May would prove, and by diverting troops from Africa to Greece the British temporarily saved the Axis position in Libya.

Hitler's attack upon Yugoslavia began on a typical note of personal vengeance. He felt humiliated by Yugoslavia's about-face decision on the Tripartite Pact. At the end of March Hitler told Mussolini to take no precipitate action against the Yugoslavs, for he needed a few days for preparation. On April 6 the Germans attacked Yugo-slavia. Hungary and Bulgaria took part in the campaign. The Hungarians had earlier signed a friendship pact with the Yugoslavs, and Count Pál Teleki, the Hungarian

Prime Minister, was so upset by the Hungarian betrayal of that pact that he committed suicide. The accession of Bulgaria to the Tripartite Pact had occurred in February. This cooperation allowed the Germans to bring troops into Greece via the Vardar Valley, thus outflanking Greece's strong "Metaxas Line." The regular Yugoslav army was crushed in a matter of days, though the birth of the Yugoslav resistance under Tito would prove that the Yugoslavs were true to their traditions as a warrior people. By the end of May the Germans had taken the island of Crete after a difficult campaign in which, for the last time in the war, they made major use of paratroopers in a purely military engagement. Their paratroop units were badly decimated in this campaign.

As Hitler had predicted, the Yugoslav state was completely destroyed. A Fascist Independent State of Croatia under the "Poglavnik" Ante Pavelić emerged by the end of April. Hungary and Rumania made various claims upon Yugoslav territory as did Italy, Germany, and Bulgaria. The Soviet Union watched these German moves in the Balkans with growing mistrust. This mistrust had at first been awakened in September and October, 1940, when the Germans sent a military mission, then hundreds of thousands of troops into Rumania. When Molotov visited Berlin in November, 1940, his attitude can best be described as reserved or even hostile. There is no doubt that Stalin and Molotov now knew that it was in their interest for the British to continue their heroic resistance in the face of the Nazi onslaught. The Soviets were seriously upset over German pressures on Bulgaria. Ribbentrop made a half-hearted attempt to deflect this hostility by turning the Soviet Union against the British in Central Asia. Indeed, he would have preferred a continuation of the Russian alliance and some sort of "Continental system" until the British had been brought to their knees. Adolf Hitler had other ideas, however.

5. Barbarossa

Historians have long argued over whether the Balkan campaign delayed or irreparably damaged Hitler's strike against Soviet Russia. It is true that he had originally planned to attack Russia by the middle of May, at the latest. Conditions of weather and terrain, however, would have made such an early attack impossible. Spring thaw would have made the land impassible for tanks and other heavy equipment. In the long run the burden of having to keep so many divisions in the Balkans did hurt the German war effort in Russia and elsewhere, but Hitler's decision to attack the Soviet Union had been made in the summer of 1940. Once it was decided to attack the Soviet Union in 1941, it was predictable that the attack would begin sometime in June. Napoleon, after all, had invaded Russia on June 22, 1812, for highly similar, Anglophobe reasons. The German offensive in 1941 began on June 22, in 1942 on June 28, in 1943 on July 5, while the Soviet summer offensive of 1944 commenced on June 22. The fact that all these attacks began almost the same time of year seems to indicate that Hitler's Operation Barbarossa was not seriously delayed by his attack on Greece and Yugoslavia.

Hitler was a strange ally. He did not tell his allies more than they needed to know for the specific tasks which he assigned to them. Thus, he informed Admiral Horthy, the Regent of Hungary, of the attack on the Soviet Union on June 22. He gave the Finns and Rumanians some advance notice because he badly wanted their participation in the campaign. The Japanese were deceived until the very end. When the Japanese signed the Tripartite Pact on September 27, they seriously thought that Germany would be useful in mediating a rapprochement between Japan and the Soviet Union. When Japanese Ambassador Oshima or Foreign Minister Matsuoka broached this issue with Hitler or Ribbentrop after that time, the Germans responded in a dilatory fashion, either urging the Japanese to move south against the British position at Singapore, or mumbling something to the effect that German relations with the Soviet Union were good but would bear watching in case of aggressive moves by the Russians.

The Japanese were as duplicitous as their German allies. Through a good part of 1941 the Japanese appeared ready to bargain away the Tripartite Pact if the United States would make major concessions to Japanese ambitions in East Asia. Hitler, Ribbentrop, and the German ambassador Ott in Tokyo were well aware of this Japanese attitude. In early April, when German-Russian relations were seriously deteriorating because of the new German military role in the south Balkans, Foreign Minister Matsuoka visited Berlin. On his way back to Japan he signed a Neutrality Pact in Moscow, one which the Russians and Japanese faithfully observed until August 8, 1945. This pact was the last thing Hitler and Ribbentrop had wanted. At this point they would have liked a Japanese attack on the Soviet Far East, on the British in Singapore, or perhaps both. They certainly did not want the Japanese to (1) sign a neutrality pact with Stalin's Russia, and (2) act as if the Tripartite Pact had been signed in order that the Japanese have a bargaining lever with the anti-German Americans over such issues as China, Indonesia, and Indochina. There was a powerful anti-Soviet faction in the Japanese army which, particularly in the Manchurian Kwantung army, would have looked upon an attack on the Soviet Far East in a friendly fashion. Civilian and naval elements, however, did not favor this course, and Japan faithfully observed the Neutrality Pact throughout the time of its existence.

Nazi propaganda heralded the attack upon the Soviet Union as a European crusade against Bolshevism, albeit one in which Germany played the primary role. Hitler told the world that he attacked the Soviet Union because of the aggressive diplomatic and military attitudes of Stalin. Actually, he attacked Soviet Russia in order to bring Britain to her knees, frighten the United States and keep her out of the Atlantic war, and win "living space" for the German master race. Hitler did have a timetable for conquest until the attack upon Poland spiraled into a European-wide war. Now all sense had departed from such a timetable. Hitler had never assumed that he would win living space for the German people while engaged in a struggle with the greatest maritime power in the world—Great Britain. As far as the crusade against Communism was concerned, Hitler had a lot of nerve in pressing *that* point. It was he, after all, who had signed the friendship pact with Stalin in 1939, thus enabling the Russians to absorb much of independent Eastern Europe. The Germans looked the other way when the Finns begged them for help in their defensive Winter War against Soviet Russia in 1939-1940. German occupation authorities had even temporarily allowed the Communists to publish their newspaper in Paris after the fall of France.

Mussolini took this anti-Soviet crusade seriously. He argued that unless the Italians played a major role in it, their claims would not be considered by Hitler at the peace conference. Thus, despite his problems in the Balkans and North Africa, Mussolini dispatched a sizable expeditionary force to Russia in the summer and autumn of 1941. The Finns and Hungarians took part in the campaign several days after it had begun. The Rumanians were a major ally from the very beginning. Spain, Croatia, and Slovakia sent volunteer legions, as did France and other European nations. From the beginning, however, the project was a German one. The overwhelming bulk of the German army and Luftwaffe now faced the Red Army.

Operation Barbarossa was the greatest offensive in the history of the world. Nobody, not even the beleaguered British, gave the Russians much of a chance. Hitler and his generals expected that the Soviet Union would collapse in a matter of weeks, though Hitler occasionally confessed to private fears. After all, how could a structure built by "Bolshevik Jews" survive an onslaught by the world's greatest military power? Although relations with Germany had been deteriorating, Stalin stubbornly clung until the end to his alliance with the Nazis. He brushed aside evidence that clearly pointed to German hostile intentions, ascribing such reports to the scheming of British imperialists. For some days after the beginning of Barbarossa, Stalin was not to be seen. When he later emerged, he was still in Moscow, and this was a tremendous encouragement to the Soviet people. He said that the enemy was "cruel and implacable," and that the Soviet peoples must use every means in order to destroy the Fascist aggressor.

From the beginning there were differences of opinion in the German leadership as to the major goals of the Russian campaign. Everybody assumed that the destruction of the Red Army in western European Russia was both desirable and possible within a few weeks. Beyond that, however, there were differences. Hitler wanted the Ukraine and the Crimea because they were the core of the future German "living space" in the East. Moscow, a great center of industry and communications, the capital of Soviet Russia, was also an important goal. To the north, the Finns wanted to destroy the Soviet Union as a Baltic power. This meant besieging and taking Leningrad. Hitler wished to accomplish this, but beyond that he wanted to raze Leningrad to the ground. By August the Germans had driven deep into European Russia. Certain disconcerting factors, however, emerged. The Russians fought hard, not collapsing as had other European armies. Observers all over Europe noticed this, and the Japanese lay low and made no move against the Soviet Union in the Far East. Churchill and Roosevelt were determined to help Soviet Russia as best they could. Most of the German generals, men such as von Brauchitsch, the Commander in Chief of the army, Franz Halder, the Chief of the General Staff, and Fedor von Bock, Commander of the vast Army Group Center, wanted to concentrate upon Moscow, but Hitler was disconcerted by the

slow progress that von Rundstedt was making against the
Soviet armies in the Ukraine. It was not until September
30 that the Nazis were able to take its capital, Kiev, after
a vast battle of encirclement.

The Germans were only able to advance this far in the
south because Hitler had transferred several powerful
armored Panzer striking forces from the center to the
south. Before they had been transferred, the necessary
maintenance work had been done on the tanks. This cost
the offensive in the center precious weeks, and by the
time the offensive against Moscow was resumed, it was
October and the muddy season was beginning. The German infantry of Fedor von Bock's Army Group Center
had to trudge along as best it could, lacking the amount
of Panzer striking power that it had possessed in July.
Vast (and misleading) victories at Vyazma and Briansk
led Hitler to believe that it was still possible to take Moscow before the onslaught of winter. The cold season set
in early, however, and by early December it was clear that
Russia was going to suffer the worst winter since the days
of Napoleon's invasion. By November all but the wildest
optimists in the *Führerhauptquartier* realized that the
Blitzkrieg against Russia had failed. The Red Army had
not been crushed, and Moscow would not be taken before
the winter. Although the Germans had made tremendous
territorial gains, especially in the rich expanses of the
Ukraine, a German army would have to winter in Russia.
Von Rundstedt, Commander of Army Group South and
a cautious man whom Hitler soon branded a defeatist,
argued that it might be best for the German army to pull
back to the Polish frontier in order to spare the troops
a Russian winter. Then a new offensive could be
launched in the spring or summer of 1942. Hitler would
not hear of this.

Mussolini was delighted by Hitler's dilemma in Russia.
The more Germany was stalemated, the more significant
Italy would appear both to its ally and to its enemies, or
so thought the Duce. All over Europe strong resistance

movements now sprang up, inspired largely by the Soviet example. Communists played a major role in most of these movements as, for example, in Greece, Yugoslavia, and France. The Germans had to commit more troops to internal security, which in turn bolstered the size and authority of Heinrich Himmler's SS. The entire *raison d'être* of Hitler's New Order in Europe now became the destruction of Soviet Russia. He and his spokesmen (such as Alfred Rosenberg) openly stated that the punishment or rewards of various European countries would depend upon their contributions to this German war effort. Mussolini had to look on sullenly as Hitler demanded and received more and more Italian laborers for Germany's hard-pressed factories. Europe was mercilessly looted and exploited in order to win "living space" for the German people in the East. What began as an indirect attack upon Great Britain and a grab for *Lebensraum* in the East now took on the dimensions of a struggle for the very existence of the National Socialist regime, and, as Hitler said, for the "future of the German people."

6. Victory Eludes Hitler

In the second half of 1941 almost all of Hitler's attention was absorbed by the problems of the eastern front. In the Atlantic, however, the situation was also deteriorating. Roosevelt had issued orders to American ships that they could shoot German submarines on sight. He agreed that American warships could serve as convoy escorts in international waters for British vessels engaged in trade with the United States. The United States was actually engaged in an undeclared naval war with Nazi Germany. Roosevelt grew bolder as it was clear by November that the Nazi Blitzkrieg had stumbled badly in Russia. At the same time the Americans were negotiating with Hitler's Japanese ally. If Roosevelt had agreed to concessions at the expense of the Dutch, the French, the Chinese, and the British in the Far East, there was no doubt that he could have avoided a war with Japan, at least for the immediate future. The only thing that concerned Hitler at this point was a reckless fear that he would become involved in a war with the United States in the Atlantic while the Japanese remained neutral in the Pacific. This is, after all, exactly what the Japanese had done in regard to the Soviet-German war. Hitler badly misunderstood American intentions and potential capabilities, and he did not care if he were involved in a war with the United States as long as the Japanese pinned the Americans down in the Pacific. He was convinced that it would be years before the Americans had serious military potential, and that by then the fate of the world would have been decided on the battlefields of Russia.

In this European-centered viewpoint, which totally overlooked the roles of sea power and of the American economy, Adolf Hitler betrayed his provincial origins and his lack of education. There is no indication that the Japanese would have immediately declared war on the United States if Hitler had become involved in a war with the United States in the Atlantic. Indeed, the Japanese gave Hitler no advance warning of their attack on the American fleet at Pearl Harbor. This oversight was typical of Axis diplomacy. When Hitler heard of the attack, he looked at the report and quietly asked Otto Dietrich, "Is this true?" When he was told that it was, he walked in a daze over to the staff quarters of his aides in order to give them the news himself. After some consideration, Hitler was relieved by the Japanese move, since it now appeared that he would not be the only one involved in the "limited" but annoying American war effort. He felt that as a matter of prestige he had to gratuitously declare war on the United States, which had been aiding England for two long years. This he did on December 11, 1941. Italy of course followed suit, for Mussolini had long since lost his freedom of action.

A few days before the Japanese attack upon Pearl Harbor, the Soviet Union had opened a tremendous counteroffensive against the frozen German armies encamped before Moscow. The Germans had not made serious preparations for a winter campaign. Many of their troops were clothed in uniforms which were more adequate for a campaign in southern France than in Russia. Frostbite was common, and men froze to death in effective temperatures of 60 and 70 degrees below zero. At first Hitler would not agree to German withdrawals. "Where the German soldier puts his foot, no other soldier will stand." Certain German commanders, such as General Hoepner, made withdrawals on their own initiative—Hitler never forgave Hoepner. Finally, however, Hitler was forced to agree to some "rectifications of the front." These partial withdrawals saved Army Group Center and probably enabled the Germans to resume the offensive in the south in 1942. It was only by a dazzling display of nerve and will that Hitler held the German army together in Russia in this dreadful winter of 1941-1942.

The Soviet troops went into battle screaming, "Za rodina! Za Stalina!" "For fatherland! For Stalin!" They now realized that a German occupation of their country would mean mass slaughter and pillage. The Soviet Union could call upon twice the manpower available to Hitler. Soviet espionage agents, particularly Richard Sorge, had determined by October in Tokyo that the Japanese would not attack the Soviet Far East. This enabled Stalin to bring up crucial divisions for the Battle of Moscow and for the counteroffensive which followed. 1812 was on everybody's mind, including Hitler's. Hitler may have been right in his assumption that a major withdrawal would presage the collapse of the German effort in the East and the loss of the war, but given the failure of the Blitzkrieg in Russia, Hitler could now achieve a strategic stalemate, at the very best. The American presence in the war meant that the global alignment of economic and demographic forces now shifted drastically against the Axis.

Hitler, of course, did not blame this difficult situation upon himself or upon his decision to attack the Soviet

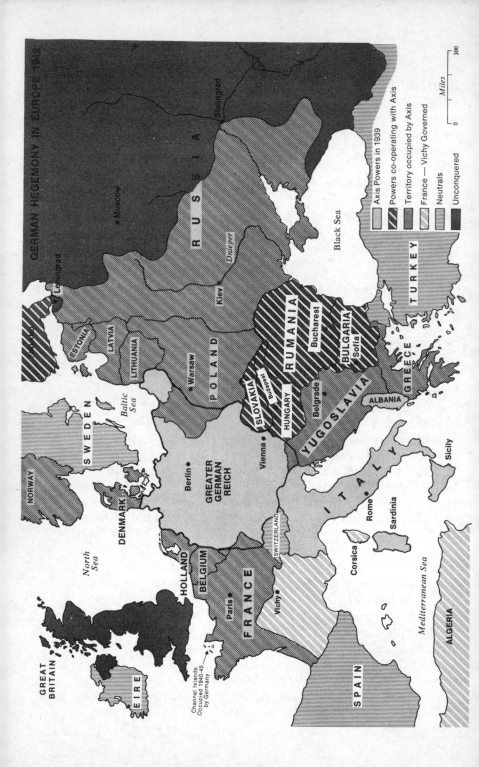

GERMAN HEGEMONY IN EUROPE 1942

Axis Powers in 1939
Powers co-operating with Axis
Territory occupied by Axis
France — Vichy Governed
Neutrals
Unconquered

Miles
0   300

RUSSIA

Moscow •

Stalingrad

Leningrad •

Dnieper

Kiev •

ESTONIA
LATVIA
LITHUANIA

Black Sea

POLAND

Warsaw •

RUMANIA

Bucharest

BULGARIA

Sofia

TURKEY

SLOVAKIA

Budapest

HUNGARY

Belgrade •

YUGOSLAVIA

ALBANIA

GREECE

SWEDEN

Baltic Sea

Vienna •

GREATER
GERMAN
REICH

Berlin •

ITALY

Rome •

Sardinia

Sicily

NORWAY

DENMARK

HOLLAND

BELGIUM

SWITZERLAND

North
Sea

FRANCE

Paris •

Vichy •

Corsica

Mediterranean Sea

GREAT
BRITAIN

EIRE

Channel Islands
Occupied 1940-45
by Germany

SPAIN

ALGERIA

Union. Rather, he took out his lust for revenge on his generals and commanding officers. There was a major command crisis in the Wehrmacht in this winter of 1941-1942. On December 19 Hitler made himself Commander in Chief of the German army. He replaced von Leeb in Army Group North with von Kuechler, von Bock in Army Group Center with von Kluge, and von Rundstedt in Army Group South with Reichenau, an ardent Nazi general. By March, 1942 the German front in Russia had once again been stabilized, but Hitler was more than ever convinced that all his generals wanted to do was retreat: von Rundstedt was a good example of this. They were either fools or cowards. Franz Halder, the Chief of the Army General Staff, was now the one powerful link in the Army High Command (OKH) with the past professional traditions of the Prussian-German army. This was ironic, for Halder was the first Bavarian Catholic ever to be Chief of the General Staff. Halder tried to maintain a degree of objectivity and independence. The High Command of the Wehrmacht (OKW), in the hands of Colonel-General Jodl and Field Marshal Keitel, was not the center for broad strategic planning and execution which some foreign observers took it to be. Rather, it was a funnel for Hitler's orders, some of which, such as his notorious order for shooting all commissars on sight, were clearly against the rules of war. Keitel countersigned anything, however, which Hitler ordered.

By September, 1942 Hitler had informed Halder that "his [Halder's] nerves were shot" and that he needed a rest. He dismissed him and replaced him with Colonel-General Kurt Zeitzler, a younger man who was presumably more enthusiastic about and less critical of Hitler's methods of waging war. Hitler now interfered in every decision on the eastern front. He not only planned ground strategy; he involved himself in points concerning local tactics and the use of artillery and tanks. Thus, Hitler tried to be a political leader and field captain at the same time. He believed in his own infallibility, and mistrusted his generals, for Hitler did not believe that they could or would adequately carry out his orders. One of his few allies (or generals) whom Hitler respected was Field Marshal Antonescu of Rumania. Antonescu dazzled Hitler with his stories about the Dacian or Roman background of the Rumanian people, and with his anti-Slav and anti-Semitic utterances. For a while Hitler even thought of giving Antonescu a major command in southern Russia. Such trust, however, was the exception. Hitler hated Admiral Horthy of Hungary and he did not trust Finnish Commander in Chief Mannerheim.

Hitler understood domination or destruction to be the alternatives in this life. The Germans, so typically given to a self-pitying obsequiousness when defeated or to arrogant, brutal sadism when victorious, were responsive to Hitler's psychological quirks. The world, however, reacted quite differently. Perhaps as early as December, 1941 Hitler knew that he could not win the war. But as he had told Hermann Rauschning many years earlier, "If it appears we will lose, we will drag the whole world down with us. There will never again be another 1918." Such attitudes set the tone for the spirit of Hitler's New Order in Europe.

CHAPTER VII

Adolf Hitler's New Order in Europe, 1939-1945

DESPITE his reversal before the gates of Moscow, despite the terrible implications of the declaration of war upon the United States, Adolf Hitler stood at the zenith of his German and European power early in 1942. German troops reigned supreme from the Ukraine to the Pyrenees, from the North Cape to the deserts of Egypt and Libya. Hitler had proven himself to be the last of the great territorial conquerors, a man in the tradition of Alexander, Caesar, and Napoleon. What vision did he have of the European New Order which was coming into existence? What was the nature of German occupation policies? How did they affect the peoples involved? To what extent did they take account of the peculiar national traditions and psychologies of the peoples of Europe?

1. Nazi Policy in the Protectorate of Bohemia and Moravia

Nazi occupation policies were far harsher in Eastern Europe than in Western Europe. This was largely because of traditional German contempt for the Slavs, but the difference also had its roots in the fact that the outside world had less knowledge of what was going on in Eastern Europe than in, say, France. In Hitler's brutal vision

there was no room for independent states in Eastern
Europe. He did not intend, after October, 1939, to allow
the rise even of a satellite Polish state. The Czechs would
never again be free if Adolf Hitler had his way. The
Slovaks would be a third-rate satellite firmly under German control. Bohemia and Moravia were a "Protectorate"
of the German Reich, at first nominally governed by
Reich Protector Konstantin von Neurath. They were
juridically incorporated into the Greater German Reich
in 1939.

The Germans controlled or suppressed every aspect of
Czech life. The Czechs were made to feel strangers in
their own land. The Nazis closed down the universities and
sent the Jews to concentration camps. They waged an
unrelenting war against the Czech intelligentsia and
bourgeoisie. If anything, the working class and peasantry
were treated somewhat better. Bohemia and Moravia
contained rich agricultural lands, hence, compared with
other areas of occupied Europe, there was little outright
starvation. The Germans looted whatever they wanted
and centralized all administrative and financial activities
so that Berlin became the effective capital for the Czechs.
The Acting Protector until June of 1942 was the notorious "hangman of Prague," Reinhard Heydrich, head of
the SS Reich Security Main Office (RSHA), who carried
out a policy of calculated brutality spiced with presumably
seductive bribes for "cooperative" segments of the Czech
population.

Surprisingly, the Germans left President Emil Hácha
in office as head of a nonexistent Czech "state" after
March, 1939. They even toyed with supporting a Czech
Fascist movement under General Gayda, but soon
dropped it. The Germans looked askance at the formation of the National Community, an all-embracing political alliance which collaborationist Czechs themselves had
formed after the absorption of Bohemia and Moravia by
the Reich. At first the Germans had favored this project,
feeling that it would be easier to regiment the Czechs

through it. Most Czechs, however, saw the National Community as a means of asserting their nationhood, even though it did not give them any political or social power. The Germans saw this, and soon suppressed the organization. Czechoslovakia was not one of the centers of resistance to German rule. Perhaps this was because of the relatively open terrain in the area where most Czechs lived, perhaps it was owing to the policy of passive resistance to external oppression which the Czechs had followed for three centuries. This was the "Good Soldier Schweik" syndrome. Even the assassination of Reinhard Heydrich in 1942 was the result of a plot engineered by the British and Czech exile authorities, not an uprising of the Czech population.

In Slovakia the situation was somewhat different. Slovakia was an "autonomous" state under German protection. It was headed by a clerical Fascist, Monsignor Josef Tiso. In the beginning a majority of Slovaks probably supported or at least agreeably tolerated the Tiso regime. When the nature of German exactions and occupation policies became clear, however, many Slovaks grew restless and looked back longingly to their old association with the "oppressive" Prague regime. In August, 1944 there was a major uprising against the Germans in Slovakia, which was suppressed with customary German brutality.

Just a few months earlier, Hitler had expressed his gratitude to President Emil Hácha. Writing on the fifth anniversary of the "reunion" of Bohemia and Moravia with the Reich, Hitler had offered his appreciation for the loyal attitude of Hácha and the Czech people. He said that while other nations allowed themselves to be provoked into hopeless resistance by British and Bolshevik forces, the Czechs had behaved honorably. The Germans held onto Bohemia and Moravia until the very end of the war, that is, until the second week of May, 1945. Except for the assassination of Heydrich—which was followed by the infamous Nazi extermination of the village of Lidiče—and the Slovak uprising, the Nazis were pleased by the behavior of the Czech and Slovak populations.

2. The Nazis at Work in Poland

An observer looking for the true essence of National Socialism should probably turn to wartime Poland. The Germans had completely obliterated the Polish state in 1939. Large parts of western Poland were absorbed into the Reich in a *de facto* manner. A Governor-General, the Nazi lawyer Hans Frank, was appointed to the post soon after the conquest of Poland. He made clear from the very beginning that his policy would be one of brutality, typified by measures such as low-calorie rations and the exploitation of Polish labor. Frank ran the General-Government of Poland from a castle in the ancient Polish crown city of Cracow, in western Galicia. At the beginning of the occupation, certain Wehrmacht officers had protested against the brutality of the SS and of Hans Frank's General-Government officials, but they soon learned to hold their peace. The brutality and the extermination increased as the demands of the war grew greater, for the Nazis had special plans for Poland. The western provinces, including areas such as Poznan and West Prussia, the old Polish Corridor, and Polish Silesia would be reabsorbed into the Reich and completely Germanized. Their Polish and Jewish inhabitants would be expelled or reduced to the status of helots. The area would be Germanized by importing Germans from areas like Alsace-Lorraine, the South Tyrol, or the Balkans. In October, 1939 Himmler became Reich Commissar for the Consolidation of German Folkdom, and it was his job to carry out these gruesome policies.

Between 1939 and 1941 it was Nazi policy that the German minorities in Southeastern Europe be brought "back" into the Greater German Reich. They would be examined racially, medically, and politically, and those most desirable would resettle the former Polish areas of the newly annexed eastern provinces of the German Reich. Those less desirable would be resettled within the territory of 1937 Germany (the *Altreich*). This program of human classification was basically a failure, for Himmler did not have enough time to carry it out. After 1941, with the rapid expansion of German power into the Ukraine and western Russia, the Nazis became more ambiguous about the wisdom of the withdrawing of German nationalities from satellite states such as Hungary, Croatia, and Rumania. By 1944 the incoming tide of the Red Army forced the German minorities in Southeastern and East-Central Europe to flee to the Reich as refugees. This chaos, of course, had not been part of the original resettlement idea. The Nazis had intended in 1939-1941 to expel all Poles and Jews from the former western provinces of Poland, driving them into the General-Government and into provinces which had formerly been part of eastern Poland or western Russia. In the case of the Jews this process was completed. In the case of the Poles, however, the Germans found they needed Polish agricultural and industrial labor in order to loot western Poland with maximum efficiency.

Millions of Poles died during the war because of calculated Nazi policies of undernourishment and starvation. Poland was divided up by the Nazis in such a way as to erase all traces of its former political existence. The eastern provinces of Poland became part of the Reich Commissariat of the Ukraine or the Reich Commissariat of White Russia. The Nazis made an attempt to exterminate the spiritual and intellectual leadership of the Polish people and they humiliated Polish national pride in every possible way. The Poles were told that Copernicus was not Polish but German. An exhibition of German art was opened in Cracow by Hans Frank with great ceremony. Polish self-government ceased to exist except at the most primitive communal levels.

During the First World War General Erich Ludendorff and other important figures in the Reich had contended that Germany must dominate Poland politically and economically. This German dream, based upon a lust for exploitation of other peoples and a particular contempt for the Slavic peoples, was now a reality, in a manner perhaps more brutal than even Ludendorff had envisioned.

3. The Fate of the "Little Nordic Brothers"

When German forces occupied Denmark and Norway in April, 1940, the Nazis did not anticipate any major difficulties with those two peoples. They were, after all, "little Nordic brothers." They would surely understand that they had been taken under German protection in order to forestall British moves against them. In the beginning, German rule in Denmark was relatively lenient and unobtrusive. The Danes were permitted to retain their monarchy and their democratic parliamentary system. Economic shortages caused by Nazi plundering were more obvious to the Danish people than were the signs of political oppression or extermination so obvious from the beginning to the Poles and the Ukrainians. By 1943, however, the attitude of the Danish population had undergone a degree of radicalization.

There were widespread protests against the forthcoming deportation of Denmark's 6,500 largely assimilated Jews. In an amazing feat of heroism the Danes succeeded in disappointing the Nazis by robbing them of their Jewish prey. Almost all the Danish Jews escaped safely to Sweden. King Christian X showed his solidarity with his persecuted Jewish brethren by openly affixing at one point a Jewish star to his breast. By 1943 it was clear to most Danes that either Germany had lost the war or the war would be inconclusive in its results. Parliamentary elections demonstrated the failure of the Danish National Socialist collaborators under Fritz Clausen, while a mounting wave of strikes and acts of sabotage, some of them furthered by British agents, brought about a German crackdown. From then until the end of the war Denmark was governed in a more repressive fashion. This, of course, was more in line with Nazi policies elsewhere on the Continent. Norway was of great strategic and economic importance to the Germans. Its air and naval bases put the British Isles and its eastern waters within striking range of German U-boats, destroyers, battle cruisers, and bombers. Norwegian fjords were excellent for the concealment of naval bases. Indeed, the battleship *Tirpitz* hid out in one of these fjords until November, 1944, when British bombers were finally able to locate and sink it. Swedish iron ore was of vital importance to the German war effort, and the Germans' control of the Straits of Skagerrak between Norway and Denmark meant an uninterrupted flow of such ore from Sweden to the Reich. There were a few convinced National Socialists and a few more opportunists in Norway who were willing to collaborate with the Germans. Vidkun Quisling, for example, had contacts with the Nazis going back to the early 1930's.

As was the case in so many other European countries, however, the Nazis did not pursue a consistent policy viz-à-vis Norway. Alfred Rosenberg, the head of the Nazi Foreign Policy Office (APA), believed that the Germans should go all-out in their support of ideological brethren such as Quisling and Albert Hagelin, while Joseph Terboven, Hitler's Reich Commissar in Norway, rigidly adhered to an exploitative political and economic line as laid down in occasional directives from Hitler, Keitel, and Ribbentrop. In September, 1940 Rosenberg won a seeming victory. All Norwegian parties, except Quisling's National Assembly Party (Nasjonal Samling) were outlawed.

The way seemed clear for Quisling to form a National Socialist government in Norway. This did not come about, however, until February 1, 1942, and even after that, as the war grew more desperate for the Germans, Quisling was allowed little real power. His countrymen overwhelmingly rejected him and the treasonous course which he pursued, and Norwegian opinion remained pro-British. The Nazis tried to make great propaganda out of Quisling's occasional visits to Berlin. He would be shown with Hitler in German weekly newsreels, and Hitler would talk enthusiastically to him about future "Nordic collaboration" between Norway and Germany. Privately, however, Hitler indicated to his intimates that Norway would never regain her independence, that she would be permanently part of the Greater German Organization of Territory (*Grossdeutsche Raumordnung*) to be carried out by the Greater German Reich through men like Quisling. In Denmark and Norway the Germans were dealing with small, sparsely populated nations. Thus, despite heroic resistance movements in both countries, they were able to maintain their military occupation there until the very end of the war.

4. German Policy in the Low Countries

Holland had been neutral in the First World War, and for the next twenty-three years, following the principle of political asylum enunciated by its Socialists and subscribed to by the other major parties, it had given a comfortable place of refuge to the former German Emperor William II. Germany repaid Holland by the Blitzkrieg of May 10, 1940. Within a few days Holland had been overrun by the Wehrmacht. The Nazis went further towards bringing about a *de facto* annexation of Holland by the Reich than they did in the case of Norway, though the measures taken in Holland were not so obvious or extreme as those taken in the western provinces of the former Polish state.

On May 18 the Germans stated that Holland would be governed by a "High Commissioner of the Occupied Netherlands." On May 29 they announced the appointment of Artur Seyss-Inquart, a dedicated Austrian Nazi lawyer, to this post. Seyss-Inquart would have dictatorial powers. The term Reich Commissar or Reich Commissariat, as applied to diverse areas such as the Ukraine, White Russia, Baltic Russia, Norway, and Holland, had overtones of a total reorganization of these areas by German political and military authorities. It did not imply outright political annexation, but it meant that these territories, which reached beyond and strategically surrounded the immediate lands of the new Greater German Reich, would be subject to the unclarified principles of a Greater German Organization of Territory.

In the early days of the occupation, German propaganda told the Dutch people that their former democratic governments had been responsible for the disasters which overtook them in May, 1940. It is questionable if many Dutchmen subscribed to this interpretation. Soon after the occupation certain Dutch leaders formed the Netherlands Union, the aim of which was to "promote the solidarity and cooperation of the Dutch people." The Nazis paid little attention to this organization, which reminds one of Hácha's National Community in Bohemia and Moravia, formed in 1939. The Nazis did not want to have to deal with a mass organization, even if it was collaborationist in nature. They preferred to exploit Holland directly, aligning its currency with that of Germany, robbing it of agricultural goods, and coordinating its industries so that they might be of greater use to the German war effort.

The Dutch National Socialist Movement, or NSB, led by a Dutch Nazi named Anton Mussert, ran up against a solid wall of hostility from the Dutch people as its hoodlums went about beating up and robbing Jews. The revulsion felt by the Dutch people for the NSB astounded the Nazis, for at the end of 1941 Seyss-Inquart had openly announced that henceforth the NSB would be the only legal political party in Holland. Here he paralleled the action reluctantly taken by Terboven in Norway a year earlier in regard to Quisling's party. In the Netherlands there was no legally recognized civilian government to stand between the Dutch people and their German exploiters and expropriators. In December, 1942 the Nazis proclaimed Mussert the Führer of the Dutch people. This action meant very little, as little, in fact, as had the proclamation of Quisling as Norwegian *fører* late in 1940. Mussert had no power, and the Nazi economic exploitation of Holland did not diminish as a result of his role as "leader."

Belgium was even closer to the German zone of war operations than was Holland. After the Wehrmacht over-ran the country in May, 1940 the Germans appointed a military governor with the title of Military Commander in Belgium and Northern France. The title itself was symptomatic of German policy in Belgium and elsewhere in Europe. Though contradictory on many crucial points, this policy generally did not overlook the possibility of sowing dissension among subject peoples by various polit-ical, economic, and ideological stratagems. The French departments of the Pas-de-Calais and the Nord were detached from France and were made part of the respon-sibility of the military commander in Belgium and north-ern France. This was an economic and political rather than a military measure. It further divided defeated France and made easier German economic exploitation of the industrial areas of northern France and Belgium. The Germans, given certain of their more unpleasant traits of a cultural and psychological nature, did not realize that in pursuing "clever" devices such as this they awakened hopes which were soon cruelly dashed and which ultimately caused their victims to rise up in arms against them. Even in the short run, the supposed "beneficiaries" of such divisive tactics realized that they were part of a general, undifferentiated, exploited mass. Hence, the rise of the maquis in France and Belgium from 1942 should not have come as a great surprise to the German conquerors.

Hitler intended to secure German control of the Chan-nel ports, northeastern France, and Belgium for all time to come. This was not a novel German aspiration. It was present in the minds of Germany's civilian and military leaders during the First World War. Hitler had to be circumspect, however, in going about the realization of this aim. Thus, it was a cardinal point of Nazi policy in Belgium to divide the Flemish-speaking Flemings from the French-speaking Walloons. In Wallonia the Nazis patronized the Rexist Fascist movement of Léon Degrelle. Hitler had no choice but to admire Degrelle, a Fascist leader who supported the New Order to the end, a man who fought as an SS volunteer on the eastern front. Personally, however, Hitler often had doubts about him, referring to him, ostensibly because of his looks, as that "half-Jew."

Even during the First World War, many Flemings, dissatisfied with the French political and cultural orientation of the Belgian monarchy, had collaborated with the Germans. The Nazis found ready collaborators in Belgian Flanders during the Second World War. In areas of northern France and Belgium, where the Flemings were in a minority, the Nazis encouraged them to develop their own newspapers and assert themselves against "Gallic domination." For awhile Hitler acted as if the German government would deal with an autonomous Belgian regime under the continued rule of Leopold II, the man who had infuriated the Allies by capitulating to the Germans at the time of the Dunkirk evacuation. The experiment with Leopold was short-lived, however. During most of the war he was a comfortable prisoner of the German authorities. After the war the Belgians voted in a stormy plebescite to allow him to return.

5. France in Hitler's New Order

France was the greatest nation to be conquered by the Germans in the Second World War. From the very beginning German authorities paid special attention to *la grande nation*. They knew that the entire world was interested in the fate of France under the German occupation. The armistice between France and Germany, signed on June 22, 1940, was the key to Franco-German relations for over four years. The Germans had seemingly been "lenient" in their treatment of France. After all, they only occupied three-fifths of the nation and did not demand that France's colonies be handed over to Italy or Germany. Nor did they request that the French fleet be delivered to the victorious Axis powers. These lenient aspects of the armistice were misleading, however. The reparations burden which France had to bear between 1940 and 1944 was far more all-encompassing and disastrous than the reparations about which the Germans moaned so much between 1919 and 1932. What the Germans did not loot in France they "bought" legally by an artificially high quotation of the mark in relation to the French franc. They bought their way into French industry and forced the coordination of French industrial and agricultural production along the lines of Axis war needs.

The Germans recognized the government of Marshal Henri-Philippe Pétain. Pétain was the last Premier of the Third Republic, and when the Third Republic was "dissolved" by the National Assembly early in July, Pétain became Head of the French State, a post which he retained until the end of the occupation. The octogenarian marshal was a humane, if vain individual. His character was somewhat warped by a desire to be revered by his countrymen and be listened to by the political powers of Europe and the world. Pétain was lucid a few hours a day; at other times he would forget what had just been told him and would not recognize familiar faces.

The regime which Pétain headed was based upon a hope for renewal, self-hatred, and fear of the Germans. Pétain was a conservative man whose idea of France was patriarchal and pastoral in nature. Military men like Pétain, who had long resented the French left and the French democratic tradition, blamed the defeat of May and June, 1940 upon these forces. Now they were joined by many of their countrymen in an orgy of self-abnegation and denunciation. Anything connected with the Third Republic had to be evil. At the same time, although Pétain was willing to cooperate with the Germans by following the letter of the armistice, he saw himself as a "shield" between the more outrageous German demands and the "little people" of France. The Germans knew that in dealing with Pétain they were dealing with an authority who could speak for the French state and the French economy. The administration of France, so centralized from the prefectures to the Ministry of the Interior, made it mandatory that there be a legally recognized political power in France. The Germans needed such a power in order to communicate their orders to the relevant authorities. Pétain and his ministers performed this task quite well. The Germans would never give them much credit, always suspecting treason and continuing to harbor deep resentment and hatred of France. Nevertheless, France was the richest plum in Hitler's New Order, and the Pétain regime was instrumental in the exploitation of French resources and manpower by Berlin.

As in other countries, so in France the Germans played a double game. The territory which Pétain directly ruled consisted of about two-fifths of France, and the poorer part of the country at that. In the rest of France the word of the Military Commander, who was located in Paris, was law, though legally the French administration continued to enjoy its civil prerogatives everywhere except in Alsace-Lorraine. The Germans pursued policies calculated to keep the pressure on Pétain and Vichy so that France would collaborate with Germany along lines prescribed by Berlin. In Paris a motley array of hangers-on and convinced French Fascists and Nazis edited newspapers and made speeches while in the pay of the *de facto* German ambassador, the "Francophile" Otto Abetz. The Germans only became blatant in their support of French Fascists such as Marcel Déat, Joseph Darnand, Philippe Henriot, and Jacques Doriot late in 1943. Before that time they were content to keep these men in their pay and allow them to write and broadcast outrageous attacks against Pétain and members of his government—men such as the wily but self-deluding opportunist Pierre Laval.

In 1940 Pétain and Laval lulled Frenchmen into thinking that France was dealing with a lenient conqueror who would not exact endless tribute and would not cause any more suffering than was inevitable. Pétain and Laval gave the impression that the Germans, along with French public opinion and the leaders of the French government themselves, realized that it was the criminal politicians of the Third Republic, men in the pay of England, the Freemasons, and the Jews, who had led France down the primrose path to a hopeless war in the wake of the British Empire. Pierre Laval, a man with boundless confidence in his own ability to "con" other statesmen into following his wishes ("*Je l'ai fait*," he would boast), believed that he could manipulate men such as Abetz, Ribbentrop, and even Hitler. Laval and Pétain pursued the policy of appeasement and collaboration as a team. This policy seemed to be bearing fruit in October, when, in a dramatic "world-historical" gesture, Hitler met Pétain on October 24 on a train halted near a railroad tunnel at Montoire.

French resistance figures in London, led by General De Gaulle, and the British government itself thereupon responded with an unparalleled intensity of vituperation against Pétain and the Vichy "traitors." The French collaborationist press played up the meeting as the inauguration of a new era of friendship between France and Germany, the end of the historic millennium of enmity that had done so much to destroy Europe. Nothing concrete came out of the Montoire meeting, for Hitler was incapable of a truly generous act. Indeed, within weeks of the meeting the German attitude toward France was demonstrated by the expulsion of over 100,000 French Lorrainers and other "undesirables" from their homes in a territory annexed *de facto* by the Germans. These people were dumped unceremoniously into the already desperate hands of the Vichy authorities. Pétain had declared that he would "enter with honor onto the path of collaboration," but as months passed it appeared that collaboration was a more and more dishonorable venture, one which did not spare France the ravages of the Nazis, all the while committing France to a Reich whose victory no longer seemed certain.

Pétain was disgruntled by early December because Laval was not obtaining results. He also disliked Laval personally, finding his cigarette smoke offensive, his personal habits repulsive, his secretiveness disconcerting. Without notifying the German authorities in advance, Pétain dismissed Laval on Friday, December 13. When Hitler learned of Pétain's action, he flew into a rage. He believed that the British or the Gaullists were behind the whole plot. Hitler was particularly infuriated because two days later, in one of his grand historical gestures of "reconciliation," the body of the Duke of Reichstadt, the son of Napoleon, was due to be reinterred in the Invalides beside the remains of his father. This was a sign of Germany's will toward friendship with France, for the Duke of Reichstadt had been buried in Austria in 1832.

Although Laval returned to power in April, 1942, Franco-German relations were never the same, or rather, they were henceforth stripped of the hopes which the Germans had encouraged in the French before December 13, 1940. Although Pierre Laval seems to have had some doubts about a German victory as early as 1942, he argued that unless the Germans won the war "Bolshevism would install itself everywhere." In a famous radio address in 1942 he stated, "I desire a German victory." Earlier, in discussing the address with Marshal Pétain, Laval had included the phrase, "I believe in a German victory," whereupon the aged marshal turned to him and said, "You're not a military man. You know nothing of these affairs." Thus, as a concession to Pétain, Laval changed the phrase from "I believe in a German victory" to "I desire a German victory"! This phrase alone seemed to justify Laval's execution in the emotional, vindictive atmosphere of the Liberation of 1944-1945.

Pétain dreamed that Vichy France might be a mediator between the Axis and the Allies. This seemed a viable alternative between the time of the Battle of Britain and the destruction of the German Sixth Army at Stalingrad (1940-1942). Pétain felt that the war would be long and drawn out, possibly ending in a stalemate, but more probably in an Allied victory. Perhaps France could shorten the war and enhance her own prestige in a postwar world by acting as mediator. Laval's hopes appeared to have been more extreme: He expected that if France collaborated with the Germans in every reasonable way she would ingratiate herself with the Reich and displace Italy as Germany's number one satellite. In this way France would emerge from a peace conference and a German victory without undue losses. The entire Vichy regime, based upon resistance to social change and an all-corrosive defeatism, showed a fantastic sense of unreality. Even the harshness and occasional sadism of German occupation measures did not completely open the eyes of Vichy's leaders, at least not until 1943.

6. Resistance and Collaboration in Greece and Yugoslavia

In France the Nazis had obtained a collaborator with universal prestige—Marshal Henri-Philippe Pétain. In Greece and Yugoslavia they had no such good fortune. Hitler had indicated that in undertaking military action against Yugoslavia he intended once and for all to smash the Yugoslav state structure, an indirect product of the hated Versailles system. Greece had allowed herself to be used as a British pawn, and although Hitler expressed admiration for this "plucky little people," he had no hesitation about turning the Greeks over to the mercies of harsh German occupation authorities. Greece was essentially governed by the German army between 1941 and the autumn of 1944, though the Germans allowed a collaborationist "government" to function. The Greeks, however, had a long tradition of opposition to foreign occupation behind them. Most of their terrain was mountainous and suited to guerrilla warfare, and the brutality of the German conqueror fostered powerful resistance movements.

The Greek government in exile resided in London, but this royalist regime steadily lost support in Greece after 1941 to the Greek Communist National Liberation Front (EAM). The British were interested in restoring the status quo in Greece, for Churchill had no intention of liberating Greece only to see it become part of a new Communist bloc. Thus, the British suppressed the Greek Communists in Athens in December, 1944. The German occupation in Greece was incredibly brutal. It ranged from psychological insults such as flying the swastika over the Parthenon to a slow, calculated starvation of the Greek population. It is ironic and tragic that after the Second World War the British and Americans supported Greek regimes which looked upon those who had opposed the Germans with suspicion and gave amnesty to Fascist collaborators.

In smashing the Yugoslav state, Hitler knew that he could rely upon dissidents among the Croat population. Croat political emigrés such as Ante Pavelić, who had been the ward of Mussolini for years before 1941, were only too willing to set up a pro-Axis, Fascist Croatian state. In the middle of April Ante Pavelić and his colleagues proclaimed the "Independent State of Croatia." This state was under the domination of a paramilitary, protofascist force known as the Ustascha. The Ustascha was violently anti-Serb. It hated the Orthodox Church and anything having to do with Russia or Bolshevism. In a sense it was a caricature of Croatia's pre-1914 cultural and political orientation toward Vienna. The Ustascha was afraid of renewed Hungarian claims upon the Independent State of Croatia, since Hungary had controlled Croatia before 1918. The Ustascha was anti-Semitic, and the atrocities which its followers committed against the Jews were only equaled by their genocidal measures against the Serbs. Indeed, Croatia was practically the only satellite state during the Second World War to pay full transportation costs for the deportation of Yugoslav Jews to the Nazi death camps in Poland. By 1942-1943 Pavelić and the Ustascha had largely fallen under the control of the Germans. Originally, it had been understood that Croatia would fall within the Italian political sphere of influence; there was even talk of the Duke of Spoleto becoming King of Croatia, but this never came to pass.

Part of Croatia fell within the Wehrmacht zone of operations, part within that of the Italian military authorities. As the Italian position in the war weakened, the Germans assumed an ever greater role. Mussolini and Ciano could only look on impotently as Pavelić and his Ustascha more and more turned to the Germans for support. Pavelić was very concerned about events in neighboring Serbia. There, an anti-Communist, nationalist, partisan force under Draža Mihailović was collaborating with Italian authorities in combating Tito's Communist National Liberation Front. This collaboration upset Pavelić and the Croatian Ustascha and drove them further into the arms of the Germans. By 1943 Tito had emerged as the only clearly national force in Yugoslavia. Mihailović had discredited his reactionary loyalist partisans by collaboration with the Axis powers against the Communists. The brutality of the German occupation authorities caused thousands of Yugoslavs to join Tito's partisans, and by 1943 the Greek and Yugoslav partisans were pinning down many Axis divisions. The Italian army was an unenthusiastic partner in the German attempt to suppress the Greek and Yugoslav peoples. The brutality of the German New Order in Greece and Yugoslavia turned (or reconverted) two morose, defeated peoples into fierce, warrior nations, fighting for their right to life and liberty.

7. *Lebensraum* and Extermination in Russia

In *Mein Kampf* Hitler had stated that *"We stop the endless German movement to the south and west, and turn our gaze toward the land in the east. . . .* If we speak of soil in Europe today, we can primarily have in mind only *Russia* and her vassal border states." For Adolf Hitler the German people could only survive if it won vital living space in the East. It would have to turn the existing Slavic inhabitants of areas such as Poland and Russia into serfs, occasionally exterminating large groups of them in order to maintain a demographic balance suitable for the realization of German plans. Hitler's image of Russia and Eastern Europe was a confused mixture of fear, contempt, and envy. Hitler wanted the vast spaces of European Russia for the future development of the German *Volk*. He felt the Slavs were generally subhuman types who were good for manual labor—but who also had a frighteningly high reproductive rate. Hitler was firmly convinced that the Bolshevik Revolution had represented a "revolt of inferior, underworld elements against the Germanic state structure" built up by the "German Romanov dynasty" and its German bureaucrats and generals. Behind this "revolt of the underworld" (*Aufstand der Unterwelt*) was the ubiquitous Jew, whom Hitler knew was numerically strong in many areas of western Russia and Poland.

Hitler's anti-Semitism appealed to many nationalist and reactionary groups in areas such as the former Baltic states, Poland, and the Ukraine. Some of the first troop trains pouring into Poland in September, 1939 had chalked upon them the slogan "We come into Poland in order to rid it of the Jews." Nazi anti-Semitism was highly popular among some strata of the population in Latvia and the Ukraine, where native auxiliary volunteers took part in the work of rounding up the Jews and serving the SS in various gruesome ways. In the beginning of Operation Barbarossa against the Soviet Union the Nazis made a conscious attempt to play upon these anti-Semitic sentiments. Hence, a German newsreel in the summer of 1941 showed "Lettish nationalists" burning the great synagogue in Riga, which "had been used with impunity by the GPU (Soviet Secret Police) as a prison and torture chamber for Lettish nationalists." The general brutality of Nazi occupation measures, however, soon vitiated the German appeal to most nationalist and anti-Semitic elements among the populations of the conquered Eastern peoples.

On July 16 Hitler convened a conference of several leading Reich figures. Hitler told Göring, Keitel, Rosenberg, and Bormann, among others concerned with Germany's Eastern policy, that "In principle we now have to face the task of cutting up the giant cake according to our needs, in order to be able: first, to dominate it; second, to administer it; and third, to exploit it. . . . This partisan war again has some advantage for us; it enables us to exterminate everyone who opposes us." Exploitation and extermination were the keys to Hitler's *Ostpolitik*. Although Hitler saw Operation Barbarossa as a lightning strike against the Red Army, destroying it in European Russia, he felt that Germany might have to wage sporadic war against the Russian Slavs for another century. This appealed to his imagination, for it reminded him of the stories of Karl May, who had delighted German readers for half a century with his tales of the struggles between cowboys and Indians in the American West. Hitler felt the Germans should territorially dominate Russia to a line stretching from Archangel in the north to Astrakhan on the Caspian Sea in the south. Even beyond this line, however, the Germans would have to launch raids as far as the Urals, and they would have to make sure that the Luftwaffe struck far enough east so as to prevent the development of a new Soviet base for thrusts against the German *Lebensraum*. Indeed, Hitler was not at all averse to such sporadic raids; such a continued Slavic threat, he felt, would force eternal vigilance upon the armed German settlers in occupied Russia.

The vision that Adolf Hitler and Heinrich Himmler had of the future German settlers in Russia was compounded of several elements. It reminds one of the soldiers of the old Roman army, who would settle in an area for twenty-five years, fortify it, Romanize it, and populate it. Himmler dreamed of *Wehrbauern* or armed peasant militia settlements in Russia. Hitler and Himmler felt that the cities would be German fortresses, while Slavic serfs would till the land. As Hitler put it, *"We must never permit anybody but the Germans to carry arms!"* This harkened back to medieval European ordinances which prohibited the Jews from carrying arms.

The romantic but exploitative nature of National Socialism comes out most clearly in the dreams that men such as Hitler and Himmler had regarding the future of this Greater German "living space" in the East. Himmler, who said that he had both his "negative" and his "positive" sides—by his negative side he meant the unpleasant but necessary work of extermination—saw the settlement of Germans in the East as "positive" work. Hitler and Himmler dreamed of "re-Germanizing" the Crimea, renaming it *Gothenland* because the Goths had occupied the area in the early centuries of the Christian Era. Hitler talked about resettling the Germans from the South Tyrol or perhaps German-speaking individuals from Alsace-Lorraine in the Crimea. Hitler's romantic vision regarding the future German settlement of the East contradicted the nature of that German occupation. This was typical of National Socialist ideology, which basically appealed to atavistic, romantic, reactionary impulses in an age of rapid social change and a great confusion of values.

During the German occupation of the western provinces of Poland, rival authorities such as the SS, Göring's Office of the Four-Year Plan, the local Gauleiters, and Hans Frank's Polish "kingdom" competed in robbing the country's agricultural and industrial resources, all in the interest, of course, of the Greater German Reich.

Whether we call this "state capitalism" or semifeudal capitalist enterprise, the end result was the same. Even the German individual was lost in the shuffle, and the resettlement of Germans in the western provinces of Poland became a bureaucratic nightmare, hardly a romantic dream of expansion into living room in the East. If the Germans had conquered European Russia, this same type of confusion and brutality would have occurred on a vaster scale. The image of happy peasant German families owning land tilled by Slavic serfs while they developed their precious *Kultur* was always an improbable one. More likely, a society would have arisen in which death camps, vast collective farms, state capitalist enterprises, and various West German industrial combines all competed in raping the land and murdering its inhabitants.

In his hostility to arming the Soviet peoples, Hitler missed a major opportunity. Hundreds of thousands of Soviet prisoners of war and young men living in the occupied territories volunteered for German military service during the war. Hitler was suspicious of such enthusiasm, and neither the Wehrmacht nor the SS got a clear go-ahead from Hitler on the subject until the disastrous year 1944. The Germans also missed a major opportunity in the way they dealt with the conquered Ukraine. Modern Ukrainian nationalism went back to the middle of the nineteenth century, and the collectivization of agriculture by Stalin in the Ukraine had been carried out with ferocious brutality and had met dogged resistance. The Nazis, however, instead of undoing the collective farm system, merely wished to exploit the harvest of 1941 for their own purposes. The most efficient way to do this was to keep the present *kolkhoz* system in existence. Posters of Hitler appeared all over the Ukraine with the caption "Hitler the Liberator," but within a few months it was clear that the Germans had not come to Russia in order to free the Ukrainian people.

Ukrainian nationalists hoped that the Nazis would create an anti-Great Russian Greater Ukraine. On August 1, 1941, however, Hans Frank, the notorious Governor-

General of Poland, took over the administration of Eastern Galicia, which had an enormous Ukrainian population. This was a clear sign that the Nazis were pursuing their typically divisive tactics even in regard to a sympathetic Ukrainian nationalism. A memorandum by a Foreign Office official noted that "The news of the assumption of civil administration in former eastern Galicia by Governor-General Dr. Frank had already become known in Ukrainian circles even before August 1. . . . It caused *great disappointment* in these circles. . . ." Ukrainian nationalists also considered the northern Bukovina and Bessarabia part of the greater Ukraine, but in 1941 the Germans returned these areas to the Rumanians.

Ever since Hitler's seizure of power, Alfred Rosenberg, a Baltic German refugee and theoretician of National Socialism, had been interested in securing a major foreign policy post for himself in the German government. He was, after all, one of the *alte Kämpfer* of the Party. Although he was head of the Nazi Foreign Policy Office, he had no major role in making or implementing German foreign policy between 1933 and 1941. In 1941 Hitler appointed Rosenberg Reich Minister for the Occupied Eastern Territories. Rosenberg would presumably know something about the Russians and the other peoples of the Soviet Union. In the early 1920's Rosenberg had served as a contact between White Russian emigrés and Adolf Hitler. It was from sources such as these that Hitler probably picked up his theories of the revolt of the Slavic underworld and the Jewish origin of the Bolshevik state. Rosenberg sympathized with Ukrainian aspirations while Hitler did not, for Rosenberg was consistently anti-Bolshevik and anti-Great Russian. He felt it should be the role of the Germans to offer some independence and some hope for a better existence to oppressed Soviet nationalities such as the Ukrainians, Lithuanians, Latvians, and Estonians. Rosenberg wanted to break up Stalin's collective farms, and he wished to create a Ukrainian state under German protection. This is what the Germans had done briefly in 1918, between the time of the Treaty of Brest-Litovsk and the November armistice.

Hitler responded to the idea in the following way: "In the opinion of the Führer, an independent Ukraine is out of the question for the next decades. The Führer is thinking in terms of a *German protectorate over the Ukraine for roughly twenty-five years*." Despite the impressive title of his ministry, Rosenberg had little administrative authority in the East between 1941 and 1945. His attempts to reach the Führer on behalf of his ideas regarding the treatment of occupied nationalities in Russia met with an increasing wall of contemptuous silence, a wall manned by men such as Hitler's Personal Secretary Martin Bormann. Rosenberg was an idealist of limited intelligence. As he put it in 1946, shortly before he was hanged, "National Socialism was the content of my active life. I served it faithfully, albeit with some blundering and human insufficiency. I shall remain true to it as long as I live."

There was no room for such a tactless idealist in the complicated Nazi hierarchy which was governing Russia. Hans Frank governed Eastern Galicia. A large part of the Ukraine became a Wehrmacht operations zone under direct military control, yet even in such areas the SS operated as a law unto itself, occasionally demanding and receiving army cooperation in the massive extermination of the Jews. On other occasions the SS acted on its own. The large part of the Ukraine which was not a Wehrmacht zone of operations fell into the hands of the brutal *alte Kämpfer* Erich Koch, Gauleiter of East Prussia. Hitler wanted tough, cruel men for the unsavory work of breaking the Slavic peoples and preparing living space for the German *Volk*. For this reason he selected old veterans of the Party and the SA. Erich Koch, who later distinguished himself by fleeing beleaguered Königsberg while thousands of his fellow countrymen perished, became Reich Commissar for the Ukraine. He established his capital at Rowno, which was far to the west, rather than at Kiev, which was looked upon by Ukrainian nationalists as the natural capital of a reborn Ukraine. Koch despised Rosenberg, with his dreams of Ukrainian intellectuals. This is the way Erich Koch described himself and his mission: "Gentlemen, I am known as a brutal dog; for that reason I have been appointed Reich Commissar for the Ukraine. There is no free Ukraine. We must aim at making the Ukrainians work for Germany and not at making the people happy." Both Hitler and Koch felt that the Ukrainians should only know how to count to 100 and that the capital of the Reich was Berlin. Hitler cynically mentioned that Germans in Russia would encourage abortions and would allow the Jews to sell contraceptives to the Ukrainian and Russian peasants. This was the true spirit of National Socialist rule in Russia.

The Germans regarded the Baltic area as part of the Greater German Reich or as part of the Greater German Organization of Territory. They set up a Reich Commissariat, *Ostland*, which embraced the whole region. This was reminiscent of the Army Command of the Upper East of Ludendorff during the First World War. In the Baltic states the Nazis did make use of native administrators, but they had no intention of granting political freedom to the Latvians, Lithuanians, or Estonians. Before long a vigorous resistance movement emerged in Lithuania, the southern part of which was crucial to German supply lines to the eastern front. Adolf Hitler's attitude toward the Ukrainians and other peoples of the "former Soviet Union" was akin to that of Erich Koch. Hitler wanted periodic exterminations. He saw the Ukrainians as animals, and Hitler wanted to foster ignorance and a high mortality rate among them. As Hitler put it, "We are the masters. We come first." By 1942 this brutal German policy in the East was reaping a grim harvest. In the Pripit Marshes, behind the lines of Army Group Center, a resistance movement emerged which eventually had the strength of an entire army group. A vigorous partisan movement emerged from the Ukraine and White Russia all the way up to Estonia. These partisans recognized the intentions and brutality of the German conquerors, and they realized that the alternative to a victory by Stalin was extermination at the hands of the Nazis.

8. Himmler and the SS at War

The major Nazi administrative and political beneficiary of the German war effort was Heinrich Himmler's SS. The SS administered and staffed the death camps of Poland. It provided political security for the Nazi regime within all of occupied Europe. It was a major factor in military espionage and counterespionage, achieving domination in this field even over the army by 1944. The SS recruited and led a huge army, the Waffen SS, which by the end of the war numbered some thirty-eight divisions. As it became clear to Hitler that the war would last a long time and might not even end in a German victory, he became more obsessed by the memory of 1918, when the Germany home front had "shamefully collapsed" due to "machinations of Communist Jews, Socialists, and pacifists." Hitler vowed that there would never again be another 1918. The main mission of Himmler's SS in 1939-1942 was to see that such a shameful capitulation never recurred.

Hitler was morbidly suspicious of his generals, and when certain SS units distinguished themselves in battle on the eastern front in 1941-1942 and in the retaking of Kharkov in March, 1943, Hitler gave Himmler the green light for the unlimited expansion of the Waffen SS. Hitler had earlier promised the army that the SS would never become a mass, armylike organization on the level of the old SA of Ernst Röhm. He now broke his word in this matter, but the army had little choice but to cooperate. Even before 1943 army generals had admired the training, bravery, and determination of SS units, which sometimes had more up-to-date equipment than their colleagues in the Wehrmacht. Although Waffen SS units fought under army command, certain of their commanders had direct access to Hitler and Himmler, thus giving them important political and military leverage against the Wehrmacht in their areas of conflict.

Himmler dreamed of establishing a multinational SS under German leadership, one which would pick the cream of the Nordic crop from the countries of occupied Europe. Most volunteers for the SS from Western Europe soon realized that they were fighting for the establishment of a Greater German Reich, not for a multinational collaborative effort based upon a common anti-Bolshevism and a desire for a better life for all the peoples of Europe. This disillusionment was not so evident in the East, where volunteers joined the SS out of a variety of motives, few of them idealistic. The SS was never a truly European organization, though Himmler advertised it as such. Only a small number of young men from the occupied countries ever volunteered for the SS. The motives of the Germans in recruiting these foreigners were not particularly idealistic, though insofar as he was capable of such "internationalist" idealism, Himmler probably personified this current in the Waffen SS. A contrasting and more typically heartless viewpoint was expressed by SS Gruppenführer Gottlob Berger: "For every foreign recruit who falls no German mother weeps." This was typical of the spirit of the SS and the Nazi regime, reminding one of Himmler's statement in 1943 that he didn't care how many Czech or Russian women died while building an antitank ditch in order to stop Soviet armor. One might estimate that about 125,000 Western Europeans volunteered for the Waffen SS. By 1945 there were more foreigners than Germans in the Waffen SS, but given the populations of the occupied areas this was hardly a startling amount of foreign volunteers. One of the problems was that the SS recruited in occupied countries through collaborationist and National Socialist movements such as Mussert's NSB in Holland and Degrelle's Rexists in Wallonia. Since these movements were viewed with contempt by most people in the countries involved, such recruitment was self-defeating.

One of the ironies of the Waffen SS is a myth that has grown up among its former members that it was somehow a multinational forerunner of NATO! After all, it was anti-Communist, consisted of recruits from several nations, and hence was the forerunner of the contemporary European army. Insofar as there was any truth in this, it is a ghastly, slanderous commentary on the North Atlantic Treaty Organization. The distortion involved, however, so outweighs whatever minuscule grain of truth might lie within the assertion, that it is hardly worth bothering about except as one more example of the infinite German capacity for self-deception.

The rise of Heinrich Himmler was one of the startling German events of the Second World War. In 1936 he had become chief of the German police, in 1939 Reich Commissar for the Consolidation of German Volkdom, in 1943 Minister of the Interior, in 1944 head of the Home Army. Later he became Commander of Army Group Upper Rhine, then Commander of Army Group Vistula. Heinrich Himmler was a pedantic bureaucrat who constantly urged his underlings to "combat the bureaucratic spirit." He was also a racialist romantic who did not view his victims as human beings, but who somehow sensed, perhaps because of vague but deep-rooted ethical memories, that the work of extermination was necessary but "negative." This, indeed, is the most striking thing about Himmler and his extermination empire in the SS: Ultimately the men involved (except perhaps at the most primitive levels of putting bodies into ovens and converting their remains into fertilizer) remained outwardly "normal" individuals. As Himmler put it in a speech to his SS men in 1943, which I paraphrase, "To have had to see what you have seen and yet remain decent fellows, that is the great thing." No phenomenon more typifies the schizophrenic German personality of the twentieth century than these SS men, particularly Heinrich Himmler. Outwardly they cultivated comradely loyalty as a cult unto death. These SS men were generally courtly, helpful to children (so long as they were Aryan), and kind to animals. Himmler shook his head in disbelief, not understanding how Göring could shoot innocent animals for sport, yet his personality was so split that he viewed his victims as animals or as criminals. In Hitler's terms they were "bacilli" or "bacteria" which no healthy body could assimilate and then remain at one with itself. Hannah Arendt has described Adolf Eichmann and the SS personality in general as the "banality of evil." This definition is true so far as it goes. One side of the personality of Himmler was indeed banal, but the banality which the SS man displayed was merely the stolid display of traditional German or Central European manners and virtues. The other side of the SS personality was a feverish commitment to murder and degradation. The banality was not a screen for this other, "negative" side of the SS personality, rather it was, in the typical case of Himmler, an alternate personality, his *better side*. What deep paralysis of feeling, what psychic or historical shock in a culture produced such schizophrenic personalities? No adequate answer has yet been forthcoming to this question, and I cannot offer one here.

9. The Final Solution

Before the beginning of the campaign against Russia, Nazi policy in regard to the Jews had been forced emigration with a minimum of property. By the summer of 1941 this policy had changed. The continuation of the war had hardened Hitler's will, and he now knew that the forced emigration of the Jews from Europe was an impossibility. He also had more Jews within his reach than ever before: the five to six million Jews living in Poland, the Baltic States, and the western Soviet Union. By the middle of 1941 Hitler had decided upon the policy of exterminating European Jewry. Somewhat later Heinrich Himmler suggested to his Finnish masseur Felix Kersten that Goebbels had been largely responsible for this policy, that

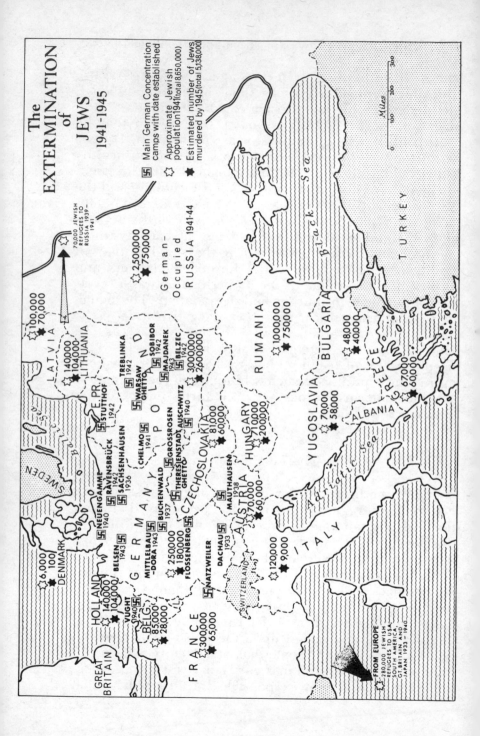

The
EXTERMINATION
of
JEWS
1941-1945

⌂ Main German Concentration camps with date established

✩ Approximate Jewish population 1941 (total 8,650,000)

★ Estimated number of Jews murdered by 1945 (total 5,138,000)

Miles
0   100   200   300

GREAT BRITAIN

SWEDEN

DENMARK
✩ 6,000
★ 100

HOLLAND
✩ 140,000
★ 104,000

⌂ VUGHT 1940
BELG. ✩ 85,000
★ 28,000

FRANCE
✩ 300,000
★ 65,000

⌂ NEUENGAMME 1940
⌂ BELSEN 1943
⌂ RAVENSBRÜCK 1942
⌂ SACHSENHAUSEN 1936

GERMANY
⌂ MITTELBAU–DORA 1943
✩ 250,000
★ 180,000
⌂ BUCHENWALD 1937
⌂ FLOSSENBERG 1938

⌂ NATZWEILER

SWITZERLAND

⌂ DACHAU 1933

AUSTRIA 1938
✩ 70,000
★ 60,000

⌂ MAUTHAUSEN

ITALY
✩ 120,000
★ 9,000

E.PR.
⌂ STUTTHOF 1942

LATVIA
✩ 100,000
★ 70,000

LITHUANIA
✩ 140,000
★ 104,000

70,000 JEWISH REFUGEES TO RUSSIA 1939–1941

POLAND
⌂ TREBLINKA 1942
⌂ CHELMNO 1941
⌂ WARSAW GHETTO
⌂ SOBIBOR 1942
⌂ MAJDANEK 1943
⌂ BELZEC 1942
⌂ GROSSROSEN
⌂ THERESIENSTADT GHETTO
⌂ AUSCHWITZ 1940
✩ 3,000,000
★ 2,600,000

German–Occupied RUSSIA 1941-44
✩ 2,500,000
★ 750,000

CZECHOSLOVAKIA
✩ 81,000
★ 60,000

HUNGARY
✩ 710,000
★ 200,000

RUMANIA
✩ 1,000,000
★ 750,000

Black Sea

BULGARIA
✩ 48,000
★ 40,000

YUGOSLAVIA
✩ 70,000
★ 58,000

ALBANIA

GREECE
✩ 67,000
★ 60,000

TURKEY

Adriatic Sea

FROM EUROPE
✩ 280,000 JEWISH REFUGEES TO USA, SOUTH AMERICA, GT. BRITAIN AND JAPAN 1933 – 1940.

Goebbels had all along been the one high Nazi leader who had insisted upon the necessity of actually *exterminating* the Jews.

Whatever the truth of this, the orderly implementation of the policy of extermination began early in 1942, though perhaps a million Jews had already been murdered in areas under Nazi rule. In the Soviet Union the SS often rounded up thousands of Jews and shot them on the spot, such as occurred at the ravine of Babi Yar outside of Kiev. In other areas they were put to work as virtual slaves of the army and of the SS. In Poland the Jews were rounded up into ghettos and sent to extermination camps such as Treblinka and Auschwitz.

In Western Europe the Nazis were more circumspect. In areas which had governments of their own, such as Vichy France, the local administration could sometimes aid its Jews and save most of them when it wished to do so, by protecting them through various administrative and police measures deviously directed against the German authorities. In Poland over 90 percent of the Jews were exterminated. German industrial firms, realizing that murder was a lucrative business, were most interested in the contracts for objects such as gas chambers, ovens, and Zyklon B gas. The SS empire was a business organization, and Himmler and his minions turned the concentration camps into profitable enterprises, producing everything from army uniforms to soap made from the remains of gassed victims. This policy of the extermination of the Jews was the one action of the National Socialists that will probably be remembered long after many of its leaders have been forgotten. Six million Jews perished at the hands of Nazi death squads, but the Nazis also exterminated millions of other victims, ranging from Polish priests and the intelligentsia to Russian prisoners of war to wandering Gypsies in Bohemia and Germany to political prisoners of all sorts. Indeed the history of National Socialism after 1939 could be written in the form of one long obituary, but the morbidity of this excercise would not necessarily lead to historical enlightenment.

At various times and places the Jews rose up in heroic revolt against their exterminators, the most famous such occasion being the revolt of the Warsaw Ghetto in 1943. Some Jews escaped as a result of such resistance, but by and large it was a futile gesture, the preponderance of surprise and of force being so great on the side of the murderers.

10. Albert Speer and the German War Economy

It is now generally recognized, thanks largely to the researches of men such as Burton Klein and Alan Milward, that it would be inaccurate to speak of a German economy geared toward total war before 1943-1944. The Nazis, for example, made far less use of women in war industries than did the British and the Americans. This was largely because of ideology and reactionary social prejudice: The place of the German woman was in the home, as a German mother. Fritz Todt, Hitler's First Minister of Armaments and Munitions, had outlined a policy of total war before his sudden death in February, 1942. Yet the economic policy of total war only came to fruition during the ministry of Todt's successor, Albert Speer.

Speer was not only confronted by the necessity of increasing economic production after the frightening winter (1941-1942) before the gates of Moscow, he also had to manipulate the jealous and feuding potentates involved in the German war effort: industrialists, the German Labor Front, Göring's economic empire, the Party, the Wehrmacht, and the SS. All these competed for a limited amount of goods and services, for the results of an industrial production which remained fairly static until 1942. In Alan Milward's words, "Consequently, although the size of the sector committed to war production did not change, there were violent switches of priority within that sector. Such violent switches of priority were all right as long as the Wehrmacht only needed a preponderance of specific weapons for a brief campaign. For a war of attrition, however, the rapid augmentation of total production was more necessary than German industry's fabled capacity for switching from the production of one type of weapon to another in a short period of time."

The output of most consumer goods was relatively stable in the Reich through 1940 and 1941. This seems particularly incredible if we contrast the German experience with that of Great Britain. Despite Göring's famous statement, Hitler's policy was definitely one of guns *and* butter. There were political reasons for this, particularly the Party's fear of alienating the proletariat. Hitler himself paid little attention to the job of organizing war production, and there was no systematic planning for a new economic order in occupied Europe. One has the impression that the Germans plundered occupied countries in order to support the comfortable status quo in the German economy. Early in 1942, despite the harsh winter before Moscow, Hitler was reluctant to change the economic order of things. In 1940 Hitler had still been thinking in terms of a major demobilization and a return to an emphasis on consumer production.

If the Germans had earlier rationalized their economy and increased war production at the expense of their own consumer production, they might not have been as brutal in plundering occupied countries for labor, raw materials, and industrial finished products. This in turn might have meant that armed resistance in countries such as France and Belgium would not have been as troublesome as it became by 1943-1944. Such internal tranquillity would have released a number of German divisions for operations in crucial sectors of the Mediterranean and eastern fronts. The Nazis, however, did not think this way. In 1942 Hitler appointed Fritz Sauckel General Plenipotentiary for the Allocation of Labor. Sauckel descended upon occupied Europe and uprooted millions of people, forcing them to work in Germany. Wherever Sauckel's minions appeared, hundreds or even thousands of young men fled to the hills and joined the resistance. The weakness of the German war economy before 1942 was thus related to the revolt against German rule after that year.

Albert Speer came from an upper-middle-class family in the city of Mannheim. He was a talented but not brilliant architect who had long been a personal favorite of Adolf Hitler. Speer passionately believed in the need for a total war economy, a conclusion which his predecessor, Fritz Todt, had also reached. Speer dedicated himself to this task with amazing diligence and passion. He was a convinced believer in Adolf Hitler and the National Socialist system. It is interesting that he admits in his memoirs that his lack of political background (the apolitical or "good" German) made it difficult for him to criticize Hitler's "ideas" when he first heard the Führer speak at his university before 1933. Indeed, Speer does not seem to have questioned Hitler or his motives until the last months of the Second World War.

Albert Speer proved to be an excellent choice, for he more than tripled German armaments production in less than three years. He created a centralized war machine for the total mobilization of German industry. Speer was even able to prevent the conscription of certain categories of key industrial workers, thereby saving them for German military production. He succeeded in establishing factories in France that did not lose their workers to Sauckel's recruitment gangs. But in his memoirs Speer makes it seem as if he had very little to do with Sauckel, and that when he did have contact with him it was as a hostile supplicant protecting skilled workers in occupied countries from Sauckel's impressment gangs. Actually, without the labor with which Sauckel provided Speer and the industrialists with whom he collaborated in preparing the German economy for total war, Germany would have had to surrender by 1944.

Before 1943 Hitler had paid little attention to new

areas of military research such as rocketry, atomic science, and jet aircraft. By late 1943, as Speer points out, Hitler realized that the tide of the war had turned against Germany, and that in order to recoup his position he would have to come up with some "miracle weapons," devices which would both restore the confidence of the German people and bring about a military victory in the West and/or the East. Hitler's government had not consistently supported scientific research in these advanced areas in the years before the war. Even after the crisis year 1943, Hitler saw these weapons in terms of retaliation (*Vergeltung*) and destruction (*Vernichtung*), rather than in the light of their intrinsic strategic or tactical possibilities. Thus, he wanted jet engines used in *bomber* aircraft in order to retaliate for the bombing of German cities which, by the end of 1943, had grown catastrophic. Hitler did not realize that given the failure of the German fighter defense and antiaircraft, the jet could only save Germany if it were an effective fighter. Hitler had an amazing technical grasp of questions concerning tanks, artillery, and the implements of the infantryman, but anything beyond this was strange territory to him. It is amazing that Speer accomplished as much as he did considering such Hitlerian prejudices, overlapping authorities, and the jealous, often ill-informed, machinations of various Nazi officials.

11. The Radicalization of the New Order, 1943-1945

In 1943 and 1944 Nazi measures in the occupied countries became increasingly brutal. Thousands of young men fled the cities and joined the resistance, harassing the German military authorities and their native collaborators. The war, which was going increasingly badly for the Nazis, led to a stiffening of resistance on the part of formerly collaborationist regimes. By 1943 Pétain and Laval had become more open in defying the Germans on the questions of deporting French workers to Germany or "evacuating" assimilated French Jews to death camps in the East. In Rumania Foreign Minister Mihai Antonescu was in secret contact with agents of the Western Allies, and Admiral Horthy in Hungary was interested in bringing about an Anglo-American presence in the Balkans and Central Europe in order to extricate Hungary from the war and prevent a Bolshevik seizure of power in the reactionary countries of Central Europe. Mussolini and Ciano realized late in 1942 that unless Hitler concluded peace with the Soviet Union at the expense of the Western Allies in the Mediterranean, a crisis of the Fascist regime in Italy would come about. The Finns were increasingly restless as President Ryti and Field Marshal Mannerheim looked about for ways of extricating themselves from the war with a minimum of tragedy for Finland. They now regretted having involved themselves in the "War of Continuation" as an ally of Nazi Germany.

Until 1944 Adolf Hitler's New Order had no coherent ideology. It was merely a synonym for the German exploitation of occupied Europe. Politically, the regimes of collaborators such as Pétain in France and Antonescu in Rumania, with their reactionary rural, patriarchal, and military foundations, had little in common with the revolutionary mass dynamism and "egalitarianism" of National Socialism. By 1944 the Nazis were in desperate straits, and there is a certain logic in the fact that it was in this year that a common theme seems to have emerged in the New Order. Conservative, timeserving collaborators such as Pétain and Horthy became virtual prisoners of the Germans, while the Nazis replaced them with more radical, desperate men, types who were committed to Nazi ideology and who realized that they could not survive unless the Germans won the war—an increasingly remote possibility.

By the end of 1943 both Pétain and Laval in occupied France were looking with more sympathy upon a transition back to the despised Third Republic. There was talk of reconvening the National Assembly in order to hand power over to De Gaulle. Ribbentrop and Hitler, who never trusted the French, knew of these Vichy machinations. By the end of 1943 and early 1944 the Germans forced the French government to publicly disavow such ideas and accept into its very bosom Paris-based Fascists and Nazi collaborators such as Jacques Doriot and Marcel Déat. These radical French Fascists constantly quarreled among themselves, and they had not even achieved any kind of unity by the time of Doriot's death early in 1945. Yet the logic of this radicalization of the New Order in France was such that by the end of 1944, after the Allies had liberated France, Pétain and Laval were virtual prisoners of the Germans, who now used a "French Liberation Committee" led by a paid Fascist collaborator, de Brinon.

One generally thinks of Mussolini's Italy as the archetypal Fascist regime. Actually, Hitler was aware by 1942 that Italian Fascism did not have strong roots. In July, 1943 a clique consisting of diplomats, military leaders, and courtiers of King Victor Emmanuel III overthrew Mussolini, thereby proving the correctness of Hitler's attitude. At this point the tired and ill Mussolini merely wanted to be left alone, but in a daring commando raid a group of SS men under Otto Skorzeny liberated the Duce in September. Soon thereafter, Hitler was instrumental in Mussolini's proclamation in northern Italy of the "Italian Social Republic." This was a puppet state existing on the suffrance of the German authorities. It was constantly humiliated by the Germans, for it could do nothing without the permission of the Wehrmacht or the SS.

There were certain interesting developments in this Italian Social Republic, one of them being Mussolini's apparent return to elements of his radical ideology of the pre-1920 years. Evidently feeling that he had been overthrown by the corrupt Anglophile upper bourgeoisie and by traitors and opportunists in the court, the army, and the Fascist Party (in this he was not entirely wrong), Mussolini now began to hearken back to the anticapitalism which had dominated his political life before 1920. Although the Germans paid little attention to these Mussolinian ruminations, the Duce's attacks upon the Italian bourgeoisie and the traditional elements directing Italian society paralleled a statement which Hitler made to Bormann in 1945. Hitler said that he had made a mistake in allying himself with the "corrupt French bourgeoisie," rather he should have revolutionized the French workers and brought about an uprising of the Arabs in North Africa. In this he would have dislocated the French Empire and gained valuable allies in his struggle against Great Britain. Hitler's social impulses were anything but liberationist and radical, however, and his musings in 1945 should be taken with a grain of salt. As an ideological parallel to the course of the New Order in Europe in 1944-1945 they are valuable, however, for in their radicalism and their desperation they were similar to the mood of men such as Doriot, Déat, and Mussolini.

This radicalization of the New Order was not merely a phenomenon in occupied or Axis-allied Europe. In Germany itself, the propaganda of Dr. Goebbels took on increasingly desperate and strident tones. Goebbels had made a famous speech in the Sportpalast in Berlin on January 18, 1943 in which, before cheering thousands of Nazi officials, he called for a "total war" effort (Stalin had called for such an effort in July, 1941). This meant closing down restaurants and night clubs (much to Hermann Göring's disgust), and it promised the further mobilization of almost all Germans for the economic, military, and political aspects of war work. As in so many other matters of crucial importance, so in the question of total war Adolf Hitler moved quite slowly. It was only after the attempt to assassinate him on July 20, 1944, which further disgraced the army and other conservative elements in the eyes of fanatical Nazis, that Goebbels actually received major administrative responsibility for the total mobilization of the German people.

How was this radicalization reflected in German society in 1944 and 1945? The year 1944 saw the reemergence of the Party as a major factor in German society. In the threatened border provinces the Gauleiters became Reich Defense Commissars. Rallies were held in order to show the solidarity of the Party with the army and the state. "Party, State, and Wehrmacht" became the slogan which was everywhere used. It symbolized the determination of all elements of the German nation in the crucial stage of the war. On October 18, 1944, the anniversary of the battle of Leipzig in which Allied forces had defeated Napoleon in 1813, Goebbels and Himmler proclaimed the formation of the Volkssturm. The Volkssturm would be a militia consisting of old men, young boys, and those otherwise unfit for military service. The Volksgrenadiere divisions, which Himmler had founded as head of the Reserve Army, were a recent precedent but also a more serious, better equipped fighting force. In most cases the German economy could no longer even provide these Volkssturm men with uniforms, much less with adequate weapons. On November 9, the anniversary of Hitler's Beerhall *Putsch* of 1923, the Volkssturm men took their oath of allegiance. This act turned into a propaganda orgy typical of Dr. Goebbels. Here, after all, was the mobilization of the broad masses of the German people, or, as the Nazi propaganda slogan put it: "A people rises up: A storm breaks loose!" In an increasingly desperate situation the German nation would rise up against its tormentors and break their will to continue the war. This is how Goebbels and Himmler saw the Volkssturm, a radical emanation of the last stage of National Socialism.

Events in Rumania and Hungary in 1944 were typical of the radicalization of the New Order. Hitler had always respected Marshal Antonescu, but as in Italy, so in Rumania there existed a situation in which a sympathetic figure had to deal with a reactionary monarchical clique, in this case consisting of King Michael and his mother. In August, 1944 the King, in collaboration with bourgeois opposition parties, overthrew Antonescu and signed an armistice with the Allies, including the approaching Rus-

sians. Hitler was predictably furious, having no sympathy
for his threatened ally. For several years Germany had
played host to members of the radical Fascist Iron Guard
movement in Rumania. Men such as its leader Horia
Sima had been forced to flee Rumania early in 1941 after
an unsuccessful attempt to overthrow the regime of
Antonescu and Michael. The Germans had supported the
military dictator, because at that point ideological consistency meant less than the continued flow of Rumanian
oil and wheat to the Reich. As soon as Antonescu had
been overthrown in Rumania, Hitler suddenly discovered
an ideological affinity with the Iron Guard, an organization that he had ordered his diplomats *not* to support in
1939-1944. Certain of the Iron Guard leaders were even
taken out of German concentration camps and were
brought together in order to form a "National Government" of Rumania in Vienna. It had no power and no
troops at its command, but it issued grandiose proclama-
tions indicating that Rumania would continue to struggle
on the side of Germany until victory over Bolshevism had
been achieved.

The situation in Hungary in 1944 was somewhat more
complex. Admiral Horthy was a counterrevolutionary
who was interested in preserving the existing social structure of Hungary in the face of any form of social change,
particularly that represented by the hated Bolsheviks.
Horthy, however, had a degree of humanity and decency
which annoyed Hitler. In addition, Hitler suspected
Horthy and his clique of pro-British sympathies, and in
this he was not altogether mistaken. Horthy had supported the successful attempt of Prime Minister Kállay
to give protection to about 800,000 Jews in Hungary during the course of the year of extermination, 1943. Hitler
had railed against Horthy, denouncing his Anglophile
leanings, seeing him as a collaborator with the British,
attacking him for protecting the Jews. By March, 1944,
when it was clear that Horthy was about to seek an armistice with the Allies, the Germans descended upon Hungary without any warning and occupied the country.

Horthy, nevertheless, remained the figurehead regent. In October he actually broadcast a statement which indicated that Hungary would sign an armistice with the Red Army, thereby removing the country from the war. At this point Horthy became a prisoner of the Nazis, who installed a National Socialist government in Hungary under the fanatical Arrow Cross leader Ferenc Szálasi. Szálasi, whose ideology was known as "Hungarism," was a fanatical chauvinist and anti-Semite who believed in close collaboration with the Nazis. He also saw himself as a charismatic leader destined for a great role in the history of his nation. Szálasi was a theoretician devoid of any sense of political reality. Men such as Szálasi cast their lot with the Nazis late in 1944, and in dealing with figures such as Doriot, Szálasi, and Horia Sima the Nazis knew they were dealing with people who, even if they had not been so sympathetic to National Socialism on the basis of temperament and ideology, had no choice but to stick with Germany until the end. They were, after all, desperate men with no place else to turn, despised outlaws in their own countries.

CHAPTER VIII

"We Will Never Capitulate": The End of National Socialism, 1942-1945

1. The Road to Stalingrad

BY the end of 1941 it was clear that Adolf Hitler could no longer win the Second World War; at best he might achieve a stalemate. He threw away even this possibility by his declaration of war upon the United States on December 11. By the end of 1942 Germany was losing this greatest of all wars of attrition on both the strategic and economic levels.

The year had not begun inauspiciously. By the late winter of 1942 Hitler and his commanders had succeeded in stabilizing the eastern front. They were involved in feverish preparations for a great offensive against Russia, which began in the Ukraine on June 28. This was the last offensive on the eastern front in which an element of strategic surprise lay with the Germans. Yet even here the Soviet reaction was far more elastic and troublesome than it had been at the time of the beginning of Operation Barbarossa one year earlier.

Hitler had begun his 1942 offensive against Russia in the south for two reasons: (1) He wanted the rich oil resources of the Caucasus, and (2) he had dreams of a strategic linkup with two other forces, that of Rommel proceeding towards Cairo and Suez into the Middle East, and possibly even with the Japanese if they were successful in Burma and India. In a vaguer sense, Hitler thought that after seizing control of the lower Volga and Soviet oil reserves near the Black and Caspian seas he would link up with the Finnish and German troops besieging Leningrad in the north. There would be offensives against Archangel and Murmansk and eventually a vast encircling pincer operation around Moscow, which would cut off the Red armies so successfully defending that city.

These plans were not well thought out. In part, indeed, they were just strategic musings. The more modest goal of Hitler's 1942 offensive as compared with that of Barbarossa in 1941 was itself indicative of Germany's changed position in the war. In 1941 Hitler's military planning, following Clausewitzian lines, aimed at the destruction of the Red Army in European Russia. In 1942 he was thinking in terms of territory and raw materials, but Hitler still daydreamed about linking up with the Japanese or with Rommel or mused about vast encircling movements around Moscow. He had to have his offensive dreams, but they were little more than that at this point. For awhile, the German offensive of 1942 went well, and vast amounts of territory were conquered. Because of manpower shortages, however, the Germans had to increasingly rely upon undependable allies such as the Rumanians, the Hungarians, and the Italians. These allies were not well supplied and their morale was indifferent.

On November 19, 1942 the Soviets began a great counteroffensive against the Axis armies fighting near Stalingrad on the Volga. In September and October the Nazis constantly announced they were about to take or had taken Stalingrad. The very name itself became a mania, a fetish for German propagandists and for Hitler himself. Hitler ignored reports of a vast buildup of Soviet reserves on the east side of the Volga. The Soviets first struck at the positions of Hitler's Axis allies. On November 22 they cut off an entire army, the German Sixth Army under

General Friedrich von Paulus, which was besieging Stalingrad. Hitler, convinced of the power of will and of his own infallibility, refused to allow von Paulus to attempt to fight his way out of the Stalingrad pocket, a move which at this point might have been at least partially successful. Hermann Göring promised Hitler that the Luftwaffe would be able to drop more than enough supplies to supply the Sixth Army during its siege until the newly formed Army Group Don under Field Marshal Erich von Manstein could come to the rescue in December. While the Sixth Army slowly died in Stalingrad, Hitler's allies, the Hungarian Second Army, the Italian. Eighth Army, and the Rumanian Third and Fourth Armies, were smashed by this vast Soviet counteroffensive in southern Russia. It appeared that the German Army Group A, fighting to the south in the Caucasus, might be cut off. Hitler's strategic justification for ordering the Sixth Army to hold out at Stalingrad was that such an action prevented a complete collapse of the front of von Weichs' Army Group B in southern Russia. Such a collapse would have isolated Field Marshal von Kleist's Army Group A in the Caucasus.

Hitler's reaction to the Stalingrad debacle was a typical one. He reorganized the command of the German armies in southern Russia, forming a new Army Group Don under Field Marshal von Manstein, a man he did not like but whose abilities he had to respect. Hitler's argument was that while von Paulus tied down "enormous numbers" of Soviet troops around Stalingrad, Manstein, reorganizing German forces in the Ukraine, would come to the rescue of von Paulus, thereby preventing the collapse of the crucial Don front by an act of will and rescue. Manstein, however, was not able to reach von Paulus and his Sixth Army cauldron. By January von Paulus could not have fought his way out even if Hitler had given him permission to do so. A few days before the end of the Battle of Stalingrad Hitler had a field marshal's baton flown to von Paulus. Evidently he had in mind the fact that "no German field marshal had ever surrendered."

By February 2, however, von Paulus had surrendered and the pitiful remnants of the Stalingrad garrison went into Soviet captivity. Von Paulus later emerged as a major spokesman for Free Germany, the Soviet propaganda group formed among German prisoners of war.

Adolf Hitler said: "I alone bear the responsibility for Stalingrad." While this was indeed the case, he seems to have learned little from the catastrophe. Hitler, who could be daring and innovative in terms of offensive strategy, believed in a traditional defensive strategy. He tried to hold all territory that he had gained instead of conducting an elastic defense of maneuver on the vast fields of Russia, which were ideal for such a strategy. Again and again he ordered German soldiers to hold territory unto death. Hitler thus permitted entire garrisons, divisions, or army groups to be cut off from the main bulk of the German armies. He believed that "strong points" or "fortifications," of which there were an increasing number in 1944 and 1945, "pinned down" numerous Allied troops and allowed the Germans to reorganize their forces for counteroffensives. While this possibly made some sense in the case of Stalingrad after Manstein had failed (this is controversial), it made no sense at all in 1944 and 1945.

2. The Axis Collapse in Africa

At the very time when the Red Army was massing over a million men for its counteroffensive against the German Army Group B around Stalingrad, the Axis suffered a major reversal of fortunes in the Mediterranean. In the summer of 1942 Hitler and Mussolini had high hopes that Rommel's Africa Korps and its Italian allies might enter Cairo within a very short time. Mussolini even had a white horse ready for his triumphal entry into the city. By July and August it was clear to Rommel that, given the difficulties of supply across the Mediterranean, he would have to go over to the strategic defensive. Hitler had recently promoted Rommel to the rank of field marshal in a pompous ceremony typical of the Nazi hierarchy, and he expected that Rommel would soon reach the Suez Canal. Rommel knew by October that the Allied forces under Alexander and Montgomery were preparing for a tremendous offensive against the Germans and the Italians. The British now had some of the new American Sherman tanks to throw into the fray, and since the British controlled the sea-lanes of the Mediterranean, they did not suffer from the shortages of petrol, equipment, and replacements which so crippled the Axis forces.

On October 23 the Allies began their counteroffensive at El Alamein, and by early November they had completely smashed Rommel's positions. Hitler had earlier told Rommel that this would not be the first time in history when a stronger will prevailed over the larger battalions. He had wired Rommel that there were only two choices confronting him, that of "victory or of death." In October and November Rommel retreated on his own initiative, surmising that if he did not, the entire Africa Korps would be destroyed. Although this was contrary to Hitler's orders in both letter and spirit, Hitler took no more than temporary action against Rommel, voicing his displeasure at the time but later appointing the field marshal to sensitive military posts in the West.

As the Axis armies retreated across the deserts of Cyrenaica and Tripolitania, Mussolini and Ciano grew increasingly fearful of the next Allied move. Winston Churchill, thinking in terms of the British Peninsular Campaign in Spain against Napoleon in the early nineteenth century, constantly looked for ways of attacking the Axis by pinpricks against the supposedly vulnerable peripheries of the New Order, but the Allies finally determined that their next move would be an attack on Sicily. A few days after Rommel's forces had been broken, American and French forces were in control of Algeria and Morocco. The Axis forces struggled to build up a defensive position in Tunisia, for they were now caught between the American attack in the west and the British forces under Montgomery rapidly advancing from the east. In heroic language typical of the National Socialist mentality, Hitler told Mussolini, "With your help, Duce, I will turn Tunisia into the Verdun of the Mediterranean." Mussolini, showing an interesting historical imagination, referred to this struggle for the Mediterranean as the Fourth Punic War.

Churchill, with his mania for attacking the peripheries of Europe, was thinking in terms of an attack on the Balkans. In 1943 and 1944 he was obsessed with the idea of bringing Turkey into the war against Germany. Churchill also was interested in preventing the extension of the Soviet system into Eastern Europe. He was intrigued by the offers of Mihai Antonescu in Rumania and Kállay and Horthy in Hungary, all of whom desired separate surrenders exclusively to the *Western* powers. The eastern Mediterranean, after all, was a traditional sphere of *British* (rather than Russian or American) naval influence. Churchill sensed that the role of American tanks against Rommel and of American forces in Algeria and Morocco symbolized the fact that the star of the British Empire was in eclipse. Britain would survive the Second World War, but it would never again be a great power. Churchill hoped to redress this balance, using British naval power and a traditional British sphere of influence in order to support his claims to continued great power status. The Americans, however, were committed to the early opening of a second front in France. Although they were not able to do so in 1943, they did not wish to get bogged down in remote theaters of war which would mean little to American public opinion and would make American forces overly dependent upon the British.

Italy, which Churchill had mistakenly called "the soft underbelly of Axis Europe," was chosen as a logical target. The British received the supreme command, but the Americans gained far more. They had prevented Churchill from going into the Balkans and they had received a firm commitment in regard to opening up a second front in France in the spring of 1944. German forces fought stubbornly in Tunis, but by May, 1943 their cause was hopeless. Over a quarter of a million Axis prisoners fell into Allied hands in another stunning German defeat. Mussolini realized that the Fascist regime in Italy was now at stake. His advisers tried to shore up his courage so that he would forcefully demonstrate to Hitler that unless the war in the East was ended by an armistice between the Axis and the Soviet Union, Italy and Fascism were lost.

3. July, 1943: Crises in Russia and Italy

Hitler was not used to listening, and he had no intention of terminating his "holy crusade" against Bolshevik Russia on any other terms than that of a total German victory. All over the world the balance of power seemed to be turning against the Axis. As early as June, 1942 there were disquieting signs (which the Japanese concealed from their German ally) that American forces were more than a match for Japanese naval strength in the western Pacific. In 1943 Hitler refused to follow the defensive advice of his despised generals, particularly that of Manstein, who urged that the Germans construct an *Ostwall* or eastern wall using the Dnieper as a logical front. The Germans would then create an elastic defense and hopefully hold the Red Army to a stalemate. This could conceivably have led to a compromise peace in the East. Hitler refused to countenance such maneuvers. As Keitel wrote in August, as usual faithfully reflecting his master's views, "There cannot be peace until the Bolsheviks have been brought to their knees. How long this will take, no one knows."

Between the time of the Stalingrad disaster and midsummer 1943, the Germans achieved a remarkable stabilization of their front in southern Russia. But instead

of building upon this in the manner suggested by Manstein, Hitler thought in terms of a renewed offensive. On
July 5, 1943 the Germans opened their last great
armored offensive in Russia, the battle for the Kursk
Salient ("Operation Citadel") in southern Russia. This
time the Soviets were not taken by surprise. The offensive
was extremely costly to the Germans, and this plus
dramatic events occurring in Italy forced them to break
off the offensive on July 19. From July until the end of
the year the Germans lost enormous amounts of territory
in Russia, particularly in the Ukraine. This was a five-
month rout for the mighty Wehrmacht.

The news from the Mediterranean theater was, if anything, even worse. On July 25 Mussolini was overthrown,
and anxious jockeying began in Italy for control of the
peninsula. The new government of Marshal Pietro
Badoglio wanted to get Italy out of the war as soon as
possible. Badoglio knew, however, that new German
troops were massing at the Brenner Pass, and that the
Germans had forces in southern Italy and were surrounding Rome. If he acted too precipitously, the Germans would occupy most of the peninsula, especially
since the Allies showed no signs of reaching Rome at this
point. The fall of Mussolini did not turn into a military
disaster for the Germans, even though Badoglio pulled
Italy out of the war early in September and declared war
on the Germans in October. By then, thanks in part to
Allied inactivity beyond southern Italy, the Germans had
secured most of the peninsula. Although this seemed to
be a tactical victory for the Germans, it proved a somewhat misleading one. If they had not tried to hold on
to so much Italian territory, but had concentrated upon
fortifying the Alps, Lombardy, and the Apennine Mountains, they would have made the Allied advance even
more difficult than it was. Even so, Churchill's statement
about the "soft underbelly of Europe" seems somewhat
incredible in the light of the fact that the Germans held
out in northern Italy until the very end of the war.

4. Adolf Hitler as Man and War Leader, 1943-1945

The overthrow of Mussolini and the "defensive" mentality of his generals enraged Hitler. He railed against "traitors" such as von Paulus, "who could have entered into national immortality with a single bullet but preferred Soviet captivity"; against traitors at the Italian court; against traitors among his own generals. What was Hitler like during this crisis year 1943? He was aging prematurely. As recently as February, 1942, at the funeral of Fritz Todt, Hitler still cut a dramatic figure, looking fairly healthy and vigorous. By late 1943 various drugs had taken their toll. Hitler did not get enough proteins because of his vegetarian diet, and he used all sorts of stimulants in order to reinforce his will and shore up his energy. He had a deathly fear of the common cold, taking various compounds prepared by his pharmacist-physician Dr. Morell, thereby weakening his natural powers of resistance. A tremble began to appear in Hitler's left arm and leg. Hitler's features, never attractive, grew even more sallow and puffy. He got little exercise, even though he retreated for long weeks in 1943 to the Berghof, his mountain hideout near Berchtesgaden in Bavaria. Hitler would occasionally go for walks with an old colleague such as Albert Speer, or take his Alsatian dog Blondi for a short stroll. He turned night into day, staying up half the night talking, then sleeping late. Courtiers such as Göring fell asleep in his presence, while even a lackey like Keitel had trouble keeping his head up. This did not seem to bother Hitler. He talked more and more as the German war effort crumbled before his eyes. Hitler was somewhat of a hermit even before he retreated to his Reichsbunker under Berlin in 1945.

In 1943 the Allied terror bombings of German cities increased in intensity. The raids on Berlin at the end of the year, though not as disastrous as those on Hamburg some months earlier, starkly proved that the Luftwaffe no longer had control of the skies over Germany, much less those over Western Europe. Adolf Hitler never willingly visited a bombed city or its refugees, whereas figures like Goebbels and even the discredited Göring increased their popularity by their willingness to show solidarity with the victims of Allied raids. Hitler could not bear objective discussion of these raids.

Hitler's insistence on retaking the strategic offensive between 1944 and 1945 takes on the aura of insanity, given the relatively limited means at the disposal of the German forces. By the end of 1943 Hitler and his generals knew that the major Allied action in 1944 would be the creation of a second front somewhere in France. Hitler intuitively grasped that the landings might take place in Normandy, rather than farther to the northeast in an area closer to Dover. In fact, Hitler seemed to welcome the Allied offensive, feeling that if the German troops could crush it, he might bring the Western Allies to their senses. After all, they too were anti-Bolshevik. The inconsistency of Nazi ideology came out clearly in Hitler's attitude toward splitting the Grand Alliance. Earlier, Goebbels and Hitler had insisted that international capitalism and Soviet Bolshevism were obverse sides of the same coin. They were both, after all, "internationalist Jewish" schemes for robbing and destroying the Aryan peoples.

In 1944, when Nazi propaganda was grasping at any straw in order to shore up German morale, Goebbels and Hitler began to talk about how unnatural the Allied coalition was—ultra-capitalist states ("plutocracies") allied with Soviet Bolshevism! Men such as Himmler—even the "loyal Heinrich"—began to think about and plan separate negotiations with the Western Allies behind Hitler's back. Hitler saw the situation somewhat differently. He believed—and this was true practically until the end of the war—that if the Western Allies saw that the Germans would oppose them ferociously and successfully they would come to their senses. They would see that there was no point in trying to destroy powerful German forces in the West so that the Soviet Red Army would reap the gains in the East. Such reasoning, studied from the detached viewpoint of the dynamics of its implicit diplomacy, seems also to have a touch of insanity about it. Hitler felt that if the Germans destroyed a Western Allied landing force the West might make a separate peace with Germany. But the British, who would not make peace after Dunkirk, would hardly be likely to do so now in 1944 when they were immeasurably stronger and had powerful America as an ally! Adolf Hitler was blind to such power-political factors.

Did Hitler realize before the Normandy invasion that he had irrevocably lost the war? There is contradictory evidence on this point. There is some indication that Hitler realized at the time of the Soviet counteroffensive before Moscow in December, 1941 that the Blizkrieg against Russia had failed and that Germany had thereby lost the war. In February of 1944 he self-pityingly told Field Marshal Rommel, "We've lost the war but nobody will negotiate with me." On the other hand, he and Dr. Goebbels reenforced each other's faith in and will to victory by constantly clutching at new straws: The Allied coalition will have to break up because "never in history was there a coalition with so many internal contradictions." Miracle weapons would change the course of the war.

Through most of the war Hitler was surrounded by military figures who did not openly contradict him. Colonel-General Jodl, for example, head of the Wehrmacht (OKW) Operations Staff, declared at Nürnberg that in a state based upon the personality of the Führer any criticism which would tend to undermine Hitler's confidence in himself was improper. Hitler, convinced of his hold upon the German people and of his own military infallibility, clutched at hope until March and April, 1945. He could not stand to receive bad news but when he did—which after 1942 was most of the time—he always laid the blame at the door of his generals.

There is a truly amazing story behind the capitulation of the once-proud Prussian-German army to former Corporal Adolf Hitler. Occasionally, a Chief of the Army General Staff such as Kurt Zeitzler or Heinz Guderian would stand up to Hitler's rages. But by and large, the army accepted Hitler's every whim and attempted to carry out his most insane orders, such as a counteroffensive against the Soviets in Hungary early in 1945. After making himself Commander in Chief of the army at the end of 1941, Hitler embarked upon a conscious program of Nazification of the German Wehrmacht. In 1944 he introduced the Hitler salute (*deutscher Gruss*) and National Socialist leadership officers or political commissars into an army which had earlier stated it would never accept such a humiliation.

After the attempted assassination of the Führer on July 20, 1944, Hitler's hatred for the army knew no bounds. It was significant that he made a naval figure, Admiral Dönitz, his successor as Head of State. Hitler felt that the navy had acquitted itself well in the Second World War, that it had "erased the shame" of the revolutionary naval mutiny at Kiel in 1918. Indeed, the failure of the German U-boat campaign against the British and the Americans, which was symbolized by the temporary but crucial withdrawal of German submarines from the North Atlantic in May, 1943, was not the fault of Dönitz nor of his predecessor Grand Admiral Raeder. Rather, it reflected the sloth with which Hitler pursued any consistent program of surface and undersea naval construction before 1941. Perhaps Hitler sensed this and believed that Raeder and particularly Dönitz had done their very best in difficult circumstances. Hitler would never give the army any such benefit of the doubt.

Until the very end Hitler used military terminology which was part of the Prussian tradition. Nevertheless, his hatred of the aristocratic bearers of that tradition grew as the prospects of German victory receded. Hitler must have sensed the disastrous implications of the Allied landings in Normandy when the Germans proved unable to hurl the Allies back into the sea on June 6, 1944. Hitler and Goebbels, always believing in the magic of the spoken word, had boasted about "Fortress Europe" and its Atlantic Wall defenses against Allied invasion. These defenses were rather meager, and when the Germans did not concentrate enough armor against the bridgehead at Normandy, the Allies established a firm foothold on the Continent. All was now lost in the West. Hitler, although he had correctly predicted that the Allies would first land in Normandy, felt this invasion was a feint and that the main attack would probably come elsewhere, perhaps to the north or in Brittany. Thus, he was loath to commit all his armored divisions stationed in northern France to the Normandy front. This proved to be a fatal blunder. When the Allies broke out into the plains of northern France in July the fate of France was decided. By the end of August most of France had been cleared of German troops, and it was obvious that the Germans would soon have to fight on the soil of the Reich itself.

Two weeks after the Normandy invasion the Soviets launched a tremendous counteroffensive against Army Group Center in the area of the old Polish-Russian frontier. Army Group Center completely crumbled under the hammer blows of the Red Army, which six months earlier had broken the German and Finnish ring around the heroic besieged city of Leningrad. By July 20, 1944 the German situation was desperate in both east and west. It appeared that the Allies would soon overrun France. They would take Paris in a matter of weeks, just as they had taken Rome a few weeks earlier. The fall of Rome and the fall of Paris were major propaganda defeats for the National Socialist war effort. In the east Army Group Center was scarcely worthy of the name any longer. It had been cut to ribbons.

5. July 20, 1944 and the German Resistance

At a military conference held in his secluded headquarters compound in Rastenburg in East Prussia on the afternoon of July 20, Hitler was preparing to discuss this disastrous military situation with a number of officers. Suddenly a bomb went off and bloody, screaming men were blown or staggered in all directions. Hitler himself emerged relatively unharmed, though his pants had been singed to ribbons, his body filled with splinters, and one of his eardrums blown out. This was the culminating act of the German resistance, an explosion which should have taken place many years earlier. Much has been written about the German resistance since that time, but a few comments may be useful here in furthering our comprehension of the German trauma.

Military conspiracies to destroy Hitler were nothing new. One existed before the Munich Conference in 1938, and from the time of the disaster at Stalingrad plots or tacit conspiracies among high-ranking German officers were not uncommon. As the tide of war turned against Germany, disenchanted officers such as Colonel Klaus von Stauffenberg, who placed the bomb on July 20, made contact with opposition civilian leaders such as former Mayor Goerdeler of Leipzig and Finance Minister Popitz of Prussia. Some of these men were driven by a sense of moral revulsion against the Hitler regime, though none of them was quite as saintly or courageous as two students, the brother and sister Scholl who, leading a small group called the White Rose, actually distributed pamphlets in 1943 accusing the Nazi regime of inhuman measures and mass murder.

The military leaders who attempted to kill Hitler in 1944—those privy to the plot included Field Marshal Rommel, Field Marshal von Kluge, Field Marshal von Witzleben—felt that if they exterminated Hitler, paralyzed the SS, and made the Nazi Party illegal the Allies would grant Germany favorable peace terms, perhaps the frontiers of September 1, 1939. This was an illusion, for ever since the Casablanca Declaration of January, 1943 (out of which Goebbels made much political capital), the Allies had insisted upon the *simultaneous, unconditional surrender* of the Nazi regime to all Allied powers. It is interesting that in his book *The Secret War*

Against Hitler the German officer Fabian von Schlabren-
dorff, in reproducing documents of the German resistance, carefully omits anything which might tell us what
its aims were in regard to the frontiers of Germany. Writing after the Second World War, he knew that it would
be impolitic to indicate that many of the leaders of the
military resistance to Hitler were by background and
inclination almost as chauvinistic and imperialistic as the
Nazis themselves. Of course, they were not so brutal, but
they intended to hold on to Bohemia and Moravia, parts
of western Poland, and certainly Austria. Some even
wanted to retain Alsace-Lorraine or at least have a
plebecite there. This arrogance and lack of reality, along
with a deep-rooted German opportunism which these
men were now overcoming and for which they were to
atone with their lives, was unfortunately typical of the
German officer corps. It was one of the fatal flaws which
had earlier led so many officers into the arms of the Nazi
leadership.

Hitler's fury after the attempt to kill him knew no
bounds. It was only exceeded by his feeling that "Providence" was somehow watching over him and would
guarantee that Germany had the final say in the war.
Hitler went on the air and denounced the "small clique
of conscienceless, ambitious, and stupid officers" who had
attempted to kill him, and in his broadcast he drew upon
the Prussian tradition of his would-be military murderers,
saying, "Obedience is the first duty of the German soldier." Hitler prepared a terrible fate for those implicated
in the plot. The relatives of the conspirators would be
arrested (this was the perverted Nazi interpretation of the
ancient Germanic law of *Sippenhaft* or kin's guilt) and sent
to concentration camps; the conspirators themselves
would be humiliated and cursed by the half-insane Nazi
judge Roland Freisler. Some of the accused would eventually be put on meathooks and garroted with piano wire,
dying an agonizing death. Hitler and Goebbels watched
the films of these executions, and they wanted new
officer candidates in the Wehrmacht to see them. They

had the films shown at the candidate school at Lichtefelde, though it must be said that the candidates walked out when the film began.

The obsequiousness and opportunism of the leaders of the Wehrmacht still knew no bounds, and it is extraordinary that a fundamentally decent officer such as Field Marshal von Rundstedt agreed to serve as President of the "Court of Honor of the German Wehrmacht," a hastily assembled front organization gathered together in order to justify Hitler's savage reprisals against the army. Fanatical Nazis such as Heinrich Himmler and Dr. Joseph Goebbels now saw their opportunity, and they grabbed even more power for themselves, Himmler becoming head of the Home Army, while Goebbels finally received an administrative role concerned with the total mobilization of Germany.

6. The End of the Third Reich

It is extraordinary to see newsreels of Hitler after July 20, 1944. He is but a shadow of his former self, kept going by an extraordinary if perverse will, egged on by the drugs which Dr. Morell pumped into his system. Towards the end of 1944 these included cocaine.

Churchill and Montgomery hoped that the Allies would crush the Reich by Christmas, but the Rhine proved a formidable barrier, largely because of Allied indecision and delays before early September, and the Germans fought tenaciously to guard it and the crucial industrial Ruhr basin. The Germans still held on to most of the Netherlands, and they successfully kept the Western Allies out of the industrial heart of Germany until March, 1945.

Even now, as the Third Reich lay *in extremis*, Hitler planned a new offensive against the Allies. This would show that the German Reich was still powerful and would fight to the end in the West. This, according to Hitler's perverse psychology, would prepare the "irrational"

Churchill and the "paralytic" Roosevelt (the "greatest war criminal of all time," according to Hitler) for negotiations. Hitler's last major offensive was the Ardennes counterattack, begun on December 16, 1944, sometimes called the Rundstedt Offensive. Though less ambitious than the Manstein and Guderian Ardennes offensive plan of 1940, the Rundstedt Offensive of 1944 roughly paralleled the earlier gamble. Hitler hoped that bad weather, reducing the possibility of Allied carpet bombings, along with the element of surprise, would enable the Germans to reach Antwerp, thereby cutting off British and Canadian forces to the north while destroying the major Belgian supply port of the Allies. This offensive would show that the German Wehrmacht had plenty of life left in it. Rundstedt, who reluctantly helped plan the offensive, argued that it was overly ambitious, but Hitler was not to be deterred. The Allies *were* amazed that the Germans could launch such an offensive at this point, but by the end of the month it was obvious that the Wehrmacht had run out of steam. They did not have the resources, the air protection, or the safe lines of supply necessary to the success of such an ambitious offensive. Hitler refused to break off the offensive and withdraw, however, so the Allies encircled enormous German troop concentrations, eventually inflicting over 100,000 casualties upon the manpower-short German army. To the east the Red Army was fighting in East Prussia and would soon cross the frontiers of the old Reich in Silesia and Pomerania.

The end was clearly near, but even in these last months of the war Hitler maintained his charismatic hold over his followers. There were no longer any plots against him in the Wehrmacht. Albert Speer, who thought of doing away with Hitler because of his scorched earth directives, which would endanger the future of the German people after the lost war, talked to miners in the Ruhr and got the impression that Hitler still had the support of the German people. Speer was so hypnotized by Hitler that he was unable to act against him. Hitler's last weeks in the *Reichsbunker* under Berlin were an insane parody on the Third Reich. Men like the molelike Martin Bormann, Personal Secretary of the Führer since 1943 and effective head of the Nazi Party organization since at least 1939, scrambled for power.

When the Allies broke across the Rhine in March and the Soviets prepared for a final thrust at Berlin in April, it was clear that it really was all over. The illusions that top leaders of the Nazi Party still held, however, are truly incredible, almost matching those of Hitler himself. Heinrich Himmler, the arch-executioner, the prophet of National Socialist purity in the élite SS, actually believed that the Western Allies would negotiate a peace with him if he succeeded Hitler. Perhaps Himmler felt that if he showed his good side. . . . Count Folke Bernadotte, the Swedish diplomat, may have encouraged Himmler's fantasies since 1944 in order to save some of the victims of the National Socialist concentration camps.

Hermann Göring also believed that Eisenhower would negotiate with him. He wired Hitler on April 23, indicating from his position of refuge in south Germany that if he did not hear from the Führer by 10 P.M. he would consider himself obliged to act on Germany's diplomatic behalf as Hitler's legally appointed (1941) successor. Hitler, egged on by Bormann, flew into a rage. "That's an ultimatum," Bormann pointed out, and Hitler cursed Göring, the "drug addict," the "failure," the man who more than anyone else was responsible for the Allied bombing of German cities. Hitler removed Göring from all his Party and state offices and ordered him arrested. Thus, Hitler's successor, Göring, and Himmler—the loyal Heinrich—both attempted to jump off the Nazi ship as it was sinking. Actually, Himmler's attempts had been more prolonged, consistent, and selfish.

In the last few weeks of his macabre existence, Hitler could barely walk a hundred feet without having to sit down. His shaking left side, which had surprisingly improved somewhat immediately after the bomb blast of July 20, was worse than ever. By April he was even cursing Dr. Morell, blaming Morell for having reduced him to a shambling wreck. Hitler had even earlier declared that only Fräulein Braun, his "friend" for thirteen years, and his Alsatian dog Blondi were loyal to him. In this self-pity he was mistaken. Joseph Goebbels and his wife Magda were willing to die with Hitler, for as Frau Goebbels so eloquently put it, "Life without National Socialism is not worth living."

Hitler prepared two last wills and testaments, one political, the other personal. What is interesting about the personal testament is its provincial, petit bourgeois, Lower-Austrian emphasis, showing how much Hitler was a prisoner of the social forms and prejudices which had been impressed upon him as a young boy in the Austrian countryside. Showing that he was still living in a fantasy world, Adolf Hitler left his art collection to the municipal museum in Linz, Austria, and bequeathed enough money to certain relatives to support them "in a decent petit bourgeois life-style." His lack of a grasp of objective reality stayed with him until the end. Even in his political will and testament Hitler showed the same Machiavellian tendency to divide authority among subordinates (now successors) that he had displayed since the First World War. Although he made Admiral Dönitz, then located in a German enclave in the north, Head of State, Hitler was careful to appoint as Chancellor Dr. Goebbels, a fanatic and loyal Nazi. This device was to prove of little use, for Dönitz's authority was destroyed within a few weeks as the British occupied northern Germany.

Magda and Joseph Goebbels decided to die with Hitler. Hitler himself married Eva Braun on April 29, and a few hours later the two of them committed suicide. It used to be thought that Eva Braun had taken poison for cosmetic reasons, while Hitler shot himself through the roof of the mouth. It now appears that Hitler may have taken poison *and* shot himself. Certainly, Hitler, so conscious of historical images, myths, and the manipulation of media, realized that it would appear more heroic if he shot himself rather than if he dispatched himself with painless (and less military) poison.

Bormann made sure that the news of Hitler's death was not broadcast until he had made one last desperate attempt to achieve supreme power for himself. First he attempted to manipulate and control Admiral Dönitz, who was still at liberty in northern Germany. Bormann informed Dönitz that he would soon join him in Flensburg. This never occurred, and to the present day there is a mystery surrounding the death or disappearance of Martin Bormann. When Hitler's death was announced, it was done in the true spirit of National Socialism: false heroism and blatant lies. The slow movement from Bruckner's Eighth Symphony was played, along with Siegfried's "Funeral Music" by Wagner. Then it was announced that "Adolf Hitler has fallen at his command post in Berlin after fighting with his last breath against the Bolsheviks." This was consistent with Nazi rhetoric, for in April Nazi and SS officials had scrawled all over the walls of beleaguered Berlin: "Berlin remains German," "Our walls are broken but not our hearts," "SS believes in the Führer." If Hitler had indeed committed suicide and had not fought the Russians to the very end, it might appear as if he had irresponsibly and pusillanimously tricked and betrayed the millions who had taken an oath of allegiance to him in one form or another.

Magda and Joseph Goebbels soon thereafter committed suicide in the *Reichsbunker*, and their bodies, like those of Hitler and Eva Braun, were doused with precious gasoline (albeit in small quantities) and burned in the courtyard. Goebbels' remains, however, were more recognizable than were those of Hitler, though in 1963 the Russians publicly admitted, for the first time since the summer of 1945, that they considered Hitler to have perished in the bunker on April 30, 1945. A major means of identification were the various elements of bridgework in Hitler's teeth. The dental assistant was located, and positively identified the dental remains as those of Adolf Hitler. Witnesses tend to agree about the sequence of events regarding the suicides of Hitler and Eva Braun. One of the ghastly details of the last days in the bunker was the suicide of the Goebbels after they murdered their six children.

It is fitting that the Third Reich should have ended in an orgy of death, with Red Army shells pouring down upon a city which had been smashed to pieces by Allied bombing raids since 1943.

7. Reflections on National Socialism and the German Trauma

At the trial of the "major Nazi criminals" held at Nürnberg in 1945-1946, Rudolf Hess proved somewhat embarrassing to the other Nazi leaders. After all, this "unstable man" had parachuted into Scotland in May, 1941 on some fantastic, self-assigned mission on behalf of the Reich. He now appeared to be suffering from fantasies and amnesia, being only occasionally aware of what was going on. What would happen to the dignity of such "statesmen" as Göring and Ribbentrop if Hess made a mockery of the Nazi leadership? Yet Rudolf Hess in 1945 was more symbolic of National Socialism than were clever cynics such as Göring, a self-important but frightened dolt such as Ribbentrop, or a humorless Nazi "intellectual" such as Alfred Rosenberg.

Hess's amnesia was occasionally broken in a feverish manner by incredible delusions about himself, the stars, diet, the Jews, or the Führer. Rudolf Hess's mind, which fed upon its own sickness, was symbolic of National Socialism in 1945, except that poor Hess—unlike former colleagues such as Albert Speer—was unable to suppress his original delusions, hatreds, and fears, those which had led him to National Socialism. They emerged at this point as confused, harmless ramblings. Most Germans, even those who collaborated with the Nazis, were spared such suffering, and by 1946 it was difficult to find a single National Socialist in Germany. An entire ideology, a mass movement involving the lives and deaths of hundreds of millions of people seemed to have evaporated without leaving a trace.

Most Germans could suppress or cover up or explain away as opportunism their thoughts and actions between 1930 and 1945. Rudolf Hess, if only because of his illness, could not do this, and his sickness became symbolic of the German trauma which had so molded and shaken Europe and the world between 1914 and 1945. Most Germans could put the horrors and hopes of those years out of their minds, and in the amazing economic and political recovery of West Germany after 1948 the Germans made a tremendous effort to become one more faceless, Americanized member of the "Western community of nations" as symbolized by rearmament against Communism and membership in NATO. For these "good" Germans there was no need to go through the trauma of Rudolf Hess, for they were able to turn away and to repress.

National Socialism died with Adolf Hitler, not because of a revulsion against him on the part of the German people but because Hitler had lost the war. National Socialism emerged out of the *German defeat* of 1918, and it would have continued on its murderous course in the event of a *German victory* in 1940-1945. This should never be forgotten.

The miseries of defeat, militarism, inflation, and depression; the collapse of traditional values; urbanization—these had led hundreds of thousands to National Socialism by 1930, but certain psychological and cultural factors present in the German people, largely as a result of their peculiar historical development, made Hitler's rise to power possible: respect for established authority, self-pity in defeat, the search for scapegoats in misery, brutality alternating with obsequiousness, a willingness to take orders. Without these characteristics Hitler never would have emerged as a great political leader. He knew that when a German crowd greeted him it was not due to an intellectual approval of National

Socialist "ideology" (only a fool like Rosenberg would believe that); rather, it was a primeval mating call, a desire for mind-obliterating rape on the part of socially frightened and morally degenerate masses.

In 1919 Adolf Hitler emerged from personal oblivion, and in 1945 he returned to that same nihilism. In the years between, however, he made an entire nation the vehicle for fantasies and twisted ambitions which are almost inconceivable in any other place or time. Adolf Hitler cursed the modern world and its tendencies toward social change, but cleverly and perversely used its technology in the service of atavistic values and impulses. He made race and struggle the criteria of existence—but almost destroyed the nation which he had set out to save. This was typical of the nihilism inherent in National Socialism, and it is fitting that the Nazi regime ended under tormented Berlin in a demented but strangely logical ceremony of murder and self-immolation. Was this the end of the German trauma?

Bibliographical Essay

THE fundamental psychological and ideological components of Adolf Hitler's mind were products of an Austrian environment. August Kubizek, *Young Hitler—The Story of Our Friendship* (British edition, 1954), contains much material relating to Hitler as the author's friend and roommate in the Vienna years. It must be used with caution. Important material on the young Hitler may be consulted in Bradley F. Smith, *Adolf Hitler: His Family, Childhood, and Youth* (1967) and in Franz Jetzinger, *Hitler's Youth* (British edition, 1958). William A. Jenks, *Vienna and the Young Hitler* (1960) is a useful study of the Vienna which Hitler knew before World War I. Alan Bullock's classic biography, *Hitler: A Study in Tyranny* (revised edition, 1964), contains a good portrait of Hitler's earlier years, but some of Bullock's material has become dated or questionable in the light of more recent research. *The Habsburg Monarchy* (1948) is A. J. P. Taylor's highly readable contribution to the study of the multinational empire.

In putting National Socialism into the context of German and European history the following works may be helpful. Ralf Dahrendorf, *Society and Democracy in Germany* (U.S. edition, 1967), is a brilliant and pioneering sociological study of the structure and weaknesses of modern German mass society. Geoffrey Barraclough, *Modern Germany* (1946), relates the contradictions of modern German society to medieval and early modern catastrophes. Hajo Holborn, *A History of Modern Germany*, Vol. III (1969) is a useful synthesis. Erich Eyck, *Bismarck and the German Empire* (1950), is a good survey of a crucial period. Harry Pross, *Die Zerstörung der deutschen Politik: Dokumente 1875-1933* (1959) is a well-edited collection of documents. On intellectual currents in imperial Germany, see Hans Kohn, *The Mind of Germany: The Education of a Nation* (1960), and the Marxist interpretation of Georg Lukács, *Die Zerstörung der Vernunft* (1954). William J. Bossenbrook, *The German Mind* (1961) and R. D' O. Butler, *The Roots of National Socialism, 1783-1933* (1941) are studies of pre-Nazi German intellectual history. A. J. P. Taylor, *The Course of German History: A Study of the Development of Germany Since 1815* (1945) is a spirited political interpretation. Leonard Krieger, *The German Idea of Freedom* (1957) is a vital study of patterns in German political thought.

Karl Loewith, *From Hegel to Nietzsche: The Revolution in Nineteenth Century Thought* is enlightening on the "German spirit" (U.S. edition, 1964). Julien Benda, *The Betrayal of the Intellectuals* (1928) is an impassioned essay on the protofascistization of the modern intelligentsia. The role of German historians in deifying the state and relativizing almost everything else is explored in Georg G. Iggers, *The German Conception of History: The National Tradition of Historical Thought from Herder to the Present* (1968). On Friedrich Nietzsche's part in creating a psychic void which forces other than a displaced Christianity might fill, see Karl Jaspers' interesting essay, *Nietzsche and Christianity* (U.S. edition, 1961). Heinrich Heine wrote a remarkably prophetic work on *Religion and Philosophy in Germany* in 1834. Heine concluded that "There will be played in Germany a drama compared to which the French Revolution will seem but an innocent idyll" (U.S. edition, 1959).

Germanic racialist ideology antedated Hitler. See the famous work by Houston Stewart Chamberlain, *The Foundations of the Nineteenth Century* (British edition, 1911). George L. Mosse, *The Crisis of German Ideology: Intellectual Origins of the Third Reich* (1964) and Fritz Stern, *The Poli-*

tics of Cultural Despair: A Study in the Rise of the Germanic Ideology (1961) contribute a great deal to our understanding of racialist and "radical conservative" thinkers in the period 1870-1933. Daniel Gasman, *The Scientific Origins of National Socialism: Social Darwinism in Ernst Haeckel and the German Monist League* (1971) is a fine study of the dissemination of racialism in Germany before World War I.

On anti-Semitism in Germany and Austria, see Peter Pulzer, *The Rise of Political Anti-Semitism in Germany and Austria: 1867-1918* (1964); Adolf Leschnitzer, *The Magic Background of Modern Anti-Semitism: An Analysis of the German-Jewish Symbiosis* (1956); Paul W. Massing, *Rehearsal for Destruction: A Study of Political Anti-Semitism in Imperial Germany* (1949); and Norman Cohn, *Warrent for Genocide* (1966), which deals with the "Protocols of the Elders of Zion," a forgery purporting to be a Jewish plan for world conquest. On the Jews in pre-Hitler Germany, see Solomon Liptzin, *Germany's Stepchildren* (1944), and John K. Dickinson, *German and Jew: The Life and Death of Sigmund Stein* (1967).

On the European background and context of National Socialism, see Francis L. Carsten, *The Rise of Fascism* (1967), which also contains valuable material on the early history of the Nazi Party; Walter Laqueur and George L. Mosse, eds., *International Fascism, 1920-1945* (1966); Ernst Nolte, *The Three Faces of Fascism: Action Française, Italian Fascism, and National Socialism* (1966); Hans Rogger and Eugen J. Weber, eds., *The European Right: A Historical Profile* (1965). Also Eugen J. Weber, *Varieties of Fascism: Doctrines of Revolution in the 20th Century* (1964), which contains useful documents; S. J. Woolf, ed., *The Nature of Fascism* (1969) is an interesting symposium on theoretical aspects of Fascism.

The economic and political German imperialism which preceded and made possible National Socialism may be studied in the following works. Fritz Fischer, *Germany's Aims in the First World War* (U.S. edition, 1967), is an exhaustive treatment of the subject, and its conclusions support the thesis that Hitler's imperialism had roots in the ambitions of politicians and business leaders of the pre-1919 era. Henry Cord Meyer, *Mitteleuropa in German Thought and Action 1815-1945* (1955), gives valuable information of an ideological nature. The economic history of the imperial and post-Wilhelminian Reichs may be studied in Gustav Stolper, *The German Economy: 1870 to the Present* (revised U.S. edition, 1967). General Friedrich von Bernhardi, *Germany and the Next War* (U.S. edition, 1914), is an outspoken example of pre-Hitler German militarism and imperialism.

Andrew G. Whiteside, *Austrian National Socialism before 1914* (1962), deals with the obscure origins of Nazism in Bohemia and Austria. Dietrich Bronder, *Bevor Hitler kam* (1964) deals with the racialist *Thule Gesellschaft* and its importance for certain early Nazis. Anton Drexler, *Mein politisches Erwachen* (1919) and Gottfried Feder, *Das Manifest zur Brechung der Zinsknechtschaft des Geldes* (1919), present the "ideas" of two founders of the Nazi Party. Werner Maser, *Die Frühgeschichte der NSDAP* (1965); Reginald Phelps, "Before Hitler Came. Thule Society and *Germanen Orden*," *Journal of Modern History*, XXXV (1963), and "Hitler and the DAP," *American Historical Review*, LXVIII (1963), and Konrad Heiden, *A History of National Socialism* (1934), are important for the history of early Nazism. Alan Cassels, "Mussolini and German Nationalism 1922-1925," *Journal of Modern History*, XXXV (1963), is interesting. Ernst Röhm, *Die Geschichte eines Hochverräters* (1928), portrays the mentality of the "lost generation" of German soldiers, men who naturally drifted into groups such as the SA. Reginald H. Phelps, "Hitler als Parteiredner im Jahre 1920," *Vierteljahrshefte für Zeit-Geschichte*, No. 11 (1963), gives some sense of Hitler's role and greatness as a speaker. Ernst Hanfstaengel, *Hitler, the Missing Years* (British edition, 1957), though sensationalistic, contains valuable testimony on this same point. Fritz Thyssen, *I Paid Hitler* (1941), provides information about early ties between Hitler and German industrialists. Dietrich Orlow, *A History of the Nazi Party 1919-1933* (1969), is a useful survey. *Der Hitlerprozess vor dem Volksgerichtshof in München* (1924) is the transcript of the Hitler trial.

Werner Maser, *Hitler's "Mein Kampf"* (1966) is the best guide to the origins of Hitler's famous book. On the development of Hitler's "world view," see Eberhard Jaeckel, *Hitler's Weltanschauung* (1969). On rightist opinion and politics during the Weimar period, the following will prove useful: Lewis Hertzman, *DNVP: Right Wing Opposition in the Weimar Republic* (1963); Klemens von Klemperer, *Germany's New Conservatism: Its History and Dilemma in the Twentieth Century* (1957); Armin Mohler, *Die konservative Revolution in Deutschland 1918-1933* (1950); Kurt Sontheimer, *Antidemokratisches Denken in der Weimarer Republik* (1962); and Jean Neurohr, *Der Mythos vom Dritten Reich* (1957). Andreas Dorpalen, *Hindenburg and the Weimar Republic* (1964), and John W. Wheeler-Bennett, *The Nemesis of Power: The German Army in Politics, 1918 1945* (1953) both throw much light on the nature and politics of conservative institutions during the Weimar years.

The evolution of Nazi thought on race and "Germandom" may be followed in: Hans F. K. Guenther, *Rassenkunde des deutschen Volkes* (1922); Alfred Rosenberg, *Der Mythus des 20. Jahrhunderts* (1930), Walther Darré, *Das Bauerntum als Lebensquelle der nordischen Rasse* (1929), and *Neuadel aus Blut und Boden* (1930). For an influential example of corporative, conservative thought during the Weimar period, see the work of the Viennese theorist Othmar Spann, *Der wahre Staat* (1921). On the receptivity of the German youth movement to National Socialism, see Walter Z. Laqueur, *Young Germany* (1962). On the crisis of the German middle classes as seen through apocalyptic visions of the state and capitalism, see Herman Lebovics, *Social Conservatism and the Middle Classes in Germany: 1914-1933* (1969). For a brilliant study of German social structure in the Weimar years, see Theodor Geiger, *Die soziale Schichtung des deutschen Volkes* (1932).

National Socialism cannot be properly understood unless one studies the political and cultural history of the

Weimar Republic itself. Erich Eyck, *A History of the Weimar Republic* (2 vols., U.S. edition, 1962-1963), and Arthur Rosenberg, *Entstehung und Geschichte der Weimarer Republik* (1955), are both useful. The second volume of Eyck's work is stronger and more interpretive than the first, while Rosenberg's Marxist account is the most brilliant work of its type. Peter Gay, *Weimar Culture: The Outsider as Insider* (1968), is a well-written introduction to the subject. Istvan Déak, *Weimar Germany's Left-Wing Intellectuals: A Political History of the Weltbuehne and Its Circle* (1968), and Harold L. Poor, *Kurt Tucholsky and the Ordeal of Germany 1914-1935*, introduce us to the world of richly gifted, cynical Weimar intellectuals of the left. On the political left in the Weimar Republic, see Ossip K. Flechtheim, *Die KPD in der Weimarer Republik* (1948) and Richard N. Hunt, *German Social Democracy 1918-1933* (1964). On the role of paramilitary ex-soldiers in Weimar, see Robert G. L. Waite, *Vanguard of Nazism: The Free Corps Movement in Postwar Germany, 1918-1923* (1952). On the crucial significance of the Reichswehr in the Weimar Republic, see the following: Francis L. Carsten, *Reichswehr and Politics, 1918-1933* (British edition, 1966); Harold J. Gordon, *The Reichswehr and the German Republic: 1919-1926* (1957); Karl Demeter, *The German Officer Corps in Society and State: 1650-1945* (U.S. edition, 1965); and Harvey L. Dyck, *Weimar Germany and Soviet Russia, 1926-1933: A Study in Diplomatic Instability* (1966). On the Weimar police, see the interesting study by Hsi-huey Liang, *The Berlin Police Force in the Weimar Republic* (1970).

The years following Hitler's trial and imprisonment in 1924 saw the NSDAP expand its structure and grow into a national party. The following works throw light on this evolution: Martin Broszat, "Die Anfänge der Berliner NSDAP 1926/27," *Vierteljahrshefte für Zeitgeschichte* No. 8 (1960); Helmut Heiber, ed., *The Early Goebbels Diaries: 1925-1926* (U.S. edition, 1963); Reinhard Keuhnl, *Die nationalsozialistische Linke 1925 bis 1930* (1966); Dietrich Orlow, "The Conversion of Myth into Power: the NSDAP

1925-1926," *American Historical Review*, LXXII (1967); and Bradley F. Smith, *Heinrich Himmler: A Nazi in the Making, 1900-1926* (1971). On the appeal of Nazism to a rural population, see Rudolf Heberle, *Landbevölkerung und Nationalsozialismus* (1963). On Nazi propaganda before and after 1933, see Hamilton T. Burden, *The Nuremberg Party Rallies: 1923-39* (1967); Ernest K. Bramsted, *Goebbels and National Socialist Propaganda, 1925-1945* (1965); William S. Allen, *The Nazi Seizure of Power: The Experience of a Single German Town, 1930-1935* (1965); and J. Goebbels, *Vom Kaiserhof zur Reichskanzlei* (1933).

On the final struggle for power, see Karl Dietrich Bracher, *Die Auflösung der Weimarer Republik* (1964); Lawrence Wilson, ed., *The Road to Dictatorship: Germany 1918-1933* (British edition, 1963); Erich Matthias and Rudolf Morsey, eds., *Das Ende der Parteien 1933* (1960); Sigmund Neumann, *Die Parteien der Weimarer Republik* (1965); Thilo Vogelsang, *Reichswehr, Staat und NSDAP* (1962); K. D. Bracher, W. Sauer, and G. Schulz, *Die nationalsozialistiche Machtergreifung* (1962); Eliot B. Wheaton, *Prelude to Calamity: The Nazi Revolution 1933-1935, with a Background Survey of the Weimar Era* (1968); Fritz Tobias, *The Reichstag Fire* (U.S. edition, 1964). Useful memoirs include Otto Strasser, *Hitler und Ich* (1948); Hermann Rauschning, *The Voice of Destruction* (U.S. edition, 1940); Otto Braun, *Von Weimar zu Hitler* (1949).

No era in modern history offers such a wealth of documentation as does the Nazi epoch, 1933-1945. A great amount of material was captured by the Allies in 1945, and some of this may be consulted in the forty-two volumes of the *Trial of the Major War Criminals Before the International Military Tribunal* (Nürnberg, 1947-49). Two books of indices are included in the series. The United States government published some of this evidence, along with further documents in the summation *Nazi Conspiracy and Aggression* (7 vols., Washington, 1946). Important war crimes trials of less notorious, but often no less guilty Third Reich figures continued after 1946. Sixteen volumes of these proceedings, based on twelve trials conducted by the United States Military Tribunals in Nürnberg, appeared between 1946 and 1951.

The Western Allies collaborated in the edition of the *Documents on German Foreign Policy 1918-1945* (Washington, 1949-   ), a valuable, well-edited multivolume selection that contained English translations of documents for the period 1933-1941. It appears that documents preceding and following these years will appear only in the original German. Captured documents have generally been given back to the German Federal Republic, but an international team of scholars is still working on the 1918-1945 project, using Foreign Ministry materials now in the archives of the Foreign Ministry in Bonn, West Germany. Scholars may find microfilm copies of many documents returned to the Federal Republic in the National Archives in Washington, D.C., and the Public Record Office in London.

The National Archives, in cooperation with the American Historical Association, has published more than fifty guidebooks to its microfilm collection of Third Reich documents. These books, while unfortunately not yet indexed, tell us about the contents of each film, and indicate when a returned original document was not filmed. The guidebooks should be used along with George O. Kent's excellent guide to the Foreign Ministry records, which has not yet been completed. The Nazi records in the possession of the German Democratic Republic are much more limited in scope, but depending on one's area of research, they may be useful. They repose in the *Deutsches Zentral-Archiv* in Potsdam, and a relevant guidebook is available. The Soviet Union captured the von Dirksen papers and certain other sources relating to diplomacy in 1937-1939, and these have been published in the United States under the title *Documents Relating to the Eve of the Second World War* (2 vols., 1948).

Hitler's Speeches, 1922-1939, edited by Norman Baynes (2 vols., 1942) is helpful, as is the collection of Hitler's speeches entitled *My New Order*, edited by Raoul de

Roussy de Sales (1941). *Hitler's Secret Conversations 1941-1944* (1953) is based upon records maintained under the supervision of Martin Bormann. *Mein Kampf* should be used in the Ralph Manheim translation (1962). *Hitler's Secret Book* (1961) was a manuscript on foreign policy finished in 1928, but it was not published during Hitler's lifetime. The best edition to date of Hitler's speeches after 1932 is that by Max Domarus, ed., *Hitler: Reden und Proklamationen* (2 vols., 1962-63). This work includes brilliant commentaries by Domarus. Hitler's "political testament" was preserved by Martin Bormann: *The Testament of Adolf Hitler: The Hitler-Bormann Documents, February-April 1945* (1961).

Hitler Directs His War, edited by Felix Gilbert (1951), contains records of some of Hitler's military conferences. The important *Fuehrer Conferences on Naval Affairs* were printed in *Brassey's Naval Annual* for 1948. A part of the war diary of the Supreme Command of the Wehrmacht (OKW) is available in the *Kriegstagebuch des Oberkommandos der Wehrmacht*, ed. Percy Schramm (4 vols., 1961-1965). General Halder, Chief of the Army General Staff until September, 1942, kept a significant diary: *Kriegstagebuch* (3 vols., 1962-1964). H. R. Trevor-Roper, *Blitzkrieg to Defeat: Hitler's War Directives 1939-1945* (New York, 1964), is most useful.

A vital work on many aspects of the Third Reich is Baumont, Fried, and Vermeil, eds., *The Third Reich* (1955). Alan Bullock, *Hitler, a Study in Tyranny* (1952) is still standard, in particular for the years after 1932. Konrad Heiden's *Der Fuehrer: Hitler's Rise to Power* (1944) is still the most brilliant treatment of the subject. Hans Buchheim, *The Third Reich. Its Beginnings, Its Development, Its End* (1961), is a short introduction, as is Mau and Krausnick, *German History 1933-1945* (1959). Milton Mayer, *They Thought They Were Free* (1955) is based upon discussions with German "little people" who had been attracted to Nazism. William L. Shirer, *The Rise and Fall of the Third Reich* (1960), is a massive narrative by an outstanding journalist. Shirer's *Berlin Diary* (1942), dealing with the years 1934-1941, is also an important work by this shrewd, humane reporter.

Ernst Nolte, *Three Faces of Fascism* (1966), places National Socialism within the framework of a broad theory of Fascism. Profound philosophical reflections on the Nazi phenomenon by a German author may be found in Gert Kalow's *Hitler: Das gesamtdeutsche Trauma* (1967). A factual narrative of the Third Reich, with extensive bibliographical information, is contained in Bruno Gebhardt, ed., *Handbuch der Deutschen Geschichte*, Vol. IV (1963). Koppel Pinson, *Modern Germany*, second edition (1966), contains an incisive, interpretive history of the Nazi epoch, along with useful bibliographies. Friedrich Meinecke's *The German Catastrophe* (1950), written by an aged historian after the war, is a controversial work. It throws more light upon the origins of Nazism than it does upon the Hitler phenomenon in itself, a common failing in German works dealing with the problem. A good antidote to Meinecke is the work of the West German sociologist Ralf Dahrendorf, *Society and Democracy in Germany* (1967), which I have earlier mentioned.

Oren J. Hale, *The Captive Press in the Third Reich* (1964), contains information of great value. Siegfried Kracauer, *A Psychological History of the German Film from Caligari to Hitler* (1947), has material on the Nazis' use of film. A more sociological analysis is that by David Schoenbaum, *Hitler's Social Revolution: Class and Status in Nazi Germany 1933-1939* (1966). Hermann Rauschning, *The Revolution of Nihilism* (1939), and A. Kolnai, *The War Against the West* (1938), were two important prewar books that saw Nazism as a revolt against the values of Western civilization. A good, recent book on the Nazi leaders and their opportunistic allies is Joachim C. Fest, *The Face of the Third Reich: Portraits of the Nazi Leadership* (1970, U.S. edition). An earlier such effort, by an eyewitness, was that of Martha Dodd, *My Years in Germany* (1939).

Gregor Ziemer's *Education for Death: The Making of the Nazi* (1941) is an anecdotal account by an observer of

Nazi educational procedures. Arthur C. Cochrane, *The Church's Confession under Hitler* (1962), studies the Protestant reaction to National Socialism. Arthur Schweitzer, *Big Business in the Third Reich* (1964), deals primarily with the prewar period, but its implications in regard to "Fascism" go beyond 1939. Unlike Schweitzer, Franz Neumann was a Marxian determinist when he wrote *Behemoth: The Structure and Practice of National Socialism 1933-1944* (1966), which was published in its first version in 1942. Burton H. Klein, *Germany's Economic Preparation for War* (1959), is of importance, as is Alan Milward's brilliant *The German Economy at War* (1965), which emphasizes Todt's role at the expense of Speer's. Hjalmar H. G. Schacht, *Confessions of "the Old Wizard"* (1956), tells some of the story of the famous financier's dealings with the Nazis.

On Nazi foreign policy before 1939, see E. M. Robertson, *Hitler's Pre-War Policy and Military Plans 1933-1939* (1963); Sir Nevile Henderson, *Failure of a Mission: Berlin 1937-1939* (1940); and Paul Seabury, *The Wilhelmstrasse: A Study of German Diplomats Under the Nazi Regime* (1954).

Some of the works cited in my discussion of Hitler's writings and pronouncements are crucial for any study of Hitler as Commander in Chief and policy maker after 1939. In addition, consult the memoirs of generals such as Guderian, Manstein, Warlimont, Keitel, and those of Admiral Dönitz. Also of importance are Peter Fleming, *Operation Sea Lion* (1957), and the reflections on Nazi strategy contained in Telford Taylor, *The Breaking Wave: World War II in the Summer of 1940* (1967). Trumbull Higgins, *Hitler and Russia: The Third Reich in a Two Front War 1937-1943* (1966), and Gerald Reitlinger, *The House Built on Sand: The Conflicts of German Policy in Russia 1939-1945* (1960), are useful on the eastern front, as is the vital book by Alexander Dallin, *German Rule in Russia 1941-1945: A Study of Occupation Policies* (1957). Pierre Renouvin, *World War II and Its Origins: International Relations 1929-1945* (U.S. edition, 1969), is a fine diplomatic survey by a famed French historian. Andreas Hillgruber and Gerhard Huemmelchen, eds., *Chronik des Zweiten Weltkrieges* (1966), is the best chronology of the war now available. Lothar Gruchmann, *Nationalsozialistische Grossraumordnung: Die Konstruktion einer "deutschen Monroe-Doktrin"* (1962) is an interesting effort to interpret Nazi geopolitics and war aims in the light of German theory and American analogy. Walter Laqueur, *Russia and Germany: A Century of Conflict* (1965) is broad in scope but essential for an understanding of Nazi attitudes toward Russia and Bolshevism.

Eberhard Jaeckel, *Frankreich in Hitlers Europa* (1966), is a great study of Nazi policy in France. Walter Goerlitz, *The German General Staff 1657-1945* (1953), contains material on the Nazi period that is of great value. On the Axis, see Elizabeth Wiskemann, *The Berlin-Rome Axis* (1949), and, for the 1940-1945 period, the extraordinary work by F. W. Deakin, *The Brutal Friendship: Mussolini, Hitler and the Fall of Italian Fascism* (1962). Gordon Wright, *The Ordeal of Total War 1939-1945* (1968), is a recent synthesis which contains excellent bibliographies. Another survey is Louis L. Snyder, *The War: A Concise History 1939-1945* (1960). The last days of Hitler are dramatically portrayed in H. R. Trevor-Roper's *The Last Days of Hitler* (1962). An interesting diary covering the last years of the Third Reich is Hans-Georg von Studnitz, *While Berlin Burns 1943-1945* (n.d.). The diaries of Count Ciano, Italian Foreign Minister until 1943, Dr. Goebbels, and Alfred Rosenberg (for the years 1934-35 and 1939-40) are all of use.

On the persecution of the Jews see Raul Hilberg, *The Destruction of the European Jews* (1961), the finest work on the subject. Nora Levin, *The Holocaust: The Destruction of European Jewry 1933-1945* (1968), is less professional and is largely based upon secondary sources. Josef Fraenkel, ed., *The Jews of Austria: Essays on Their Life, History, and Destruction* (1967), contains useful material on the period 1938-1945. Jacob Presser, *The Destruction of the Dutch Jews* (1969), is both thorough and movingly written. Hannah

Arendt, *Eichmann in Jerusalem* (1963), is controversial, but its portrait of the Eichmann Nazi type is brilliant. On Himmler and his SS see the recent book by Heinz Hoehne, *The Order of the Death's Head: The Story of Hitler's SS* (1970). Nothing reveals Heinrich Himmler's bizarre personality more than his letters: see Helmut Heiber, ed., *Reichsführer: Briefe an und von Himmler* (1970). Also see Edward Crankshaw, *Gestapo: Instrument of Tyranny* (1956).

On the German resistance, Gerhard Ritter, *The German Resistance: Carl Goerdeler's Struggle Against Tyranny* (1958), and Hans Rothfels, *The German Opposition to Hitler* (1948), are both useful, as are the diaries of Ulrich von Hassel. Gilles Perrault, *The Red Orchestra* (1969) is the overblown story of an extraordinary Soviet-German spy ring in Hitler's Europe. Hoehne's book on the SS contains interesting material on that strange brew of Himmler, the German resistance, links to the West, and the possibility of a separate peace in 1943 and 1944.

How did the Nazi leaders and the German resistance leaders react to the Allied demand (1943-1945) for unconditional surrender? Did this demand prolong the war by its extremism and unreality? Anne Armstrong argues this case in *Unconditional Surrender* (1961), while the implication of P. Kecskemeti, *Strategic Surrender* (1964), is an opposite one.

The material on the Third Reich contained in scholarly journals has reached voluminous proportions. The serious research student should look into the *Journal of Modern History*, the *American Historical Review*, the *Vierteljahrshefte für Zeitgeschichte*, and the *Revue d'histoire de la deuxième guerre mondiale*.

INDEX